To my loving wife, Anne Elizon Brown, for helping with the kind of things that makes a difficult assignment such as the writing of a book possible.

PUBLISHER'S FOREWORD

David S. Brown leads an exceptionally busy life, simultaneously serving as professor, counselor, researcher, student, lecturer, world traveller, business man and family man. It is remarkable then that this action-oriented person has had the time to write about the subjects that concern him most—the management of enterprises, public and private.

The sum of his published—and unpublished—writing in the last twenty years is impressive both in its quantity and the original contribution it makes to the literature of management.

David Brown is an intellectual adventurer in search of truth. He is not disrespectful of conventional management thought and theory but he constantly tests and challenges, refines and supplements it.

Drawn together in this volume is the expression of a remarkably fertile mind, a scrutinizing observer, and a highly motivated communicator. He is a dedicated student with a missionary spirit to share his findings, which he does through an amazing schedule of world-wide lecturing and documentation.

We asked Dr. Brown to interpolate into such a busy schedule the task of assembling and arranging selected writings. He has done better than that. He has brought older pieces up to date and written new ones. He tells us that he is pleased to have noted in the process that papers he wrote nearly two decades ago are, in some instances, even more pertinent today than when he wrote them. As he himself has aphorized, constants are always changing.

It is our observation that the most challenging intellects do not take time out to document a completed comprehensive theory, and that when they do the result is a book in which the imaginativeness and the challenge have been wrung out in an effort to be sequential, reasonable and systematic. The most valuable insights are often engulfed in turgid prose. That has not happened here.

Managing the Large Organization is the first volume in a projected Lomond series to bring together in edited format the writings of unusually creative people on social issue topics during their most productive periods. Initially we intended to call it *The Management Ideas of David S. Brown* but because the focus of those papers selected for publication was so clearly large-organization oriented we believe the present title more appropriate. It contains Brown's ideas of how large and complex organizations should be managed, and enables him at the same time to put forward what he has called Theory A as an approach to be applied to uniquely American management.

In introducing this series, we are especially happy to have Brown as our first author. He is a person of integrity, curiosity, objectivity, and insight. He cares—he cares about people, about governing, about leading, and about better group and individual relationships in business and government.

We believe anyone who enters upon a study of the writing of David S. Brown will come out of the process a better manager or group leader, a more intelligent follower, a keener observer, a more astute critic, and a better human being.

Lowell H. Hattery

AUTHOR'S PREFACE

A number of the chapters which follow make use of information which appeared earlier as part of professional articles or papers by the author. Some are in their original form. Others have been revised substantially. The author wishes to express appreciation for permission to use them here.

"Power Problems at the Managerial Level" appeared first in *Human Resource Development*, a British journal. "The Bureaucracy and Foreign Policy" was originally a book review, done for the *Washington Star*. "The High Cost of Hierarchy" was published by the *Civil Service Journal*, as was "Organizational Mantrap: The Deputy Chief." Another British publication, *Leadership and Organization Development Journal*, is the original source of "The Chain of Command and What Is Happening To It."

"Staff People and Their Problems" first appeared in *The Public Administration Review* along with "Reforming Bureaucracy: What Can Be Done About It." "The Myth of Reorganizing" and "The Fifth Freedom: Freedom From Supervision" were in *The Journal of Systems Management. The Management of Personnel Quarterly* published "Shaping the Organization to Fit People." "The Manager as a Change Agent" appeared under another title in *Public Management*. "Constructive Uses of Conflict" was in *Ideas For Management,* a book of papers published by the Association for Systems Analysis. The *Public Personnel Review* is the source of "When Nothing Succeeds Like Excess." "Ideas on Demand: A New Approach to Problem Solving" and "Looking Ahead: The Manager in the Year 2000" were in *Public Power.* "Why Subordinates Don't Do What They Are Asked To Do—and Why They Do" and "Leadership and Followership: Twin Ingredients" first appeared in *Management Quarterly*.

The author is particularly indebted to Clinton A. Britt, at the time a graduate student, who did much of the research that formed the basis of Chapter II on the American characteristics as part of a master's thesis completed in 1966. Over the years, however, these ideas have been developed more fully with new materials added. My colleague, Professor Susan Tolchin of the School of Government and Business Administration at George Washington University, should be credited with suggesting the name under which they now appear: Theory A for American management. I wish also to express appreciation to Miller McDonald, formerly of the Office of Personnel, Department of Commerce for his assistance in the preparation of "Organizational Systems: Some Variables" which appeared earlier as a Department handout under another title.

D.S.B.

CONTENTS

PART I

A THEORY OF MANAGING FOR OUR TIMES

CHAPTER I

INTRODUCTION

Of the many books and articles about the managing of enterprises, only a very few have been concerned directly with large organizations, or have even acknowledged that size makes a difference.

Not only does size place new and substantially different requirements on the organization but it also has major influence on what one must do to fulfill these requirements. A change in mass is also a change in form and causes change in managerial functions as well.

It is high time we recognized that there is as great a difference between the large, complex modern organization and the smaller, face-to-face one as there is between, say, an American and a Japanese corporation, or between a steel mill and a city welfare department. We acknowledge the differences between public and private enterprises, between civilian and military, between those that involve professional and blue collar workers and between services and manufacturing, but have given little attention to the differences which size and complexity impose upon systems.

Much of what we have been taught about managing has, in fact, come from the face-to-face group, and most of that from systems which have involved simple and repetitive tasks in times substantially different from our own. While a great deal of this may be pertinent, it is by no means all one needs to know, and often misleading at that. The managing of large organizations, whatever we may have been led to believe, is hardly a multiplication by some x factor of what we have learned at first line, wage rate supervisory level.

This book addresses some of the problems which arise from bigness. In so doing, it reveals only a small part of what one needs to know as a manager. Every organization must have its own attention and study. But if the reader is encouraged to think of the large organization as requiring an approach quite different from that conventionally urged by teachers and texts about managing, it will have served a useful purpose.

The emphasis in the chapters which follow is upon the interpersonal relationships, both planned and unplanned, which organizations produce. The dysfunctions which result—and there are many of them—are far more counter-productive than is either appreciated or understood. Indeed, dysfunctionalism is one of the major costs of large organizations. Beyond a certain size, it increases. This may help to explain why, as is generally agreed, both organizational efficiency and effectiveness are likely to decline.

There is, of course, no magic formula for success. The author has a number of observations to make and not a few suggestions. These are presented within a context and an approach which I call Theory A. It is put forward explicitly in Chapter II but is the backdrop to the entire text.

It has always seemed strange and senseless to me that our organizational systems are so poorly adjusted to the more obvious characteristics of the American workman at whatever level, from professional to blue collar. It is not by chance that we must increasingly turn to those in, and from, other countries to do so much of the work our society requires.

To this point, I have referred very generally to the "large organization." How does one define largeness? What, in effect, is a large organization—and what is not?

One of the ways of assessing size is, as *Fortune* magazine has done, by the volume of a company's business or the amount of its assets. There is no denying that America's 500 largest corporations are large, but so are many thousands of other institutions of lesser financial affluence. There are also many other institutions which cannot be judged by these standards: cities, counties, towns, government agencies, churches, hospitals, educational systems and the like. Largeness is, of course, more than a matter of capital or of dollar income.

The Small Business Administration determines size by the number of employees. Over 1000 is large, under is not. The problem with this is that it fails to take into account the systemic relationships which a company or agency has with those on the outside which are so important to what it does. Some organizations whose nucleus is much less than a thousand have influence over many more than this number.

There are others who judge an organization by the number of hierarchical levels it contains. Hierarchy breeds complexity and four levels or over is hardly small, regardless of total numbers. Yet many organizations with sizable hierarchies have found ways around them, and think of themselves as small. Compared to the giants in industry and government, they are.

Still others judge the size of an organization by more practical standards: whether those in higher managerial positions know in a personal way the men and women who occupy key decisional positions in the organization, and whether those at lesser levels know and recognize the people at the top. If on both counts the answer is yes, the organization need not think of itself as large, no matter what its numbers are.

Such measures make a great deal of sense, and each undoubtedly serves a useful purpose. Size, however, is a relative thing and the elephant is small when compared to the whale. Organizations are certainly large when procedures need to be committed to writing and regularly up-dated; when systems of selection and promotion are standardized; when relationships between those at higher managerial levels and those at operational ones have become depersonalized; and when communications must be conducted through channels. Beyond this, I am satisfied to leave the definition of largeness to the reader. Size is primarily a matter of point of view, and one probably does not need to be more specific than that.

This book, as will be obvious to the reader, is concerned with ideas. It contains ideas which can be applied to managing whether the organization has 5000 people or only 50 in it, despite our emphasis on large organizations. Applicability of ideas is the criterion for their inclusion here.

This book should encourage readers to look analytically at what they are a part of, what they are now doing, and where they propose to go. One objective is to help them achieve their goals more effectively.

CHAPTER II

THEORY A: A CONTEXT FOR AMERICAN MANAGEMENT

A great deal has been said and written during the past twenty years about Theory X and Theory Y. These were ideas put forward in a very influential book by the late Douglas McGregor—*The Human Side of Enterprise*.[1]

McGregor's purpose, as he thought he had made clear, was to suggest how self-fulfilling our estimates of people, good and bad, can be. To illustrate his point, he identified two quite opposite approaches. The one he called Theory X was described, among other things, as autocratic, directive, and distrustful; and the other, Theory Y, as supportive, understanding, and democratic. McGregor recommended neither of these, although his own philosophic approach clearly favored Y.

Theory Y almost immediately caught on. It was popularized nationally as *the* recommended approach to managing. Even though McGregor pointed out in a book published posthumously, what his real intentions were, teachers and trainers up and down the land were advocating Y management.[2]

There must be something about the end of the alphabet which inspires theory-making. Recently, Theory Z has been advanced by William Ouchi which combines elements of McGregor's Y management with what the Japanese have shown us by way of new and improved work systems built upon increased worker participation.[3] This is a worthy objective but not easy to achieve. The extent of its application remains to be seen.

The philosophy this book puts forward, however, is presented as Theory A, with the A standing for American management. It is not intended to be chauvinistic. Nor does it take issue with many of the ideas suggested by McGregor, Ouchi and others. Its purpose is to suggest that whatever American management undertakes, now or in the future, must be viewed in the context of the cultural characteristics of the participants. After all, these are the values and behaviors which are brought to the marketplace, the office, the factory, the shop and the field, and they are manifest in one way or another not only in what is done but also in *how* it is done.

It is a pity more attention has not been given to American cultural patterns by those concerned with organizational performance. The mores and habits of the individual, along with the culture which has helped to produce them, have major influence on individual and group behavior. Psychology, of course, is important to the manager but so also are sociology, anthropology, history, and political science which are disciplines on which this book draws as well. The behaviors we practice as part of the process of living in the larger community we share tell us much of the men and women who make up our work systems.

The American Character

The American character is an amalgam of many elements. It derives, as we do, from many sources, often diverse and frequently contra- dictory. Ours is a gigantic land which over time has tested the mettle of those who invaded and have lived in it.

A listing of the values we hold, even the most prominent of these, is no easy task. There are substantial differences in the customs and mores of different parts of the country. There are differences also in the values and behaviors of youth and middle age, of rich and of poor, of those who serve in differing trades and professions, and those who come from different ethnic, racial, and national backgrounds. Neverthe- less, there are ideas and practices which, living together for so long, we share, and it is useful to be aware of them.[4]

We do not have to agree with Princess Bibesco that "nations are like trees—they always bear the same fruit" to recognize and take into account the differences between Americans, for example, and Mexicans and Canadians even though we share the same land mass with them; and we note with interest, amusement, concern, and sometimes envy the differences between ourselves and the Japanese, the French, the Ger- mans, and the Poles.

Recently I re-read de Tocqueville's *Democracy in America*, written in the 1830s and his notebooks (published as *Journey to America*) on which it is based.[5] The observations he made nearly 150 years ago on the nature of America and the Americans are greatly similar to what a number of experienced observers have reported of the American of this generation. There are many in fact who have written of us—among them are James, Lord Bryce, English diplomatist and scholar; Sir Dennis Brogan, a friend of America but also a critic; James Truslow Adams, Henry Banford Parkes, James Beard, Henry Steel Commager, and others, all distinguished historians; Max Lerner, journalist and philosopher; Margaret Mead and Edward T. Hall, anthropologists;

Harold Laski, English political economist; David Riesman, sociologist; Gunnar Myrdal, economist; and many more, including journalists. Still others writing for a popular market have remarked in passing of our culture and our traits. Writers such as Vance Packard (*The Pyramid Climbers*), William Whyte (*The Organization Man*) and economist John Kenneth Galbraith (*The Affluent Society*) have also contributed observations.

The Department of Defense authorized a study of the American soldier and his characteristics because, in the final analysis, the defense of the country depends upon him. Its purpose was to suggest the systems and equipment which best fitted his behavior. It was published as *The Armed Forces Officer* and for years was required reading in officer training.[6]

There is no attempt here to define precisely what these American characteristics are, simply an indication of some of the most prominent. Theory A holds only that organizational arrangements must take them into account. After all, the individual is a basic building block of the system. The organizational architect should consider such characteristics in constructing the work system, and the manager on the job will need to determine which are dominant in the specific job situation.

There is remarkable agreement on some American traits. Americans, for example, are seen as gregarious, pragmatic, materialistic, innovative, optimistic, individualistic and independent but personally responsible and, more often than not, both mobile and flexible. They are also hard workers, and although an ethic of fairly recent origin has appeared to make inroads upon this trait, it is still there, probably strong and vibrant below the surface. The American also believes strongly in equality and democracy although there are many examples where they are not really practiced.

There is less agreement on other characteristics, but a sufficient number of observers has noted the American's wastefulness and carelessness and his competitiveness-aggressiveness (which often makes association with others difficult) for these to be recorded as well.

While we pride ourselves on our individualism, we sometimes show mass tendencies towards conformity. We are often highly moralistic with respect to others, although not always applying such standards to our own actions. And, if we are to believe some of our critics, we are quick to act, quick on the draw. If we are not inured to violence, we should be. We have enough of it.

We will be examining some of these characteristics at greater length. They are important to Theory A. As we do, we should understand that many of them apply also to other than Americans. The combination of them, however, is what marks the American as fully as his dress or the English he speaks after nearly 400 years on this continent.

Gregariousness

As Andre Maurois once remarked, "When you become used to never being alone, you may consider yourself Americanized."

The trait was first observed and recorded by de Tocqueville. "Americans of all ages, all conditions, and all dispositions," he noted, "constantly form associations. . .religious, moral, serious, futile, general or restricted, enormous and diminutive. . .to give entertainments, to found establishments for education, to build inns, to construct churches, to diffuse books, to send missionaries to the Antipodes. . . ."[7] Bryce, too, has much to say about American "sociability." Undoubtedly this and the patterns of interdependence which also are a part of the American personality were derived from the need for mutual support as we invaded the unfriendly frontier. It is hard to believe that such characteristics were the genealogical forebears of what we know today as "togetherness." Of his own travels, Bryce writes: "Sociability is the rule, isolation and moroseness the rare exception."[8]

The pattern has continued. Commager observed that his countryman is a joiner, one who takes comfort in numbers.[9] The American soldier exemplifies the feeling for and the strength received from group-supported behavior. He is a man who fights best when his power is closely related to that of others. "The normally gregarious American is not at his best when playing a lone-handed or tactically isolated post in battle."[10]

That is merely one side of the equation. The other is that group action has time and again demonstrated its effectiveness. The American is at home with others socially, and professionally he knows that such associations pay off. Despite his individualism, he accepts the need for working with others.

Pragmatism and Practicality

Americans are action-oriented. William James, the father of psychology, pointed out that pragmatism is the philosophy with which we have strongly identified ourselves. John Dewey, the philosopher, later helped to refine it. Our activism is, by and large, practical in nature—"if it works, it's good." A large part of this derives from our frontier heritage which required so much by way of resourcefulness and common sense, both action-oriented ideas.

We are less moved by esthetics than by utility, which is why so many of our cities are so ugly, why we have left gaping holes in our land, but also why we have been so problem-directed. By the time a boy is a teenager, he has learned how to repair his bike, and later his car, even if he has shown himself sometimes delinquent in caring for them.

Of the Americans of his time, de Tocqueville wrote: "They will habitually prefer the useful to the beautiful, and they will require that the beautiful should be useful."[11] This is, of course, the essence of pragmatism.

Innovativeness

From pragmatism comes innovativeness. No one would deny, considering the range of goods we have given the world, that Americans are innovative. We produce 70,000 patents a year, but that is only a part of the story. This turn of character applies not only to the physical and mechanical, but also to novel ways of farming, of building our houses, of educating our children, and of recreation. Even our art has reflected the willingness to experiment. A noted Moscow critic of the ballet, by way of passing judgment on the celebrated Bolshoi group, wrote recently that the most innovative work in ballet had come from an American choreographer, Ballantyne. His book created a storm in Russia, but his remarks could apply also to what has happened here in literature, in theatre, in music, in art, in architecture, and in cinematography.

As Commager has put it:

> The inclination to experiment was deeply ingrained in the American character and fortified by American experience. America itself had been the greatest of experiments, one renewed by each generation of pioneers and each wave of immigrants, and, where every community was a gamble and an opportunity, the American was a gambler and an opportunist. . . .He was always ready to do things which had not been done before. Except in law, tradition and precedent discouraged him, and whatever was novel was a challenge.[12]

A more recent observer, the English born Henry Fairlie who has written widely of events here, relates the American to his continent in a unique and convincing way. He says:

> It is clear to me that it is not the "propitious circumstances" of the continent that have acted on the American so much as the American

who has, by his energy and ingenuity, made a place of "propitious circumstances" out of his continent; and this is the example, above all others, he has set to the world.

In this work, the trait in the American that I would put first, although it is unfashionable to celebrate it, is his inventiveness. Whether we call it gadgetry, at one level, or technology, at another, it is the one factor that is not "closed" in the world today, that is still propitious in the performance of the American, and auspicious in its promise to the rest of the world.[13]

Laski has observed, in much the same vein, that "Americans are always doing things or trying things; more, they are always seeking a shorter way of getting things done."[14] He is probably more optimistic, given the current decline in productivity, than the facts warrant but the idea that things can be done in a better way than they presently are is an idea to which most of us basically do subscribe.

Individualism and Independence

If there is any doubt about it, the American over many years has practiced both individualism and independence. Both were required on the frontier, and the habit remained. Pascale and Athos see a major distinction between the Japanese and the Americans. The former stress interdependence; the latter, independence.[15]

We like to think we are our own man (or woman) and sometimes say and do things which get us into deep trouble with those who control the resources we need to have. Our children first learn to talk and then to talk back. Without their knowing it, they are indulging a cultural pattern.

The Armed Forces Officer regards the individualism and independence of the American soldier, sailor, airman and Marine as a "contemporary virtue" and seeks to have officers understand it as such. When a company of soldiers failed to advance into the jungle during the Vietnamese War as their captain had ordered, because they saw no point to it, an investigation later cleared them. "It is good to have in our armed forces," the report of an investigation of the incident said, "young men who think." "We are an altogether unregimented people," *The Armed Forces Officer* reminds us, "with a strong belief in the virtues of rugged individualism and in the right of the average man to go about as he pleases, so long as he does not do actual injury to society."[16]

As James Truslow Adams had pointed out:

> The American loves freedom. He came from Europe to get it, has moved to frontier after frontier to get it again when he thought he was losing it. He has always wanted to be his own boss. Possibly one of his strongest traits has been that he has wanted to "go to Hell in his own way," or indeed anywhere else he chose. It shows in the Southerner; in the Yankee farmer; in the hunters, trappers, and other frontiersmen; in the Forty-niners and the cowboy; in the whaling and clipper-ship captains; in the squatters and pre-emptors of lands; in the businessmen, big and little; in a word, in all Americans, from the beginning.[17]

Such characteristics are important in the sense that they move us to "take charge" in situations where leadership is needed, but they can also lead, as they have sometimes led, to disputation, divisiveness, and, occasionally, disorder.

Responsibility

There is a strong sense of personal responsibility in the American character. One may speculate that this has derived historically from the hardships that those who braved the forests, the plains, and the waters of the continent have had to face. Whatever its source, however, a sufficient number of those of latter day generations have acquired enough of it for it to be seen as an American trait.

Those involved with the training of persons from the developing countries in the managerial arts often despair of their unwillingness to accept responsibility. While many Americans undoubtedly have the same fault, many more do not, and on such a foundation strong systems can be built.

The literature of the frontier tells of women and children who have assumed men's burdens without either the knowledge or the strength to bear them properly. Yet bear them they have because the task needed doing and because there were no other viable alternatives. "It is your responsibility" is a charge whether given by a parent or a community elder which brooks no shilly-shallying or naysaying.

Responsibility is an idea which most Americans acquire at a very early age. It is built upon in our families, encouraged by our religions, and stressed in our schools. *The Armed Forces Officer* remarks upon it as a characteristic which represents enormous latent strength in both the individual and the society. Responsibility suggests initiative, another American characteristic. It presupposes freedom and, as Richard Taylor has suggested, to be responsible one must be free to do otherwise. That alternative, alas, is available.[18]

It is to our loss that the trait of responsibility has not been built on more generally in designing and managing our work systems.

Optimism

The American is basically an optimist. This attitude has seen him through a variety of calamities and will probably serve him in many more. Bismarck once remarked that "God takes care of children, drunks, and the United States of America." The American believes with the Seabees whose World War II motto was "Can Do."

Speaking of the GI's, *The Armed Forces Officer* notes that although "their griping is incessant, their natural outlook is on the optimistic side" and urges their officers not to overlook this. Adams points out:

> We were always moving on to something new. No one knew what was ahead, what situations he might meet, what lay over the mountains. If you took a wrong turn, settled on the wrong spot, came a cropper in a business venture, well, start again, but why worry? Everybody was doing it, and somehow, after all, most people were getting somewhere.[19]

Marquis and Goldhammer, discussing American values in a textbook on administration, echo the same theme: "The belief that everything is ordered for the best and that eventually good will triumph over evil has been and continues to be a dominant value in America."[20] As Robert Heilbroner says:

> At bottom, *a philosophy of optimism is an historic attitude toward the future*—an attitude based on the tacit premise that the future will accommodate the striving which we bring to it. Optimism is grounded in the faith that the historic environment, as it comes into being, will prove to be benign and congenial—or at least neutral to our private efforts. [Emphasis his.][21]

Optimism can, of course, be excessive, but it is an important organization building block. People who believe that good will ultimately triumph and are willing to do what is required to assure it are an incalculable asset to any institution.

The Willingness to Work Hard

The "work ethic" has long been a predominant American value. Not only has work historically been essential to survival, but we have been told from the pulpit, the political rostrum, and in the classroom that it is good for us. From the landing of the Pilgrims, it has been practiced as well as preached. Small wonder that the American heritage is one of hard work.

The national motto, as Brogan has pointed out, might well be "root, hog, or die." "When convinced," he notes, "that death is the alternative, the hog roots."[22]

Recent years have seen, for a variety of reasons, a re-examination of this proposition. The advent of social security and welfare systems (the so-called "welfare state") may have dulled the ethic in some, but no less an authority than *Work in America* (1973) is convinced that the idea is still a part of the American soul, and that it is still alive and well.[23] We have amended it only to require that work be meaningful, productive, respected and properly compensated. This does not seem to be an unreasonable stipulation.

Mobility

The mobility of Americans is expressed in two ways. The first is geographic. Americans from the earliest days have shown a willingness to gather up their families and possessions and push on to new frontiers. They continue to do so. There is another type of mobility, however, and that is the ability to move from one class or level to another.

Max Lerner has written perceptively of geographic movement as being a basic part of our life. He says of us:

> Americans have always been voyagers. After crossing the ocean to find the America of their dreams, the settlers paddled, steamed, and carried freight down its network of great rivers and built canals to connect them. They proved to be good land sailors across the "sea of grass" on their prairie schooners.[24]

Our movement has not stopped. One of the problems with which American education has had to cope in recent years is that children are constantly being moved from school to school as their parents change locales. Families move on the average of once every four or five years. One of our booming industries, in fact, is the moving industry.

If we are, as has been generally agreed, a melting pot derived from many cultures, we should not be surprised that this has bred social mobility also. Young women of modest family origins can, if they are bright, attractive, and fortunate enough, marry into wealth and social standing; and, correspondingly, young men with some of the same advantages will marry well above their economic levels. The school and university systems, for one thing, enable people from a variety of economic classes to come together. Love presumably does the rest.

The American believes strongly in growth and progress, and even that growth *is* progress. "This conception of growth as everybody's business, everybody's interest," Brogan reminds us, "is deep-rooted in the American national psychology."[25]

The American accepts these ideas and voluntarily and willingly gives up the old for the new. Not to do so would be out of character. Laski says that not only change but also "adaptability is inherent in the personality of the American, and with it, there has gone a zeal for what is new merely because it is new."[26]

Materialism

The American is materialistic. No other people has shown the interest in material things, or the talent for acquiring them, as has the American. We surround ourselves with cars, TV sets, stereos, boats on trailers, and a thousand different gadgets. An Irish housekeeper who joined my family during a period of emergency came from a flat which had only two pieces of electrical equipment, a light bulb and a "fridge." With us, she had to learn how to manage nearly fifty others.

The super-abundance of material resources that the land has provided has been from the very beginning a major force in determining the nation's success and the achievement of its people. Size and spaciousness are, of course, additional descriptors of the American environment. Material abundance has been and continues to be part and parcel of American life.

The American's attitude toward abundance, as we shall see, is often one of valuing it less rather than valuing it more. This is not an insignificant point. Adams has pointed out:

> The attitude of the American toward money is quite different from that of almost any other people, if not of all. In the past the chances have been so great, the natural wealth of the country so enormous, its resources so apparently illimitable, its growth so rapid in population and industry, that the American has come to think of money in almost wholly new terms. Making it has been more exciting and more of a game than anywhere else, and when made, because made so easily, it has not been something to be hoarded and conserved but to be spent and given away. With regard to wealth, the American mind thinks in an economic world of a fourth dimension.[27]

Ours is a society built upon the notion that it is easier and in the long run perhaps cheaper as well, to get rid of something than to be burdened with the task of taking good care of it, or even repairing it. Galbraith, in fact, devotes an entire book to the implications of *The Affluent Society*. They are many. Not least among them is the fact that this affluence while widespread is not fully shared by the lowest one-fifth of the population. They, however, can learn of the life they do not have by merely turning on the TV which nearly everyone has.

Belief in Equality and Democracy

The American is strongly committed to a belief in both equality and democracy. However imperfectly these may be defined or practiced, most Americans believe strongly in them. And when such ideas are reinforced by basic documents, such as the Constitution, and by the law and judicial decision, it is only a matter of time until they are realized.

De Tocqueville noted the general equality of conditions among the American people of the 1830s. Bryce, fifty years later, saw the acceptance of the idea of equality as one of the most important factors in the American makeup. He suggested that "this has been the most constant boast of the Americans themselves, who have believed their liberty more complete than that of any other people, because equality has been more fully blended with it."[28]

While America, in European terms, may have a classless society, there is no doubt that social distinctions are constantly being made. "It does not in the American ideal," Lerner reminds us, "mean an absence of rank, class, power, or prestige. More exactly it means a class system that is casteless and therefore characterized by great mobility and inter-penetration between classes." This is better expressed, Lerner feels, by the term "open-class society."[29]

In an important sense, equality and democracy have been closely related from the start. Whether the one led to the other is of no great importance. They have, in fact, reinforced each other. At the time of the Constitutional Convention we were already 150 years old, and one cannot read the annals of this period without a deep appreciation of the demand on the part of the colonists for a voice in matters affecting them. This probably anteceded even the Mayflower Compact, and applied to spiritual as well as temporal matters. Those who chose to come here were an individualistic and assertive sort and their landing on these shores made such characteristics even more imperative. One cannot read our history, even our military and church history, without realizing that democratic patterns have long been prevalent.

This belief in democracy is not something ideal and remote—an idea

to be discussed but not really practiced. To the contrary, it is to be
lived with. Commager points out that although the doctrines of human
rights were first put forward in France, they were first put into practice
on this continent.[30] As Margaret Mead has said, Americans see—and
want—a direct relationship between what they do and what they get.
She believed that the special brand of American democracy is based on
a faith that the simple people of America "are worthy of a hearing in
the halls of the great."[31]

All of this, of course, can be carried to extremes. Whether there is a
specific "Freedom of Information Act" on the books or not, we expect
to be told—and told honestly—of the state of public affairs, even at
times in great detail. Brogan puts it this way: "The man-in-the-street
expects to get the low-down on all secret conferences, to have international decisions supplied to him before the participants have had time
to put their smiles on and pose for the group photograph."[32]

The democratic creed we have so strongly endorsed requires not
only that we be able to vote for candidates of our choice but that we be
consulted by them and, what is more, listened to. Perhaps the next
most significant step in our development as a society is embodied in the
word "consultation." "Send them a message," one of the political figures of the generation has prescribed, and a large percentage of his
countrymen is trying to do just that. Both as individuals and as people,
we expect to be heard.

What we demand of our social and political systems, we are beginning to ask of our organizations as well. Increasingly, there is talk of
organizational democracy in specifics if not always in theory.

There is to be greater democracy in the years ahead if for no other
reason that it parallels what we have experienced elsewhere.

Other American Characteristics

The above are by no means the only American characteristics—
merely those most often noted by observers. If one explores further,
one will discover that there are others, some of a provincial nature,
some of professional origin; some are habits brought here from other
countries, some of quite recent origin and peculiarly our own.

The American is often wasteful and frequently careless. Despite an
individualistic turn of mind, there are times when no Prussian foot-
soldier could conform more willingly. Our styles often underline this
point. The American is sometimes highly competitive and aggressive,
but at other times cooperative to a remarkable degree.

The American is seen by his neighbors to be "quick on the draw" and ready—all too ready, in fact—to "shoot from the hip." Such characteristics hardly generate confidence whether practiced by the individual or the group. Being quick on the draw suggests a tendency to act without thinking or from emotion or instinct rather than rationality; and shooting from the hip indicates a dependence upon agility rather than sagacity. That both characteristics have often been successful is hardly a recommendation of same save in emergencies.

Our loudness (which others frequently remark upon) is often a manifestation of individualism and independence. We tend to be moralistic (e.g., the Moral Majority), to be greatly generous in many ways, to love gadgetry, and, of course, to be acutely time-conscious. This is not the place to indicate in full detail the characteristics of Americans so much as to remind the reader that, whatever they are, they are important in determining behavior on the job. This is what Theory A is intended to convey.

Still Other Factors

Generalized American traits are not, of course, the only factors of which leader and manager should be aware.

Each profession has its own standards and mores and if one is exasperated by the lack of logic of an understanding which permits the electrician to do this but not that (because it belongs to the plumber or the carpenter), one needs only to be reminded that law, medicine, and the like have their own codes which are no less rigid and which may not be any more logical.

There are also the factors which have to do with the organization itself. Each system has its own history, and this history as a precedent influences what is done. The characteristics an individual brings to the organization are influenced by what has gone before. We accept much of this without question—"this is the way it is done here"—and soft-pedal more basic inclinations. But we reserve the right, as in labor-management disputes, to re-introduce them and even to magnify them as the situation demands. The larger the organization, and the less influential the individual in it, the more likely some of these characteristics are to emerge. They are probably close to the surface already.

Finally, there is the matter of the nature of the work to be done. There are some who have learned, for one reason or another, to accept boring and repetitive tasks with little complaint; to understand that they are going nowhere, American tradition to the contrary; to do unpleasant and degrading work for interminable periods; and to endure autocratic and humiliating supervision with bowed heads. They are, however, a minority. Many of the more than nine million unemployed prefer unemployment to work that is both beneath their competence and their dignity.

In Conclusion

Theory A is thus a collection of influences, conditions, attitudes and ideas which the manager, whether one supervises others or merely works with them in the pursuit of common objectives, should want to explore.

Theory A applies to the factory foreman as well as to the chief executive officer. This universality is its primary significance.

And because the large organization, whether factory or bureaucracy, is so likely to overlook the significance of the culturally derived characteristics within the individual, it is particularly applicable there.

FOOTNOTES

[1] Douglas McGregor, *The Human Side of Enterprise*, NY: McGraw-Hill Book Company, Inc., 1960.

[2] Douglas McGregor, *The Professional Manager*, ed. by Warren G. Bennis and Caroline McGregor, NY: McGraw-Hill Book Company, Inc., 1967.

[3] William Ouchi, *Theory Z: How American Business Can Meet the Japanese Challenge*, Reading, MA: Addison-Wesley Publishing Company, Inc., 1981.

[4] In his study of American cultural characteristics, done under the guidance of the author, Clinton A. Britt examined 11 books and several articles. In the process, he identified a number of American character traits, of which mobility-flexibility, pragmatism, equality, gregariousness, optimism, belief in democracy, and materialism were the most frequently noted in the sources he used. The results were published as a master's thesis entitled "The American Character: A Basic Value in Organizational Planning" (Washington, DC: 1966, 82 pp.), submitted to The George Washington University. As indicated in the Preface, the author is indebted to Britt for his initial exploration of the literature on this subject.

[5] Alexis de Tocqueville, *Democracy in America*, NY: New American Library, 1956; and *Journey to America*, Forge Village, MA: J. P. Mayer, 1959.

[6] *The Armed Forces Officer*, Washington, DC: U.S. Government Printing Office, 1950.

[7] *Democracy in America*, Vol. II, p. 114.

[8] James Bryce, *Social Institutions of the United States*, NY: Chautauqua Press, 1891, p. 228.

[9] Henry Steele Commager, "The Ambiguous American," *New York Times Magazine*, May 3, 1964, p. 12.

[10] *The Armed Forces Officer*, p. 257.

[11] *Democracy in America*, p. 18.

[12] Henry Steele Commager, *The American Mind*, (New Haven: Yale University Press, 1957, p. 12.

[13] Henry Fairlie, "The American Mind Can Overcome an Age of Scarcity," Outlook Section, *The Washington Post*, Dec. 22, 1974.

[14]Harold J. Laski, *The American Democracy*, London: George Allen and Unwin, Ltd., 1949, p. 42.

[15]Richard Tanner Pascale and Anthony G. Athos, *The Art of Japanese Management: Applications for American Executives*, NY: Simon & Schuster, 1981.

[16]*The Armed Forces Officer*, p. 14.

[17]James Truslow Adams, *The Making of a New Man*, NY: Charles Scribner's Sons, 1943, p. 383.

[18]"Action and Responsibility," in Myles Brand and Douglas Walton, eds., *Action Theory*, Boston: Reidel Publishing Co., n.d., p. 293.

[19]*The Making of a New Man*, p. 381.

[20]Lucian Marquis and Keith Goldhammer, "American Values," in E.G. Wengert, ed., *The Study of Administration*, Eugene, OR: University of Oregon Press, 1961, p. 50.

[21]Robert Heilbroner, *The Future as History*, NY: Harper and Row, 1960, p. 17.

[22]D. W. Brogan, *The American Character*, NY: Alfred A. Knopf, 1954, p. 162.

[23]Report of a Special Task Force to the Secretary of Health, Education and Welfare (prepared under the auspices of the W. E. Upjohn Institute for Employment Research), Cambridge, MA: MIT Press, 1973.

[24]Max Lerner, *America as a Civilization*, NY: Simon and Schuster, 1957, p. 94.

[25]*The American Character*, p. 29.

[26]*The American Democracy*, p. 11.

[27]*The Making of a New Man*, p. 378.

[28]*Social Institutions of the United States*, p. 147.

[29]*America as a Civilization*, p. 469.

[30]Henry Steele Commager, *The Empire of Reason*, Garden City, NY: Anchor Press, 1977.

[31]Margaret Mead, *And Keep Your Powder Dry*, NY: William Morrow and Co., 1965, p. 202.

[32]*The American Character*, p. 133.

CHAPTER III

THE FIFTH FREEDOM: FREEDOM FROM SUPERVISION

There is increasing evidence that one of the objectives most wanted by working men and women at all levels in our times is freedom from supervision. This has become a kind of Fifth Freedom, perhaps more important today than any of the other four freedoms—Freedom of Speech and Expression, Freedom of Religion, Freedom from Want, and Freedom from Fear—which came out of World War II.

That so large a degree of "freedom from supervision" has already been realized in many American jobs is undoubtedly a major factor in its being sought in others.

This is neither as revolutionary as it sounds nor as difficult to achieve as it seems in a large number of work situations. *Minimal* supervision, and often *no* supervision at all, is present, whether by design, practice, or chance, in many, many jobs. This is true of organizations, both large and small, as well as in the professions. There can be no doubt that it is a major factor in the choices individuals make with respect to lines of work to be followed and has major bearing also upon work inputs such as job commitment, initiative, industry, creativity, and the like.

What is being suggested here is that *the absence of close supervision* ("freedom from supervision") be recognized for the important motivator that it is and intentionally built into the organizational system. There is indeed much to recommend it.

A Matter of Common Practice

First, let us explore what is actually happening. By doing so, we may be able to lessen some of the heat which surrounds any perceived diminution of what is traditionally seen as management's "rights" and prerogatives.

There are already, in fact, many jobs in our society without supervision which perform very well. On the whole they are desirable ones, commanding, for a variety of reasons, high status and often high pay. On the professional side these belong to the doctors, the lawyers, the dentists, the CPAs, the consultants, the artists, and the writers. There are many others: small as well as large entrepreneurs; the traders, the prospectors, the artisans, the investors, and the farmers. Many of these are traditional lines of work with their duties and risks well known. There are also many elective positions. The total of all such jobs is in the millions. They have appeal not only because of large popular acceptance of and identification with them but also because of the independence of action they permit. It is not by chance that the American character has been molded by its farmers, its fisherman, its frontiersmen, and its small-business men.

When one says these jobs are unsupervised, one is saying only that in an organizational sense the majority have no real superiors. All have conditions or restraints upon them. All, or nearly all, are subject to the whims of clients, the marketplace, the law, the weather, or other factors. Many are "regulated" in the sense that government at one or another level sets conditions which must be met. The great majority demand a heavy time and work investment, often considerable risk, and many offer little prospect of great financial return.

Yet much of their appeal lies in the fact that they are not directly supervised in the sense that someone is "over" them, demanding adherence to standards of production, time schedules, attendance, and the like. No man, as Plato has reminded us, is truly free, but those holding jobs such as the above feel a remarkable sense of freedom of choice and action.

As a lobsterman on the coast of Maine once told me: "I put my traps where I want to put them. No one tells me where." He suffers willingly all the hardships of a hard life, but he feels he makes the basic decisions himself. He is his own man.

Jobs of Minimal Supervision

We have spoken thus far of individual entrepreneurship. Let us now turn to organizations, and, in particular, to large ones.

These are not the monoliths which many suppose them to be. There are, in fact, many jobs in large organizations which have little or no direct supervision (i.e., they are minimally supervised if at all) either because it is impractical or inefficient to do so, because the functions are so well known and accepted that it is not really necessary, or for other reasons. Many of these job holders go about their chores with little or no actual direct supervision by those nominally above them in the hierarchy. It is useful to understand how and why this occurs.

The Distance Factor

One of the better examples of freedom from supervision is provided by the subordinate physically separated from his superior. As Napoleon told his prefect for the Lower Alps: "You are a pasha here. Once you are a hundred leagues from the capital, you have more power than I have."[1] So it may be today in the business or governmental organization with its field offices and field men.

The best example is the lighthouse keeper. His superiors may learn later of his failures but this is well after the fact and probably too late to do much of anything about it by way of setting him right. The head of the field unit, the captain of a ship, the director of the branch store or the local representative are all in this category. But so is the fellow in another building who is fortunate enough to be situated a block or two away from the immediate boss.

Distance dulls direction. While the power and the will may still be present, the execution is limited. No one knows this better than a subordinate—except, of course, the superior.

Salesmen long ago discovered that while out on the road they are virtually unsupervised. True, on return their performance may be analyzed and criticized by those in the home office and judgments made concerning it. But they are then being *audited* rather than supervised. There is an important distinction here. The salesman accepts the criticism as the price of his freedom the rest of the time.

Law enforcement is another example of work affected by the distance factor. This applies to the patrolman as well as the FBI agent. A policeman's lot may not be a happy one but one of its merits is that the sergeant knows only in a general way where the patrolman is and what he is doing at any given moment. The TV show of several years ago which featured the plaintive call from headquarters of "Car 54, where are you?" pointed up the policeman's advantage in being on his own. The postman is similarly endowed. The newspaper reporter operates most of the time away from the newsroom and the critical eye of the editor. So do the truck driver, the garbage collector, the plumber, the electrician, and many others. Such jobs rarely go begging. Those who hold them know why, even if the management theorists appear not to know.

Well Established Programs

Many old and well-established programs with clearly delineated tasks and roles have succeeded in reducing supervision to a minimum. The best examples come from the established religions where a relatively long period of training precedes the assignment to a parish church. Religious practice varies, but priests or pastors throughout their careers will usually be very much on their own even though they may work closely with parish leaders.

There are many parallels in education. At the top is the university professor whose independence of action is underlined not only by the expertise brought to the position but also by something called "academic freedom." The professor, in fact, is more likely to go unsupervised than the dean who is often held closely in check by the college president.

What goes on at university levels is emulated in many ways in high schools, grade schools, and other schools throughout the country. Both private and public school teachers use the academic freedom argument, buttressed by their willingness to go on strike if necessary to gain or preserve a professional independence. Principals and superintendents, once the archetype of the narrow-gauged supervisor, have either gotten the message or are preoccupied with problems of student discipline, bussing, and the like.

The Unique Job

The scientist and researcher hold unique positions. Fulfilling them requires insight, imagination, the willingness to experiment, patience, and dedication. These are characteristics better served by self-discipline than by discipline imposed by others from above. Accordingly, the prevailing practice, whether in an open society like the United States or a closed society like Russia, is minimal supervision or none at all. This may apply to the technologist and the engineer as well as the scientist.

These are, of course, not the only jobs or professions that are unique, or whose occupants are permitted a large degree of personal freedom for decision and choice. The number is in fact large. Doctors (in an institution) demand and get large freedom of action. But so do other professionals, particularly if they are in short supply: psychologists, physiologists, therapists, pharmacists, and even nurses.

Jobs which require creativity are minimally supervised: writers, artists, advertising men and women, planners, architects, media people, analysts, photographers, etc. There are also jobs in which the job holder is performing a highly valued service which could not easily be replaced. One may be a machine operator of high skill; one may have acquired special knowledge because of many years of service; one may be a teacher or trainer of others. One may in fact have any of a variety of capabilities which others value.

Uniqueness applies in other ways as well. The job holder may be "unique" (and "entitled" to minimal supervision) where the supervisor is of one profession or skill and the subordinate of another. Or one may be doing a job that over a long period of time has not been supervised, such as a special assistant, an accountant, or an enforcement officer, and so, rather than face the issue squarely, arrangements continue as is. Precedent is a compelling force.

Persons with Special Sources of Power

Power is acquired in a variety of ways, only one of which is via the hierarchy. In fact, the exercise of hierarchical power often produces an opposite effect, known as countervailing power, a condition in which the nominal supervisor is now the threatened one.

If managers are not aware of the many jobs which are minimally supervised, their subordinates are. There are many advantages to occupying such positions, which is why people so often set their sights on them and refuse to move from them even though offered higher pay elsewhere. Consider the following:

The job with its own constituency. There are many of these in both government and industry. They usually developed over a period of time with clients looking to a particular individual to meet their needs. Often, as in the case of banks, advertising agencies, brokerage firms, and real estate companies, there is the implied threat that if the job-holder leaves, he or she will take the clients with them.

The employee with special information about the company or the program—information which would be of great value to a competitor or would look bad if revealed in print or to a legislative committee. This may be a form of blackmail but it often influences the degree of supervision.

The employee who makes decisions which if over-ruled would elevate him to a new level, the boss's. There are more of these than meet the eye. The Commissioner of Internal Revenue, for example, will rarely over-rule the tax judgment of a subordinate. This is a matter of long-standing practice, but there are many other cases where the superior automatically, and for very good reason, supports the decision of the subordinate even when privately disagreeing with it.

The employee with strong union support. Does this need to be developed further?

The employee who does a job no one else wants to do because it is risky, dangerous, unpleasant or tedious. There are many such jobs, both blue and white collar, which superiors are content to leave pretty much alone.

The employee who resents and resists close supervision. Unpleasant persons, like an unpleasant child, often get their own way. A supervisor quickly learns to respect their territory.

The Special Cases

There are many instances, particularly within today's large organizations, where for a combination of reasons the employee well down the line is permitted a large degree of personal freedom.

Many jobs are covered by MBO (management by objectives). These emphasize a mutual agreement on standards and periodic evaluation of progress towards them.

The job with several supervisors. Those who work for several bosses virtually work for themselves.

The "floating" job with essentially no supervision. The job holder is for the most part free to do what he or she thinks ought to be done. Liaison officers, coordinators, analysts, expediters and special assistants hold such posts, and, sometimes, so do inspectors, internal auditors, and the like.

The job which is expected to pay its own way by selling its services to other units. If it can't survive, so the theory goes, it doesn't. There is little point to such a job being closely supervised, and it isn't.

The job in which the supervisor spends much of his or her time on other matters—in travel, in cultivating outside relationships, in hobnobbing with superiors and the like. There is little time or inclination to supervise closely, and both "superior" and "subordinate" accept this fact.

Persons who are particularly liked or trusted. This is a special category but with many in it. Who has not observed the special treatment accorded to those with records of faithfulness and service? Who has not noted the larger freedom of persons well-liked or trusted, and often those with long tenure? The special reward of the king's favorites is greater freedom of initiative. The special reward of the obedient dog is to come off the leash.

The Studies Have Their Say

The purpose of the above is to demonstrate the many instances in which minimal supervision—not poor supervision but limited supervision—is actually being applied in today's organizations. It is already a reality to millions.

Being seen and savored by so many, why should we be surprised that it is sought by others? If we are conversant with the literature, we know that objections to close as well as "nosy" supervision have been listed time and again among the major complaints employees have about their jobs. Correspondingly, broad supervision, or no supervision at all, are among the goals most workers value and seek.

Such findings, however, are not always put as bluntly or given the emphasis of this essay. More often than not, worker preference for freedom from supervision is hidden among other needs, hygienic or non-hygienic, and so phrased that it is more likely to be obscured than strongly registered.

Yet if one examines closely what the researchers are saying, one will be impressed by the weight of the evidence indicating that the man and woman on the job want to organize the work to be done as they think best, set their own standards and go about achieving them in their own way. Myers summarizes the roles of a group of supervisors at Texas Instruments as: (1) giving visibility to company (customer) goals; (2) providing budgets and facilities; (3) mediating conflict; but primarily (4) *staying out of the way to let people manage their work* [Emphasis his]. The effective supervisor, he goes on to say, is one who "provides a climate in which people have a sense of working for themselves."[2] How could it be put more succinctly?

This is, in fact, quite consistent with the major findings of the Likert studies of the late fifties and early sixties. With due allowance for varietal factors which his detailed and extensive research has produced, there is a strong case for broad as against close supervision, for participation by workers in matters affecting them, and for "feeling free" to plan their own work programs, to set their own pace, and the like. Note that the great majority of Likert's research was done with lower level and often wage-rate employees both in offices and shops. The "demands" they make are much the same, although less strong, than those expressed in other ways by persons higher in the social (and also the work) system. Traditionally, of course, blue collar and clerical workers have had much less freedom (and more supervision) than their professional brothers. As Likert concludes:

> Supervision is, therefore, always a relative process. To be effective and to communicate as intended, a leader must always adapt his behavior to take into account the expectations, values, and interpersonal skills of those with whom he is interacting.[3]

Note the reference to the values and expectations of the subordinate.

McGregor's views are too well known to require repetition here. In his widely known postulate, Theory Y, he holds that "man will exercise self-direction and self-control in the service of objectives to which he is committed," and proposes a theory of management by integration and self-control.[4] Such an approach argues strongly against traditional methods of direction and control and for a "strategy" which permits individual self-development and commitment.

The idea is again supported in the extensive studies of motivational factors by Maslow, Herzberg, Vroom, Gellerman, and others. The employee, having satisfied lesser (and more basic) needs, seeks the gratification of higher ones, namely, individual development and societal contribution.

The Herzberg studies merit further attention.[5] The genesis of his approach (the Motivation—Hygiene theory) is that individual motivation is inhibited by what he identifies as the "hygiene factors." The two most important among these are: (1) company policy and administration and (2) supervision. The majority of worker complaints, he indicates, are the product of close and, from the point of view of the employee, limiting supervision. On the other hand, the real motivators are those which emphasize the ability of the individual to contribute to the organizational product. These appear in work where the employees are to a large degree on their own or where the supervision is of such a nature that they feel a large degree of individual freedom.

If more evidence is required, one need only to observe the effects of the "up-tight" supervision practiced in many industries. The automobile assembly plants provide vivid examples of what these systems have produced. Lordstown, Ohio, is a case in point. General Motors, if one is to believe recent news and magazine reports, is now diligently searching for some means of revising both its present assembly and supervisory line practices and may be finding it in an adaptation of the Swedish and Japanese experience.

Further support for a loosening of traditional supervisory practices is provided by the Department of Health, Education, and Welfare's task force on the American at work. This remarkable document known variously as the "O'Toole report" (for its chairman, Dr. James O'Toole) or *Work in America*, its published title, leaves no doubt that much of the dissatisfaction felt by today's workers is from the kind of supervision they receive. It reports:

> What the workers want most, as more than 100 studies in the past 20 years show, is to become masters of their immediate environments and to feel that their work and themselves are important—the twin ingredients of self-esteem. Workers recognize that some of the dirty jobs can be transformed only into the merely tolerable, but the most oppressive features of work are felt to be avoidable: *constant supervision and coercion*, lack of variety, monotony, meaningless tasks, and isolation. An increasing number of workers want *more autonomy in tackling their tasks*, greater opportunity for increasing their skills, rewards that are directly connected to the intrinsic aspects of work, and *greater participation in the design of work and the formulation of their tasks*. [Emphasis added.] [6]

From the Supervisor's Viewpoint

Thus far, our attention has been upon those who are being supervised. Actually, supervising is often only slightly less objectionable than being supervised. This observation is supported in a multitude of ways: by the criticism of first- and second-line supervisors by those higher up; by the need for supervisory training programs to "improve" their performance; by their failure (as seen by higher management) to carry out instructions passed down from above; by the joint problems of absenteeism and declining productivity; by non-acceptance by lower-level supervisors of increased responsibility; and by the complaint that foremen conspire in many instances with the people they are supposed to supervise.

Few quandaries are as vexing as those of lower- and lower-middle-level managers, torn between their own demanding superiors on the one hand and diffident if not hostile subordinates on the other. They discover that they are neither fish nor fowl—neither accepted members of management nor members of the work force. Even their families are sometimes troubled by the same job-related problems. The supervisor's lot, like the policeman's, is usually not a very happy one.

Even the word "supervisor" has become controversial and a substitute is sought. People at all levels have found it demeaning and obsequious. It taints the holder as well as the subordinate. At a time when egalitarianism has become a cherished value, it reminds all who are involved that there are clearly superior and inferior levels. This is why terms, such as "group leader" and "coordinator," are being experimented with.

Are There Alternatives?

The conclusion to be reached from all of this is that supervision in its traditional forms, where one person obviously—and often threateningly—oversees the work of another no longer suits the work system, nor is it acceptable to increasing numbers of those who fill the majority of American jobs.

There is a major distinction to be made here between supervising and *guiding* or *leading*, or for that matter, *monitoring* or *auditing*. Levels of responsibility exist because varying vantage points provide different vistas and carry different requirements, and they will undoubtedly continue to do so.

This is why it is so important that any change toward lessened or minimal supervision be undertaken with prudence, thoughtfulness, and careful planning.

The rationale behind it—that much that has been done under the rubric of supervising has produced greater dysfunctional than functional results—must be understood and accepted not just by those in upper managerial positions but by those at operational levels as well. Some of the strongest defenders of conventional supervision are actually among those most critical of the way it is practiced: they will claim, of course, to be demanding *better* rather than *lesser* supervision. Such a demand, however, is probably more the product of conventional knowledge and standard practice than anything else. The supervisory idea, no matter how critical we may be of the way it is performed, is deeply etched in American management.

Those who are involved must be helped to understand that what is being proposed is neither un-American, unreal, or unattainable; that it has, in fact, actually been taking place under their very noses. That is why I have given so much attention to the listing of the many professions, occupations, jobs, and tasks which function well with little or no supervision even within the framework of some of the largest and most conservative organizations.

The trend, in fact, is already well established. It has come upon us from a variety of sources piece-meal—a tribute to practitioners who, caught between organizational needs and the temper of their associates, have once more done the practical and sensible thing.

In industry after industry, the span of control has been expanded as enlightened managements have come to understand new worker-machine ratios. Spans of 30 to 50 persons are today standard in many areas. Some are higher. Both government and industry have come to recognize that the traditional "one over seven," first established by the military under Frederick the Great and reaffirmed by Graicunas, has little merit in the dynamics of today.

The example of the coal mining industry provides a useful illustration. With the advent of new types of machinery, the first-line supervisor has become redundant in many instances. The problem has been dealt with sensibly in mine after mine by leaving the workers individually and as groups to develop ways by which standards are to be met. Those who were formerly foremen are often serving as safety inspectors.[7]

The O'Toole Report provided examples of companies which have lessened the number of supervisory levels by adopting more open systems. There are innumerable instances of jobs which in practice are virtually "boss-less." It remains only for the traditionalists—among them are many of our most persuasive writers, teachers, and trainers—to see that this is so and to indicate what it means.

In those areas where minimal supervision has been most successful, it has been supported by a combination of factors and conditions which help the individual to relate his or her contribution to the contributions of others. One does not have to be a management scholar to know that this can be done in a variety of ways:

-- By lessening the number of supervisors.

- By increasing the span of supervision or control.

- By lessening the power of the supervisor.

- By delegating to others.

- By deliberately increasing the responsibilities of the subordinate or the group.

- By endorsing more democratic group procedures.

- By physically separating superiors from their subordinates.

- By helping to develop other systems for determining performance—new ways of monitoring and auditing.

– By encouraging present supervisors to take on other functions and responsibilities.

– By using systems of peer evaluation.

– By rotating those "in charge."

– By using such systems as Management by Objectives which make use of joint superior-subordinate standard setting.

Some of these steps are both obvious and easy to bring about. The supervisor with many subordinates cannot give the single individual the close—and frequently unwanted—attention that would occur if the former were overseeing only a few. The supervisor who is physically removed from subordinates cannot hover over them.

All of this, however, will not, and should not, happen without deliberate planning. The best results will probably ensue from incremental action: a pinch of delegation here, a bit of training there. The employee is encouraged to take on new tasks and, when convenient, to tell others about them.

The trend we have identified should be recognized for what it is—a growing rejection of the traditional concept of supervision. Old ideas die slowly, but the need for a greater freedom for those in the workplace from close and burdensome oversight by organizational superiors is a concept whose time has come. The new systems already developing will help to make the office and shop a more attractive as well as a more productive place in which to work.

Such approaches build upon existing American characteristics. They represent Theory A in action.

FOOTNOTES

[1] Sanche De Gramont, *The French: Portrait of a People*, NY: G.P. Putnam's Sons, 1969, p. 207.

[2] M. Scott Myers, "Every Employer a Manager," *California Management Review*, Spring 1968.

[3] Rensis Likert, *New Patterns of Management*, NY: McGraw-Hill Book Company, Inc., 1961, p. 95.

[4] Douglas McGregor, *The Human Side of Enterprise*, NY: McGraw-Hill Book Company, Inc., 1960, p. 47 and pp. 61-76.

[5] See in particular Frederick Herzberg, *Work and Nature of Man*, Cleveland: World Publishing Co., 1966.

[6]*Work in America*, Report of a Special Task Force to the Secretary of Health, Education and Welfare (prepared under the auspices of the W.E. Upjohn Institute for Employment Research), Cambridge, MA: MIT Press, 1973, p. 13.

[7]Stephen Klaidman, "Coal Miners Doing Their Own Thing," Outlook Section, *The Washington Post*, Jan. 25, 1976, p. F2.

CHAPTER IV
AUTHORITY: WHO DECIDES WHAT IT IS

On May 10, 1940, Winston Churchill became prime minister of Great Britain. He later wrote of his thoughts on that memorable occasion:

> I was conscious of a profound sense of relief. *At last I had the authority to give directions over the whole scene.*[1] [Emphasis added.]

Churchill's "need" is a familiar one. Most managers, whatever their position or level, are greatly concerned that the authority they have is equal to the job they are asked to do. The late Douglas MacGregor, in *The Human Side of Enterprise*, reminds us that "if there is a single assumption which pervades conventional organizational theory, it is that authority is the central indispensable means of managerial control." He elaborates this point with the further comment:

> The very structure of the organization is a hierarchy of authoritative relationships. The terms up and down within the structure refer to a scale of authority. Most of the other principles of organization. . .are directly derived from this one.[2]

Authority is prized for many reasons. It connotes status, legitimacy, and also power. In the words of Henri Fayol, a management pioneer, it is "the right to give orders and the power to exact obedience." It "authorizes" someone to compel others to do things which might not otherwise be done. It is "legitimized power."

Most of us, in fact, have accepted without questioning a number of ideas concerning authority. We have been taught to believe:

1. That there is something called authority which exists higher up in the organization.

2. That it was vested by some still higher authority (God, the Constitution, the legislature, the ownership, long accepted practice, etc.) on select officers or individuals.

3. That it is basically unitary in nature but can be divided and parceled out (delegated) to others by those who possess it.

4. That a part of the contract the individual makes in coming to the organization is to agree to respect and follow this authority.

5. That the manager, or someone higher up, is entitled to use it in "getting things done."

6. That failure to respect such authority can result in punishment of the offender, including firing.

On its face, this is clearly a formula for action—more specifically the kind of action those in authority want. In practice, however, it has not always worked out that way.

No one has written more insightfully—or more authoritatively—on the subject of authority than has Chester Barnard whose *The Functions of the Executive*, published in 1938, is perhaps the most important of all the books written on the managerial role. Barnard is not content to rely on definitions but wants to see how they are applied. Of authority, he writes:

> Now a most significant fact of general observation relative to authority is the extent to which it is ineffective in specific instances. It is so ineffective that the violation of authority is accepted as a matter of course and its implications are not considered.[3]

What was true of the time Barnard was writing is even more in evidence today. Strange things are happening in our organizations as well as in our society:

- Work assigned and agreed to is not being done, or, if done, not done properly or as instructed.

- Subordinates are openly rejecting the authority of their superiors and doing in many instances what they please.

- Work slowdowns and stoppages are common; there is also sabotage.

- Employees who have agreed not to strike are going on strike.

- Excessive leave is being taken; absenteeism on certain days of the week is astronomically high.

- There is "talking back," disrespect, and disloyalty.

- Superiors fear to mete out punishment even when organization rules permit them to do so.

- The right of the director to direct or the commander to command is being challenged increasingly.

– Employees are even striking against the government, something the law tells us cannot be done.

We search for explanations of all this. We argue that there are problems in communication (as there certainly are), or there are personality conflicts or differences in values. We claim that people are not as committed as they once were, that they do not work as hard, or that they are not properly trained. Many explanations are put forward. There is undoubtedly substance to all of them.

By advancing them, however, we should not overlook other reasons which may be more basic and even more in need of our attention. These have to do with the authority system itself and our expectations of it. In particular, those who are part of either large organizations or large systems—and this includes the majority of us—need to examine and understand what is really occurring.

Richard Cornuelle, a former business executive and author of *De-Managing America*, believes that "Americans everywhere are becoming insubordinate, unmanageable."[4] Senator Daniel P. Moynihan says that "we are facing a crisis of authority in American society, a crisis of legitimacy." George Berkley notes in *The Administrative Revolution*:

> Authority is becoming ever more diminished and confused. Not only are those above having an increasingly difficult time keeping abreast of, let alone controlling, those below but in a very real sense, it is becoming harder and harder to tell just who is below and who is above.[5]

Whether what is happening is due to actions of those who give the orders or those who receive them—or both—has clearly not been resolved.

The "Acceptance Theory"

Barnard, however, has some useful thoughts on the subject. His major point is that authority is *not* what we have traditionally taken it to be, and *not* on its surface what it seems to be, a "right" to command. It depends not upon its being granted, or from what source it derives, as much as upon its being *accepted*.

The word itself (authority) can be interpreted in a variety of ways. It is the root form of "authoritarian" (which describes a way of doing things) but it can also mean "authoritative," an altogether different idea. The one describes the attitude and behavior of a superior; the other suggests how a subordinate views the requests or instructions directed to him.

Barnard reminds us further that "a person can and will accept a communication as authoritative only when four conditions simultaneously obtain:

(a)   he can and does understand the communication;

(b)   *at the time of his decision*, he believes it is not inconsistent with the purposes of the organization;

(c)   *at the time of his decision*, he believes it to be compatible with his personal interest as a whole;

(d)   he is able mentally and physically to comply with it."[6] [Emphasis his.]

Put another way, Barnard is suggesting that it is the *receiver* of the command or instruction who determines whether it shall or shall not be complied with, not the *giver* as has been so vigorously contended.

Charles Lindblom says much the same thing but in a slightly different way:

> Authority is a concession from those who are asked to obey. The rule that establishes authority is a rule of behavior for the person who is controlled, not a rule of behavior for the controller. You have no authority over me until I decide to follow, for whatever reason, the rule of obedience to you.[7]

The receiver may reject for a number of reasons what someone has asked to be done. In fact under certain circumstances (e.g., the Nuremburg Rule) one is expected to do so. Directives can be refused—and the refusal defended—if they are illegal, impossible, irresponsible, or immoral. A case can also be made for rejection if they are improper, irrational, or inadvisable as well. There are those who hold, further, that orders can be refused if improperly made or if the order-giver is personally offensive in doing so.

Not only is this true of the workplace, but it is also present within the family, the community, the church, and even the military. If anyone has doubts about this point, a look around should dispel them. The traditional view of authority—the one held for centuries—is being challenged, and successfully.

"You can't just hand out orders," an Army officer is quoted as saying of an incident in Vietnam in which soldiers refused to obey the commands they had been given. The incident is reported by Judson Gooding in *The Job Revolution* who observes that "this is as true now on the factory floor as it is in the Vietnamese jungle—in fact, it is much more so." Its significance, as he sees it, is that it marks the decline of authoritarianism.

> But [he cautions] it is important to note that this change in military structure does not necessarily mean permissiveness. It is rather the substitution of another kind of authority, that of fellow workers or fellow soldiers and that of the task itself. It is a profound change.[8]

In many respects it is, indeed. But in others it recognizes at long last what has been happening all along: a development which as Barnard noted, we have stubbornly refused to recognize as we struggled to maintain the fiction if not the fact of control.

Let us examine more closely what is actually taking place, starting with the individual which is surely where one ought to begin.

The Power of the Individual

The individual at all organizational levels is expected to be more than a piece of equipment. He or she does not respond as an electrical circuit responds to the throwing of a switch or the pressing of a button. We are taught as part of our earliest training to think, to question, and to act responsibly. What can be more thoughtless or irresponsible than to do something which we know is clearly wrong?

Lord Acton's famous dictum that "power tends to corrupt and absolute power corrupts absolutely" reminds us that people with power—and "authority"—do ask things of their subordinates which ought to be questioned and sometimes not carried out. So, there are reasons for examining what one is asked to do and its expected effect. There are reasons also for trying to determine the basis on which the order is being given and perhaps the rationale behind it. In other words, is it authoritative?

The validity of the command and the "right" of the command-giver to make it can be challenged for a variety of reasons. Because someone is the head of an organization does not make that person an expert in the law. For that, we look to lawyers or judges because we know that if what we do is not legal, we can personally be held to account for it. We turn to experts in whatever field for the guidance we seek. As organiztions become more complex, the more frequently we seek the professionals of all types, whether part of the chain or not. Often they will not include the person "in ch differ, those of the expert weigh heavily with us, an

In fact, most organizations abound with authorities. Each has a claim to acceptance, and the individual chooses from among them what seems to be most pertinent. We do not, for example, necessarily look to our hierarchical superiors for *moral* authority where the propriety of a contemplated act is in question. There is also the authority of *seniority*: we recognize the years someone has contributed to the organization and are influenced by his or her views. Likewise, the *dedication* of a particular person. The willingness to give long hours to the job recommends that person for followership. There is *functional* authority, a kind of authority particularly prevalent in bureaucracies where people are sensitive to each other's territory. The whole has many components and, not wishing our own areas invaded, we are respectful of the same point of view in our associates. This is why so many persons are sometimes required to "sign off" before an action is taken.

The *union* has authority because, in certain matters, it is expected to speak for its members. Nor should one overlook the authority of the group. *Consensus* is an important value and deserves to be respected. In fact, the views of our associates often weigh more heavily than those of an immediate superior.

Now, a plea to respect God's will has very little effect on an atheist, and a plea to one to accept hierarchical authority indiscriminately when there are other, competing forms of authority that make better sense will also be unsuccessful. When hierarchical authority comes from someone the receiver believes is uninformed, wrong-headed, self-serving or incompetent, there is even less reason for doing what is asked. The exception is where punishment is likely to follow. When that occurs, it is, of course, power that is being respected, not authority. Even then, there are examples where someone feels so strongly about "rightness" that he or she will act as he thinks proper and accept the punishment.

"Zones" in the Individual

It should not be concluded from the above that "higher ups" are without influence, or that each request made of subordinates is subjected to penetrating analysis. Those in managerial positions, from the foreman to the president, carry the prestige of their offices with them. They are presumed to be acting peoperly until, by their words or actions, they give evidence to the contrary. Most of us, in fact, accept what we are asked to do as being reasonable or proper: it has usually been asked of us before. Habit is a powerful factor and it is ordinarily followed. However, where the request that is made of us is new, different, radical, or, on its face, violates those precepts we deeply respect, will be likely to question it. Doubts will also be raised when the approach violates accepted norms. We reserve the right to question and often to modify instructions given us, for the reasons given above.

Barnard describes a "zone of indifference" which he suggests exists in all of us.[9] There are always things we are asked to do which we do not particularly like, or feel do not really need to be done, but it is often simpler to do them than to refuse, and so we cultivate an indifference to them. Besides, we have contracted eight hours a day to the organization, and believe that those holding higher positions in it should clearly have a say, albeit within limits, in how we spend it.

Herbert Simon, a Nobel laureate who has written extensively about organizational subjects, identifies also a "zone of acceptance."[10] We accept many of the requests made of us because we agree with them and also with organizational objectives. If we did not, we should work elsewhere.

I would suggest a third zone which is becoming increasingly obvious as we approach the end of the century: the "zone of independent judgment." It is my observation that all of us demand of others the privilege of making independent judgments in selected areas. We also expect these judgments to be respected. This applies to the ditch digger as well as to the laboratory researcher although the nature and range of decisions may vary greatly. To deprive one of this capability (right?) is to reduce the human being to a machine part. It simply will not do.

It follows, of course, that observance by the organizational superior of the subordinate's "zone of independent judgment" will often result in actions of a different nature than the order-giver would choose. This should be expected. It is always implied when one shares the decision-making process with another. Sometimes, it is true, the results are less than satisfactory, but there are other occasions when they are better than the principal could have ordered or achieved. There is the added benefit when the subordinate makes the choice that a feeling of increased responsibility results also.

Mary Parker Follett, one of the earlier, outstanding observers of management practice, put forward her "law of the situation." Given agreement on objectives, on the facts, and on the situation, the solution to the problem being addressed will not vary greatly among those levels which concern themselves with it. This is a powerful argument for acceptance of the "zone of independent judgment." It is also an argument for suasion as against order-giving.

In Summary. . .

If authority, as this chapter has suggested, lies largely in the eye of the beholder, we should not be too greatly disturbed by such a revelation. Those of good will clearly outnumber those of other turns of mind, and a willingness to give over a large portion of one's days to an organization carries with it the desire to do what the compact calls for. The fact that one is in a subordinate role does not make one of less good will or, necessarily, have less interest in the success of the enterprise.

The development of responsibility within the individual is clearly the best guarantee of effective performance, assuming that sufficient ability and adequate training are also present. It is the responsibility of managers to encourage and develop this acceptance. That it will at times be expressed counter to some of their own wishes should surprise no one. Most of us, however, prefer cooperation to conflict.

There are, of course, some caveats. What is asked of the individual must fall within the terms of the original understanding he or she may have about duties and obligations. It must make sense, and it must be reasonable and honorable as well. Otherwise, common law, common practice and common sense hold that one is no longer bound by it. If that time comes, there is much that can and will be done to thwart those who pretend to leadership. In the end, they will usually be the losers.

"The greatest enemy of authority," Hannah Arendt has reminded us, ". . .is contempt, and the surest way to undermine it is laughter."[11]

FOOTNOTES

[1]Winston Churchill, *The Second World War*, Vol. 1, Boston, MA: Houghton Mifflin Co., 1948.

[2]Douglas McGregor, *The Human Side of Enterprise*, NY: McGraw-Hill Book Company, Inc., 1960, p. 16.

[3]Chester I. Barnard, *The Functions of the Executive*, Cambridge, MA: Harvard University Press, 1938, p. 161.

[4]As quoted in *Business Week*, July 14, 1975, p. 12.

[5]George E. Berkley, *The Administrative Revolution: Notes on the Passing of Organization Man*, Englewood Cliffs, NJ: Prentice-Hall Inc., 1971, p. 22.

[6]*The Functions of the Executive*, p. 165.

[7]Charles Lindblom, *The Policy-Making Process*, Englewood Cliffs, NJ: Prentice-Hall Inc., 1968, p. 37.

[8]Judson Gooding, *The Job Revolution*, NY: Walker and Co., 1972, p. 20.

[9]*The Functions of the Executive*, p. 167.

[10]Herbert Simon, *Administrative Behavior*, NY: The Free Press, 3rd ed., 1976, p. 12.

[11]Hannah Arendt, *On Violence*, NY: Harcourt, Brace and World, 1969, p. 67.

PART II

PROBLEMS OF SIZE AND COMPLEXITY

CHAPTER V

POWER PROBLEMS AT THE MANAGERIAL LEVEL

The preceding chapter has addressed the matter of authority—what it is, who has it, and, more importantly, who determines who has it. This chapter is concerned with *power*—and the ways in which it is expressed.

Most people think of the manager as the epitome of organizational power. Indeed, managers do have power, as their positions, duties, responsibilities, status, and salaries suggest. But others occupying lesser roles in the organization have power, too, and in both individual and collective ways this is often greater than that of those who manage.

In fact, the powers managers are granted by those higher up often will mislead them with respect to what they can accomplish. They may be given such titles as director, administrator, governor, general manager, controller, commander and the like, suggesting that their role is one of directing, governing, controlling, and commanding those at lower levels. Even the relatively modest title of supervisor has a Latin root which means "over-seer" as if to distinguish between those who labor in the vineyards and those who stand over them to make sure that they do.

The "right to command" or the "right to expect obedience" are historically part of the organizational system, and the holders of such titles—even the most innocuous of them—are distinguished from their subordinates (those in lesser or *sub*-orders) by such stipulations. The office-holder, in fact, has a compact with those "above" to see that "orders" are carried out as given.

Now the facts of the matter are, as any experienced manager already knows, that power as well as authority is limited and, depending on the time and circumstances, one is often frustrated by the limitations under which one functions. As difficulties increase and troubles mount, the manager searches for an explanation of what has gone wrong. Are subordinates at fault? Are they incapable of doing what they are instructed to do? Are they consciously trying to undercut management?

Or perhaps the system is at fault. Has it failed in some crucial element? Is it a matter of communications lapse? (Poor communications is always a convenient scapegoat.) Are we sufficiently motivating those who work with us? Have we permitted red tape to overwhelm us? Or perhaps the authority we have is inadequate to do what needs to be done?

Finally, I suppose, each of us will ultimately look to ourselves for a possible explanation. Do we really have the leadership capabilities we assumed we had? Are we meeting the new requirements of managing as we should? Are we too permissive? Too autocratic? What should we be doing we are not now doing? Have we, in keeping with the Peter Principle, already exceeded our capabilities? What should we be doing differently?

It may be that both we and the system are indeed at fault. Most of us can, in fact, do better than we are doing and most systems do need improving. But it may also be that there are other explanations; and that while changes will undoubtedly still be necessary, there is no real reason why we should have guilt feelings about what is happening.

We know that in today's world the *power* of the manager—the power to hire, to fire, to set terms of compliance, to reward, and to reprimand—is severely limited. It is limited by law, by regulation, by contract, by agency directives, as well as by custom and practice. It is limited also by time and circumstances. But so is the manager's authority limited also, and for many of the same reasons. It makes no sense to talk about abstract authority or power. None of us lives in the abstract, and if we did, the other fellow, who is also part of the system, won't accept abstraction for actual fact. The fact is, as we have seen, managers today do not have *either* the power or authority they are presumed to have and cannot do many of the things that they are expected to do.

There will be those quick to point out that in given circumstances, the power of the manager has been increased. This may be so, but what we need also to take into account is that the power of a lot of others both within and outside the organization has increased also, and often out of proportion to the power of the manager. Let us be more specific about this.

This power which others have can be expressed in a variety of ways. While many of these are negative in character—that is, they can stop an action even when they can't start one—the power is no less real.

There are the matters of tenure, of seniority, and of contractual rights which often counter the power of the manager. There are government agencies to which the employee can protest that the employer is violating his or her rights, is acting in unsafe ways, or against the public interest. There are unions to whom one can turn. There are whistles to be blown or organizational secrets to be revealed. There are those in the community to whom one can turn for support. Some of them in fact write for newspapers.

The power of the individual vis-a-vis management is increased in many subtle ways as well. As the complexity of the organization grows, as the variety of its objectives increases and the multiplicity of priorities becomes more pronounced, greater dependence must be had on the willingness of employees at whatever level to do what is asked. Those at operational levels can make decisions—or fail to make them—which have impact on not only an entire system, but on the community as well. On a more limited scale, we know how persons occupying modest positions—as secretaries, clerks, supply officers, or contract agents—can, by withholding, deferring, or revising a service, delay the enterprise. The old parable of "for want of a nail, the shoe was lost" is multiplied many-fold in our complex and interdependent industrial society. "I do not rule Russia," complained Nicholas I, known to history as the Iron Czar, "Russia is ruled by 10,000 clerks." There are times, as all of us know too well, when one of those ten thousand makes what becomes the critical decision from which there is no recourse.

Let us examine this in more detail. The superior, whether a president, a director, a manager, or the holder of any of a hundred imposing titles, asks the subordinate to perform a particular task. For reasons which will be examined in more detail later, it is not done. What are the explanations that can be offered for not doing what is asked which will prove acceptable to higher ups? (Whether they are believed is quite another matter.) What can the subordinate offer for non-compliance that will avoid major punishment—and sometimes any punishment at all?

There is first the matter of receiving and understanding the assignment. This is primarily a matter of communication. If one does not get the message, surely one cannot carry it out. Nor can it be carried out if it is received but not understood. One cannot be held culpable either if one, for a variety of reasons, cannot perform it in the fashion required.

One can offer excuses for failure to comply: that it is not one's job; that it has been delegated to someone else; that the assignment is not a legal or even a reasonable one; that it violates some other order or instruction; that tools or equipment required are not available; that it violates one's own moral code; or that it has not been properly authorized. One can claim that the job was done and leave it to others to prove that it wasn't. One can even do something different. One can do part of the job and leave the remainder undone. One can alter the time and quality requirements. All of these fall within the discretion or judgment of the subordinate.

There are even more subtle ways of non-compliance. One can do what is done once, and then not repeat it, or overcomply, or suddenly become ill or inept and leave the assignment to others. One can try to convince one's superiors that the job does not require doing, or do what one is instructed to do but at the same time set in motion actions which will nullify it. One can indicate to others, either inside or outside the organization, what is happening and leave the rest to them. If such actions are repeated, the subordinate may be dealt with severely, but the practised hand knows when to stand and when to retreat. The superior often gets no warning, however, of what is likely to happen.

Why Non-Compliance?

Why should the subordinate want to act in so negative a way? Why might he or she want to exercise, either overtly or covertly, such power? Most of us, if we stop to think about it, know the answers.

Our society teaches men and women to think for themselves. Our organizations depend for their success on their doing so. We should not be surprised when the answers they achieve do not agree with our own. Ours is a society built on the importance of rationale. As one of my children once reminded me: "I'll do it because you're making me, but making me isn't a reason why." We learn the importance of justification at an early age, and it is reinforced by both our societal and educational systems. Yet we have only to recall our own work experience to be reminded of instance after instance where instructions have been given us without a word concerning the objectives they are expected to serve or an explanation for them. Indeed, a chronic problem of today's organizations is that so little attention is given to a sharing with others of either objectives or strategies for achieving them.

There are other reasons as well for non-compliance. The order-receivers are often in a better position than the order-givers to know what ought to be done but have difficulty in making suggestions with respect to it. Or perhaps they do not like the looks or the tone of the order-giver. In fact, they may not like the person at all. They may believe the request to be improper and perhaps illegal, as well as ill-advised. Their job security is involved or their ego is at stake. For a variety of reasons, the individual is not and cannot be an automaton who responds to a command as an electric current responds to a switch. When soldiers in Vietnam refused to follow a captain's command—and were charged by him with disobeying an order—a subsequent investigation of the incident recommended that there be no punishment. "Thank God.," the investigating officer told CBS News, "we've got young men who question."[1] This is explained by John Fisher to the effect that "true obedience does not lie in carrying out the orders of your superior; the truly obedient soldier carries out the orders his superior would have used if he knew what the hell he was talking about."[2]

The Societal Input

There is in fact a whole generation of men and women who question both authority and power. This is clearly a mark of our times. Traditional authority no longer has the influence it once had. Egalitarianism is in the air and an "I'm-as-good-as-he-is" way of thinking permeates our organizational structures as well as our society. Appeals to the flag, to national goals, and even to the law do not carry with them the clout they once had. If the Vietnamese War proved anything, it proved that.

Nowhere is this better realized than among those we have previously thought to have little or no real organizational power. As both society and the organization grow more complex, it is increasingly difficult to discover what went wrong, which circuit failed to produce what was expected of it, which person put the sand in the grease box or the monkey wrench into the machine.

No one likes to feel powerless in a society that exalts power. No one relishes subservience. No one takes pride in doing inconsequential or trivial things, no matter how necessary they are. And so one turns to ways by which one's essentiality can be shown. There is a native American tendency to "show them," whether it be George III or those in the executive suite, that we can fix their wagons if we choose. And sometimes we do choose!

We turn our backs on the commander when the critical order is being given, or as Nelson did at Copenhagen, we put the telescope to the blind eye so we will not see the orders we know are being given. There are many ways of turning a feeling of powerlessness into one of actual power. The old rule that "if you don't pay the cook, he will pay himself" is applicable here. Parkinson has a law which covers the subject: "Those who have little of importance to do will regard as important whatever they do." And so it is that they will find ways of reminding us of their presence even though the organization, and sometimes they themselves, suffer in the process.

One need not dwell on the number and variety of those at modest levels, in inconspicuous positions, whose contributions are vital to but who are virtually unknown within it. They are the clerks, the machine operators, the service people, the hourly laborers, the privates and the able-bodied seamen. They live, as Professor Rosabeth Moss Kanter has suggested, in the lines of supply and support that must be present if the system is to function properly.[3] These are the obvious ones. There are many others: those in positions which appear to have power but in effect have very little (such as first-line supervisors); various staff people; and old hands whose time has passed. Like those in Solidarity, they have discovered a hidden power—the power to determine not only what does or does not apply to them (authority) but also the ability to perform or withhold action. There are few among them who have not exercised these options at one time or another. They will undoubtedly continue to do so and often at the most inopportune or embarrassing moments.

What the Manager Can Do

How does the manager deal with such situations? There are no simple or easy answers. The wise manager, however, will do several things.

One will, first of all, try to understand the nature of the situation. The fact that traditional organization theory centralizes both authority and power in the leadership of the organization does not mean that this can be assumed for our current institutions. Quite to the contrary, both power and authority have increasingly become decentralized, and in a variety of ways. This is the nature of the environment in which the modern manager must work. It must be understood and accepted. All leadership positions have limited power. Leaders can go no further than their supporters permit them.

Secondly, the manager's primary—and continuing—task is to understand the nature and characteristics of the system which produce the goods and services being offered, and the roles various individuals play in it. By doing so, one will come to appreciate the contribution of each, how that contribution is seen, and hopefully some of the values which move those who are part of the process.

All of this is basic, but it is much more easily said than done. As individuals, most of us make every effort to understand the non-human environment in which we live and work—and do a fair job of it—but tend to fall back on shibboleths, simplisticisms, old wives' tales, and sheer fantasy when it comes to noting and understanding what goes on in human systems.

Managers who know and understand the processes by which work, whether a piece of paper or a thing of aluminium and steel, is produced will often have little or no grasp of the human feelings and behaviors which are involved in their production. On the one hand, we seek to know all there is to be known of chemical composition, of tensile strength, and of application characteristics, but we think of the human element, if we think of it at all, as if it were controllable by the mastery of some kind of organizational arrangement.

It is enormously important that the manager, at whatever level, understand the nature of the human systems that are at work both inside and outside the organization. This is the starting point. What happens from here on will be determined in large measure by the capability of these managers both as managers and leaders, and by the relationships they have with their associates at all levels.

Much has been said and written about both management and leadership that would have been better left unsaid. The manager is someone who performs an organizational role. Managers are chosen by those *above them* in the hierarchy. They are expected to represent the owners in the private sector and the governors in the public. Their role is basically one of systematizing behavior so that certain pre-selected objectives can be achieved. While managers are often leaders, their power is usually based on other than leadership skills.

Leaders, in fact, are "chosen" by those at lesser levels. What we call leadership is determined by followership. One may hold an organizational title but without those willing to follow, it is an empty thing. We are leaders because others are influenced by and elect to follow our suggestions, our instructions, and our example. Thus, *acceptance* becomes of major importance even in the most carefully structured and closely supervised organizations.[4]

Voluntarism so significant to successful followership can be, and is, achieved in a variety of ways. It is, of course, an anachronism of a society which is dominated by size and complexity that we have given much more attention to the behavior of small organizations and face-to-face groups than to large ones. Yet, despite this shortcoming, much more is known about the large organization than is put to use.

We know, for example, as the above suggests, that however competent in managerial skills managers may be, they need leadership skills as well. To be leaders, to have influence beyond the *directive* powers they already possess, they must be able to reach and convince those elsewhere—below them, above them, in other divisions, and even outside the organization—in rational, non-threatening, and persuasive ways.

An organization director might well think of himself or herself as someone continually running for office. The idea is not an unrealistic one. After all, the head of an organization must have the support of subordinates, and the "control" systems which are conventionally used have proven themselves inadequate to the task. Nor is the political analogy as far fetched as it might at first appear. Many of those at operational levels are often more receptive to the ideas the director holds than those at mid-levels, and to reach them one must use other than traditional organizational channels. I am not trying to make a manager into a politician but am suggesting that some of the approaches used in the larger society may not be inappropriate to the smaller one.

Such an approach is not really new although it is probably put more bluntly here. Philip Selznick, the sociologist, has suggested some of the things the administrative leader must do in his book on *Leadership in Administration*.[5] They are hardly what one will find in the more conventional management texts. Peter Drucker, who has written widely of the managerial role, indicates in *The Effective Executive* some of the most important leader tasks.[6] He builds upon these in *Management: Tasks, Responsibilities, Practices*, a far more thoughtful and definitive work.[7] On this subject, military management also has much to offer. The greatest commanders are not always those whose battlefield brilliance overwhelms their opponents. They are those who have sought to convey—often personally—to their troops what is going to be needed and how each soldier fits into the pattern. Alan Moorehead has provided us with a great deal of information on how one commander, in this instance Montgomery, sought to inform and encourage his troops in preparation for the cross-channel invasion which he knew to be only a few months away.[8] Montgomery's approach was unique only in the size of his army and the extent to which he went to reach his soldiers and lesser officers.

A task of the leader, as Selznick has suggested, is not only to define the purpose or objective to be sought, but also to play an active role in "value infusing" and "institution building." The true leader becomes an institutional embodiment of purpose as Montgomery became for the British Tommy. ("The task of leadership is not only to make policy but to build it into the organizational social structure.")[9] This is much more than a mere managerial assignment. As Leonard Sayles has put it:

> Leadership must be active, not passive; authority must be exercised
> to be accepted. The strong, distant, placid, and silent types idealized in
> fiction are not the leaders of the real world.[10]

I am more sure of some of the things managers ought *not* to do than what they should do. This is what the situational and the contingency approaches have in common—a recognition that different people, times, places, and work to be done, will require different approaches. And this is, of course, what managing is all about. Otherwise, things would work out as the textbooks would have them. Herbert Kaufman has reminded us:

> When managers die and go to heaven, they may find themselves in charge of organizations in which subordinates invariably, cheerfully, and fully do as they are bid. Not here on earth.[11]

Let us have no illusions. The manager's assignment is a difficult one and is likely to become even more so. The tools available, no matter how useful, are by themselves insufficient to the task. This is why the manager must discover ways beyond the conventional to obtain the followership that is demanded.

The approach I suggest, although realistic, goes to the heart of some of the most sacred and best preserved of organizational beliefs. Among them are those dealing with managerial authority—the right to expect and obtain compliance and obedience—and chain of command, which passes this authority with limitations to other levels. The evidence is, as Barnard, McGregor and others have reminded us, that this is often less fact than fiction, and it is high time that it was understood.

If organizations are to succeed in the purposes for which they exist, new approaches must be found for producing the acceptance, the commitment, and the capability of those who make up the bulk of the organization's population. Power exists at all levels but if it is not used responsibly, it will be used in other ways. A large share of the manager's time, energy, and intelligence must go to seeing that this does not happen.

FOOTNOTES

[1] As quoted by Max Ways in "More Power to Everybody," *Fortune*, May 1970, p. 174.

[2] "The Easy Chair," *Harper's Magazine*, March 1970, p. 28.

[3] Rosabeth Moss Kanter, "The Power Failure in Management Circuits," *Harvard Business Review*, July-August 1979, pp. 65-75.

[4] This point is developed in David S. Brown, "Leadership and Followership: The Twin Ingredients," *Management Quarterly*, Fall 1979, pp. 26-34.

[5] Philip Selznick, *Leadership in Administration: A Sociological Interpretation*, Evanston, IL: Row, Peterson and Co., 1957.

[6] Peter Drucker, *The Effective Executive*, NY: Harper & Row, Publishers Inc., 1966.

[7] Peter Drucker, *Management: Tasks, Responsibilities, Practices*, NY: Harper & Row, Publishers Inc., 1973.

[8] Alan Moorhead, *Eclipse*, NY: Harper & Row, Publishers Inc., 1945, pp. 92-94.

[9] Selznick, *op. cit.*, pp. 62-63.

[10]Leonard Sayles, *Leadership: What Effective Managers Really Do. . .And How They Do It*, NY: McGraw-Hill Book Company, Inc., 1979, p. 56.

[11]Herbert Kaufman, *Administrative Feedback: Monitoring Subordinates' Behavior*, Washington, DC: Brookings Institution, 1973, p. 2.

CHAPTER VI

THE IMPACT OF SIZE ON MORALITY: BIGNESS AND ITS EFFECT ON BEHAVIOR

There is substantial evidence that bigness *qua* bigness has had, and is continuing to have, a major impact on morality in America. The large size of so many of our organizations and institutions, private as well as public, is in fact shaping community *mores* in ways contrary to accepted national patterns.

For years we have believed that being big is also beautiful, that it is more efficient, and that we must be big in order to survive. We are a big country, with a large population and very large needs, and organizational bigness follows automatically. Further, by their nature, large organizations are likely to be more "business-like" than smaller ones. They can afford better facilities, more sophisticated equipment, and greater expertise than their smaller counterparts. Their names are familiar, and the fact that they are suggests permanence, predictability, and respectability. This, however, is only one side of the coin.

The other is that large organizations have larger, more vital interests to protect; are more likely to see their own survival as essential to the society; are themselves cultural centers not always consistent with the culture of the larger community; and seek to pursue these interests by extending their influence in a variety of ways into the society. Being large, their effect is pronounced.

A book, *Organizational America*, by William Scott and David Hart, two eminent and scholarly observers, has recently appeared to remind us that we are, in fact, part of an organizational society and, ergo, the victims of it.[1] What best serves these organizations, they suggest, is what we are most likely to get. This is the matter of the *effect* which distinguishes the elephant from the cricket. The impact of large organizations, from governmental agencies to giant corporations, is substantial, dwarfing smaller institutions.

"Modern organizations," Professor Scott himself had written earlier, "have influenced us profoundly, but so quietly and so benevolently that we are scarcely aware that they are the major agencies of value change in our country."[2] How could it be otherwise? How can such institutions as the Army, the Internal Revenue Service, General Motors,

IBM, the church, the American Medical Association, the AFL-CIO and the National Rifle Association *avoid* having influence? How, indeed, given the size of their memberships, their resources, what they produce, and what their leaders believe? In fact, it is their business to have influence.

However, large organizations do not necessarily serve us better than smaller or medium-sized ones. Nor should we overlook the fact that size has its price, and that often it is a price we cannot afford to pay. While they may practice, as has often been observed, a microcosmic integrity, they are open to macrocosmic practices of a quite different character. Though they may act in good faith, this does not mean these actions square with conventional *mores*.

Organizations by their very nature are self-serving, and large organizations, for many reasons, are surely the most self-serving of all. The values they pursue may be at odds with those of client, community, nation, and even their own employees. And because of the resources they control, large organizations have more influence than do their smaller prototypes. Let us examine these issues further, in relation both to business and to government.

The Private Sector

In the private sector, there is documentation of a variety of behaviors that are contrary to American values, ethics, morality, propriety and responsibility. They include: product misrepresentation; production of inferior and/or dangerous goods; bribery of officials; kickbacks; despoliation of the environment; lying and cover-up about company misdeeds; and in-house practices which affect officials, employees and others.

If one looks only to the last two decades, the list of large and prestigious organizations which have violated the norms of a reasonably tolerant society is relatively long. We are treated to the sorry spectacle of companies knowingly—admittedly knowingly—loosing wastes into our rivers and streams, polluting the air with chemicals, bribing prospective customers, accepting kickbacks, and then having their senior officials lie about all this. One does not have to be an admirer of Ralph Nader and his associates to know that all is not well.

Government Also

The private sector is not the only offender. If bigness is indeed the villain, its effect is apparent in the public sector as well as in institutions which are neither public *nor* private. A government agency composed of some of the best educated, most highly skilled and dedicated individuals may be guilty of many things that violate conventional norms. Of these, bribe taking and misappropriation of funds are probably among the least consequential. What is of far greater moment are individual and institutional practices which violate not only individual rights but basic rules of decency as well. Large public organizations and the individuals who act for them have been found guilty of: knowing misrepresentation and outright falsehood; destruction of evidence; improper uses of authority; collusion with those they were created to regulate; wastefulness, profligacy and redundancy; indifference to individual rights; and in-house practices not greatly different from those cited against private companies.

We do not suggest how often each of these actions occurs; nor do we point to specific guilt. We simply observe that things are done in large organizations that would not as likely be done in small ones, and that because these organizations are large they have greater impact on the society as a whole.

That our governmental system is able to deal with some of these improprieties should not blind us to the fact that they exist, and that it is likely the majority go unpunished and very often unnoticed. The tragedy of Watergate was not so much what happened as it was the revelations from the playing of the tapes of the ways which high level persons, including a president and an attorney general, were approaching the business of governing.

No less a person than a former Secretary of Defense, Robert A. Lovett, himself a veteran of nearly 25 years of governmental service, testified before the Jackson Committee (U.S. Senate) that he had found it prudent never to "use any governmental statistic without checking the source. Skepticism," he went on to say, "is the most essential quality in evaluating military intelligence, or indeed, any governmental statement, diplomatic or otherwise." It is a sobering commentary.

Size and Its Effect

. There is something about bigness which titillates the American soul. We are a large country with a large population. We deal in large figures, whether dollars, distances, goods, or equipments. E.F. Schumacher in his *Small is Beautiful*[3] had much to say about the virtues of smallness, but the traditional American view is that being big is even more beautiful—and essential as well. We have, in fact, a love affair with bigness as long as we do not look too carefully into what it contains.

We know that bigness offers many advantages. It means (to some, at least) power, affluence, capability and survival. But it can produce side effects which we neither want or need. Bigness, for example, creates its own moral codes. High among these is loyalty to the organization. The late Professor Charles Frankel, after a stint as Assistant Secretary of State for Cultural Affairs, observed that organizational loyalty "is the source of the richest pleasures of public life, and it is also one of the reasons for the curious phenomenon which shows up so often, of governmental imperviousness to external influences,"[4] Weisbrand and Franck agree. In *Resignation in Protest*, they point out:

> The person who sacrifices team loyalty in order to pursue a competing value, such as integrity, is likely to have brought to bear against him the coercive weight of that society's historically conditioned sense of self-preservation. Societies, groups, organizations, systematize the process of making value-judgments. Indeed, they systematize the very process of perceiving reality. Woe to the individual who contradicts the organization's values and perceptions.[5]

The matter of loyalty—and to whom—is a troubling one, made more complex by the large organization and its various hierarchies. It is easy in the large organization to mistake loyalty for propriety and zeal for good judgment. It is easy also to apply loyalty selectively and, conveniently, to overlook others. The conventional approach, however, is to show loyalty primarily to one's immediate superiors, rather than to higher-ups. This is probably the safest course of action, but it leads sometimes to inappropriate results.

The consequences of actively opposing those in executive positions, or for that matter, the company norm, is a dangerous piece of business even when one is right about the facts. It seems as though no one likes the informer; and that most people will prefer to see the whole business swept under the rug than revealed in public.

The large organization increases the power of those who speak for it. Like a microphone it magnifies their effect, and encourages them to do things which they might not otherwise risk. This is evident in law enforcement agencies where policemen, tax collectors, inspectors and others clothed with bureaucratic authority often seem to take a personal delight in bullying others. It is a phenomenon which is less likely to be practiced by those who speak only for themselves or for small organizations.

Bigness increases the stakes for employees. It is the case of the frog in the puddle: the bigger the puddle, the more it offers the frog. A characteristic of the modern large organization is the potential it holds out to those who are "climbers." They do the things which propel them to the top, proper or not.

Those who follow unethical as well as illegal practices undoubtedly do so for a variety of reasons. Many of these are already familiar to the public. On the surface, they may be persuasive enough. The international corporation is tempted to bribery because in Country X "everyone does it"—which may, indeed, be true. The large corporation, because so many people depend for their livelihood on it, may see an unsavory deal as one which truly prevents unhappy economic consequences. Or a company which permits an untested product to go to market—or worse permits one which initial testing has shown to be inferior or unsafe—can do so under the guise of needing more "road experience" to make it what it ought to be. Experts can be counted on, like lawyers, to disagree. Risk-taking is always a requirement of modern management, and it can be argued with considerable logic that if one were to require "proof positive" of the wisdom of every venture before it were undertaken, very little would ever be done. Thus are rationalizations devised.

The large organization offers opportunities also for game-playing where units work in ignorance of each other or pretend to do so. Subordinate managers may "take the blame" for concealing malfeasance from the head of the organization who, like the queen bee, is protected by their doing so. This, of course, undercuts traditional ideas of responsibility but it often gets the company or government agency off the hook. It is a characteristic of large organizations that no one knows fully what goes on. Some may pretend that they do, computer printouts being what they are, but one who believes this is only deceiving himself. And, of course, even if it could be known, it could not be controlled.[6]

Those who may have actually made a decision in question, deep down in the bowels of the ship, are free to find other ways of escaping responsibility. It is not really difficult. The fleeing criminal loses himself in the crowd, and the decision maker who wishes to remain anonymous has only to hide behind the record. Hannah Arendt has put it this way:

> Bureaucracy is the rule of an intricate system of bureaus in which no men, neither one nor the best, neither the few nor the many, can be held responsible, and which could properly be called rule by Nobody. (If, in accord with traditional political thought, we identify tyranny as government that is not held to give account of itself, rule by Nobody is clearly the most tyrannical of all, since there is no one left who could even be asked to answer for what is being done. It is this state of affairs,

making it impossible to localize responsibility and to identify the enemy, that is among the most potent causes of the current world-wide
rebellious unrest, its chaotic nature, and its dangerous tendency to get
out of control and run amuck.)[7]

Yet in many respects, large organizations have a tighter hold on the
individual than do smaller ones. The mid-career executive certainly, and
even many of those in the upper levels, is at the mercy of those in
executive positions. Most such people are tied by profession to certain
lines of work and by years of service to retirement systems which may
be open to company manipulation. "The company man," Michael
Maccoby has reminded us, "bases his sense of identity on being part of
the protective organization. At his weakest, he is fearful and submissive,
seeking security even more than success."[8] He is often as fully inden-
tured to the institution as the serf to the land.

The larger the organization, the more secure it can become. The old
axiom that "you can't fight City Hall" has its modern equivalent in
either the large public or private agency. Most organizations, private
and public, which have been criticized for various forms of malfeasance,
have gotten off with modest fines and mild scoldings. Rob the local
liquor store and you're likely to go to jail, but bribe an official whether
of this or another government, put sub-standard products on the market, participate in large-scale collusion, or participate in the big lie, and,
with a little luck and the right kind of lawyers, nothing very dire will
happen. After all, you can't put either a corporation or a Government
department in jail.

The bigger the organization, the greater the possibility of its setting
its own standards.

The Effect on the Participants

There is another side to large organizations which has major effect
on the *mores* of the community—the inside. This may well be one of
the more important by-products of the organization and may have the
more permanent moral effect. Weber himself is authority for the point
that "as bureaucracy develops the more perfectly, the more it is 'de-
humanized,'" [9] Argyris, Bennis, Hummel, Downs, Thompson, Presthus
and many others have written despairingly of it. Hummel puts it this
way:

> Bureaucracy, then, separates human beings in two ways: (1) it sep-
> arates individuals from other individuals with whom it was supposed to
> provide a link; (2) it separates individuals from themselves. This in-

volves two forms of separation—separation between roles, and the detachment of roles from an integrating self.10

Not only is the human fit a poor one, but many of those who serve large organizations over long periods of time develop such characteristics as frustration, lethargy, cynicism, dependency, and other types of what Thompson calls "bureaupathic" behavior. These are communicable social diseases, and one does not have to be a part of the bureaucratic process to suffer from them. In the mass, they produce a malaise which trusts neither government nor anything else and by spawning a kind of "every man for himself" philosophy undermines the basis for effective cooperative action.

A generation ago, V.O. Key, Jr. had this to say:

> A seasoned bureaucracy, without heroic measures to the contrary, tends to become attached to the time honored ways of doing things, hostile toward innovation, lacking in initiative, and timid. These qualities are admirable at the right time and place, but the next few decades in the United States will hardly be the time and place for pleasant habituation to the customary.11

What Can Be Done?

If we conclude, as it is sensible to do, that large organizations, private as well as public, will be with us for some time to come, we must be prepared to tolerate many of the things they are currently doing. But that does not mean that we should cease our efforts to make them more our tools and less our masters. If largeness leads to unwanted patterns of morality, then we should certainly try to address the things that cause them. The good news is that there is increased awareness of large organizational effect on the part of a young, new group of corporate as well as political leaders who feel a greater consciousness of the social ethic. They can be expected to make a number of useful changes in old ways of doing things.

There is also an increased interest in the study of large organizations to which the small but growing literature attests. Most of those writing of it are also critical of it. The Freedom of Information Act of 1970 is an effort to bring into the open what had previously been hidden. Legislation to provide protection for "whistle blowers," those brave souls who have gone public with information which the public clearly needs to know about, is a further example. A 1981 statute has gone so far as to set up a reward system for those who report examples of mismanagement, waste and wrongdoing. We do not yet know, of course, how well it will work.

One of the more positive things which can be done is to understand the relationship between the size of organizations and how they behave. We cannot dispense with large organizations but surely we can be reminded not to make them larger or more pervasive. And we can also seek ways to limit those behaviors which we neither want nor need.

This may not be as difficult as, on its surface, it seems. As organizations grow in size, they tend to become in many respects more decentralized. With the local office, the retail outlet, the profit center, and the project group, one may find even in those organizations which emphasize a top-down management approach the rudiments of democratization. This does not by itself assure the achievement of a new ethic, but it is a reminder of the existence of pluralistic forces which will make themselves felt in new and diverse ways.

The shape of organizations is changing in other ways as well. No company today of any size and few public agencies are without computer systems. While these are primarily for internal use, they affect what the organization does by the records they create. Internal audit systems, while slower to materialize, are becoming more commonplace. They can be found throughout much of the Federal government and in most large corporations. State and local governments have lagged far behind. Internal audit is better able to deal with problems of a micro than macro nature but, by its existence, is a reminder that conventional forms of wrong-doing will at least be investigated. Because of their nature, however, they cannot be expected to deal with many of the kinds of transgression earlier identified.

The ombudsman (where it exists), the investigative journalist, the Congressional committee, the university researcher, and the interested citizen or consumer group are all likely remedies. Each has a potential for discovery and disclosure which will at least alert the proper persons to what is happening. They are in themselves hardly sufficient, but in concert they are capable of triggering a process which has made itself felt in many ways. That they have focused upon the specific instances rather than upon the sources is hardly cause for criticism.

Legislation which makes available to reporter and citizen alike records which have previously been hidden from them in the vaults of bureaucracy has made those who work there more fully aware of the implications of what they do. There are few things which the wrong-doer finds more ominous than public exposure. The fact also that the courts have shown a greater willingness than heretofore to look into organizational processes is having its effect. The class action suit opens both private corporations and government agencies to the possibility that they may have to pay for their transgressions.

Such events cannot fail to have their effect upon what the organization does and also upon its form and behavior. New patterns are needed which will make the individual, so often anonymous in our vast institutions, responsible for what he or she has a hand in doing. New devices must be found by which citizens/clients, so important a factor in the system, can better protect themselves from it.

There needs to be also a larger sensitivity on the part of those who provide organizational leadership to the impact of what they and their associates are doing upon the society as a whole. There is some evidence that this is already occurring but the process is slow. Even though many of these men and women have a far greater awareness of their social responsibilities than their predecessors, they have yet to understand fully and sensitively the inverse relationship between size and morality.

FOOTNOTES

[1]William Scott and David Hart, *Organizational America*, Boston: Houghton Mifflin Co, 1979.

[2]William Scott, "Organicism: The Moral Anesthetic of Management," *Academy of Management Review*, Jan. 1979, p. 21.

[3]E.F. Schumacher, *Small is Beautiful: Economics as if People Mattered*, NY: Harper & Row, Publishers Inc., 1973.

[4]Charles Frankel, *High on Foggy Bottom*, NY: Harper & Row, Publishers Inc., 1968, p. 54.

[5]Edward Weisbrand and Thomas M. Franck, *Resignation in Protest*, NY: Grossman Press, 1975, p. 3.

[6]For more on this, see Anthony Downs, *Inside Bureaucracy*, Boston: Little, Brown & Co., 1967, pp. 132-143.

[7]Hanna Arendt, *On Violence*, NY: Harcourt, Brace and World, 1969, pp. 38-39.

[8]Michael Maccoby, "The Corporate Climber Has to Find His Heart," *Fortune*, Dec. 1976, p. 100.

[9]For further comments on the same theme, see B. Bendix, *Max Weber: An Intellectual Portrait*, NY: Doubleday, 1960, pp. 455-456 *et seq*.

[10]Ralph P. Hummel, *The Bureaucratic Experience*, NY: St. Martin's Press, Inc., 1977, p. 48.

[11]V.O. Key, *Politics, Parties and Pressure Groups*, NY: Cromwell Publication Co., 1958, p. 763.

CHAPTER VII

THE BUREAUCRACY AND FOREIGN POLICY

In one of his more spontaneous and garrulous moments, Calvin Coolidge said "the business of America is business." In the same vein, the business of Washington is government. Anyone who can help make that government better understood has made a welcome addition to both the literature and the system.

This is what Morton H. Halperin and his two associates have done for foreign policy. In doing so, they have provided an insightful overview also of what goes on in large organizations. Those who would understand what happens in these organizations, and why, are referred to their book, *Bureaucratic Politics and Foreign Policy*.[1]

We are particularly enlightened by the "why." The men and women described in this book and often quoted are among the brightest, most dedicated to be found anywhere. They believe strongly in the specifics of what they are doing, which is part of the problem.

Halperin's concern with foreign policy began as a participant, first in the Defense Department's Office of International Security Affairs and later as a National Security Council staffman in the White House. He has accordingly had considerable opportunity to observe and think about bureaucratic behavior. The book's sources are primarily the published work of those who have served the government—or observed it—at the highest levels. Now, freed of their obligations, they have told it in their memoirs, their autobiographies, and their private conversations the way they actually saw it. Halperin's achievement is in the generalizations he and his associates have developed. While their primary concern, as indicated earlier, is with the making and carrying out of foreign policy, this is also a study in large organizational behavior.

The book is divided into three major sections, the first of which deals with the participants and the interests they represent; the second, with the actual making of foreign policy decisions; and the final one with how they are acted upon—or, sometimes, as the evidence indicates, not acted upon.

The policy designers include not only the President and his major advisers—names every schoolboy knows—but many lesser officials as well. It is the latter who make intelligence reports, write papers, send telegrams, devise institutional positions and conduct day-to-day business. The viewpoints of these technocrats not infrequently collide with national interest, and may or may not prevail over it.

The Navy has dragged its keels more than once when both White House and Congress wanted a new or different approach to a problem than it was prepared to give but so have other agencies. Many an inter-bureau fight has marred relationships between CIA, Defense, and State and on a number of occasions it has looked as though the participants were more interested in protecting their rears and their careers than in supporting national goals.

"An organization," Halperin reminds us, "will accept new functions only if it believes that to refuse to do so would be to jeopardize its position with senior officials or if it believes that the new function will bring in more funds and give the organization greater scope to pursue its 'own' activities." Or again: "An organization resists functions which it believes may interfere with career patterns. . .;" and ". . .bureaucrats give close attention to the likely effects of any change of policy or patterns of action on the morale of the organization, and they shun changes which they feel will have a severe effect on morale." Finally: "Organizations are vigilant not only about their absolute share of the budget but also about their relative share of a larger budget."

There are many ways of gaining the ear and eye of the President, some straightforward and well-established, others imaginative, still others devious and dubious. The press, as everyone must know by now, is important as a means of getting one's views across at all levels. Foreign governments sometimes serve a similar purpose. Occasionally, Halperin relates, an American ambassador in the field can stimulate the government to which accredited to make a request that will influence U.S. policy making.

The decision that is made is often not the end of the matter but merely a new and different phase in the process. The decision has to be carried out and unless those responsible have reason to agree with the decisions, there may be further difficulty. The Kennedy order to remove missiles from NATO bases in Turkey was not carried out, as the President himself belatedly discovered during the Cuban crisis, and for very good reason. Those with this assignment felt that they had been given conflicting directives, and in the face of Turkish opposition (after all, Turkey was a pact member) sought additional instructions. They also added their own arguments.

The experienced bureaucrat has many options. Subordinate levels, Halperin reminds us, often fail to pass down orders they have doubts about (as with the Turkish bases); they may change the "cosmetic image" but not the reality; they may do something else (yes, it can usually be defended); they may delay or obfuscate; they may obey the letter but not the spirit of the orders; and much else.

Observations of this kind may seem mild stuff when compared to Watergate but those who concern themselves only with enuciating policy should make note.

This is not presented by Halperin by way of either criticism or exposure; his purpose is to provide understanding. "A government," he says, "is not, in fact, a single individual with a single purpose and an ability to control completely his actions. Rather, each government consists of numerous individuals, many of them working in large organizations. Constrained, to be sure, by the shared images of their society, these individuals nevertheless have very different priorities, and are concerned with very different questions." This may bring the book to a close but it does not, of course, end the matter.

The professional arm of the government, the bureaucracy, whether it likes it or not, is, along with the President and the Congress, suffering from public disesteem these days. It is in fact on trial. (If you doubt this, see what the press, the polls, and the politicians are saying, or better still, listen to your neighbor.) Many will read the Halperin report as a further indicment of the bureaucratic system. It behooves those who are a part of it, therefore, to look not only to their own performances but to the way the public sees them.

This book, serious and thoughtful though it is, will probably make few people sleep more easily.

FOOTNOTE

[1]Morton H. Halperin (with the assistance of Priscilla Clapp and Arnold Kanter), *Bureaucratic Politics and Foreign Policy*, Washington, DC: Brookings Institution, 1974, 340 pp.

CHAPTER VIII

ORGANIZATIONAL SIZE AND WHAT CAN BE DONE ABOUT IT: IS BUREAUCRACY THE ONLY WAY?

There are few ideas more likely to arouse negative responses today than those having to do with bureaucrats and bureaucracy. What Weber hailed as the system having "technical superiority over any other form of organization" has over the years fallen seriously in public esteem.[1] Whatever their other differences, people in all countries are in substantial agreement that bureaucratic systems, for a wide variety of reasons, are not performing in ways they find acceptable.

The seriousness of such criticisms is emphasized by the distinguished pollster, Louis Harris. Of the Federal government, Harris reports:

> By 69-18 percent, a majority do not think that the best people are attracted to serve public life. By 84-10 percent, a landslide majority think we do not have a federal government that is almost wholly free of corruption and pay-offs. By 61-26 percent, a majority do not think the guiding principles of the federal government are to put the good of the country above special interests. . . .By 51-36 percent, a majority do not think that most public officials are more dedicated to helping the country than being out for themselves. Most serious of all, by 48-38 percent, a plurality feels that most public officials do not really care what happens to the people.[2]

Admittedly, these figures lump political appointees with civil servants but other studies show that, when taken separately, the latter stand no higher with the public. At state and local levels, there is an even greater lack of confidence in those who carry on the day-to-day business of government.

Yet despite the negativism of these judgments, Harris believes that something can be done to improve both the current performance and the image of those who make up our bureaucracies. First, however, they must recognize the extent of negative public feeling and be ready to respond to it. He concludes:

This is not cynicism by any measure. It is tough talk; it is talk from a constituency that probably is many leagues ahead of its leaders. I say to you, seize this positive opportunity while there is still time. For time can run out. *Please, seize it now, before it is too late.* [Emphasis his.] [3]

What Price Bureaucracy?

The Harris survey was of public agencies, but the results of other surveys of large private sector organizations have produced some of the same kind of criticisms. Because public confidence in and support for our institutions is essential, this has to be of great concern to all of us.

The starting point is obviously the large organization itself. This suggests several questions:

-- Is what we call bureaucracy either in its present or future forms adequate to the demands being placed upon it?

- Are large organizations, in fact, the only way in which goods and services can be delivered in quantity?

- Can their behavioral patterns be modified to bring them more in harmony with our needs?

- If not large organizations/bureaucracies, what is there?

These are serious questions which clearly must be addressed. But before this can be done, there needs to be some agreement on what we mean when we use the terms bureaucracy and bureaucratic.

Common usage holds that a bureau is an agency of government. Hence, bureaucracy for government as a whole. Both the noun, bureaucrat, and the adjective, bureaucratic, have taken on pejorative colorations. They apply also to the private sector where they mean much the same thing that they mean in government.

The connotations that such terms produce—remote, officious, bungling, expensive, self-serving, etc.—are by no means confined to modern times. There is little difference between the functionaries described by Balzac in *The Civil Servant* over a hundred years ago ("Bureaucracy is a giant mechanism operated by pygmies") and those caricatured in modern society. Charles Dickens wrote at length about them in *Little Dorrit* (who was deeply involved with the Circumlocution Office) and Anatole France had similar observations to make in *Penguin Island*. Franz Kafka's writings (*The Trial*, for example) are of a more sobering nature. "File clerks," an Iranian observer has noted, "after a while may even have trouble finding themselves." [4] They certainly do in Kafka.

Most of us have been greatly frustrated in our dealings with large organizations, and for a variety of reasons. We find it difficult to reach the right persons, and when, at long last we do, we find often that they cannot help us. In fact, dealing with a large bureaucracy is a little like walking through a swamp on stilts. Charles Frankel in writing of his experiences a few years ago as a very frustrated Assistant Secretary of State, speaks of "apoplexy at the center and anemia in the extremities."[5] Adlai Stevenson has suggested that "your civil servants serve you right."

The bureaucratic form has been identified for us and a rationale provided for it by Weber, although, as Jacoby has indicated, it has a much longer history than his writings would suggest.[6] Simply stated, bureaucracy is a formal, rational, structured organizational arrangement in which units and individuals are related in pre-determined ways; boundaries are set; there is a uniform pattern of superior-subordinate division of authority; roles are specified; tasks are laid out; and careers fashioned in systematic ways.

Those filling jobs are selected on merit, having met pre-established requirements of the office. The job itself becomes the chief source of income of the incumbent who is given training in order to insure continuing competence. The organization follows prescribed rules so as to eliminate arbitrariness.

Most large organizations today, of course, fulfill Weber's requirements. Perrow has remarked that he cannot imagine one which is not bureaucratic in nature.[7] Neither can I.

Because rational patterns of behavior have been established, however, does not mean that the system itself will function in either effective or efficient ways.[8] As Herbst has suggested in *Alternatives to Hierarchies*:

> The bureaucratic model is a good theory in so far as it provides a simple logically consistent model, and this is also the reason for its potential inadequacy. If implemented the organization may not be able to function and survive without the development of informal practices and relationships. Where this happens, it is possible to spend large amounts of time in organizational planning and change projects which operate in terms of theory, but may not relate to the way the organization actually functions or may need to function.[9]

There are, of course, many factors which bear upon the manner in which those within the organization perform their functions. Four of these which are of particular importance are:

- The problem of size.

- Complexity.

- Escalating client demands.

- The deficiencies of conventional organizational theory.

1. *The Problem of Size.* One of the most pressing problems of our times is the management of bigness. Large organizations, of course, pose much more difficult problems than small ones, but the matter does not end there. We must also be concerned with large and interdependent systems which extend beyond the organization proper; with large (albeit limited) resources; and with large numbers of clients and others who either participate in or need to be satisfied by what is done.

Being big has a fascination about it and most Americans are attracted by it. Bigness means many things and has many advantages. It means power, affluence, capability and often survival. But largeness does not necessarily equal either greatness or goodness, nor does being big mean being more efficient, better organized, or more economical. It may not even mean being more effective, although it usually represents a greater availability of resources.

Smallness, in fact, is sometimes more powerful, and often more influential. It is usually more flexible and often more resourceful. It makes better use, for one thing, of the individual organizational member. There are many examples which bear out this point.

Bigness may be needed to cope with bigness, a not inconsiderable point. But there are occasions when smallness—or at least middle-sizedness—may be much more useful for such a purpose. In fact, large organizations have given considerable attention to ways of creating smaller, semi-autonomous operational units while at the same time remaining large. Thus, a kind of federalism results.

2. *Complexity.* Bigness, of course, leads to complexity, and complexity to a variety of problems which greatly affect organizational performance. This requires a quite different approach to managing than we have traditionally followed. What we are involved with is the guidance and coordination of multiple systems within the larger community. These systems are concerned not only with difficult and variable problems which reject conventional ideas of control but each is likely to be of a highly technical nature understood in its entirety—if at all—by only a few.

A recognition of the growing complexity of social systems has become increasingly one of the preconditions of modern management. A study, for example, conducted by the Center for the Study of Social Policy, a division of SRI International in Menlo Park, California, produced a number of hypotheses which managers of the future will face. These include the diminishing relative capacity of given individuals to comprehend, let alone deal with, the overall system; a decline in public participation in decision making; a lessening of public access to decision makers; growing system rigidity and dehumanization; a declining legitimacy of leadership; and the increasing vulnerability of the system itself to outside forces.[10] The recent nuclear plant difficulties at Three Mile Island near Harrisburg, Pennsylvania point up some of these problems.

"What with the tendency of one thing to lead to another," E.B. White has written, "I predict a bright future for complexity." That time has already arrived.

3. *Escalating Clientele Demands*. If they did nothing else, the spaceship voyages to the moon and beyond have left the man and woman in the street with the idea that nothing is any longer impossible. The tolerance they might once have had for bureaucratic imperfection has disappeared in a wave of new demands on already overloaded systems. Imperfection is seen as incompetence and fallibility as intolerable and unacceptable.

If we can send a spaceship to Venus or Jupiter, why can't we deliver a letter across town in less than three days? Why aren't the police doing more to prevent crime or catch law-breakers? Why do we continue to have huge potholes in our streets? Why must we tolerate roads blocked by snow? Why can't rebates and due bills be paid with the same efficiency as tax notices?

Needs and expectations for a variety of reasons have multiplied faster than our ability to deal with them. Not only do we need the material things of life—goods and services—but as Americans we are also redefining our rights and expectations. Equity is taking on a new meaning, and so is fairness.

We "need" to be informed, we "need" to participate, we "need" the opportunity to develop, we "need" to be heard. However reasonable these needs, they have their costs. They place severe burdens on delivery systems already overloaded. We are not really tolerant of systemic failures, but we expect performance on demand. As a former Air Force Secretary once wearily remarked, "The only one who can help us with some of the administrative problems we've gotten ourselves into died nearly 2000 years ago—and anyway, He's been preoccupied with other things."

4. *The Deficiencies of Conventional Organizational Theory.* Despite the major changes that have taken place in society over the past half century, we are still trying to solve many of the problems we face with approaches designed for other periods and other problems. This is particularly true of much of organization and management theory.

There is nothing, of course, sacred about organizational forms. They are merely systems by which people relate to each other. Yet, not only have we reified many of them but we have often deified them as well. I continue to be amazed by the fervor with which so many of my associates defend organizational patterns which are basically adaptations of earlier drill squad or factory floor models. We are today a white collar society which persists in following blue (or khaki) collar prescriptions. Some of even the best organizational minds of our times have shown themselves incapable of divesting themselves of established master-servant ideas.

Although the past half century has witnessed more spectacular change than any previous period in human history, we still cling fiercely to static organizational arrangements and to ideas which continue to be concerned primarily with authority and control. Our approach to managing has been increasingly humanized, but it is not greatly different in its basic concepts than that devised by Frederick the Great.

Barnard observed that "organizations of complex character grow out of small, simple organizations." In doing so, they continue to perpetuate characteristics of the shop, the store, or the office. We have added to them, of course, new levels and introduced new functions as the organization has grown, and have tried to deal with the problems which have arisen by the use of new equipments and the introduction of new roles—those of coordinator, expediter, liaison officer, auditor, and most recently *ombudsman*—in order to make things work at all. We move from one reorganization to another when what really is needed are viable new concepts for the managing of the large systems and the large organizations which are endemic to our times.

The sociologist Daniel Bell has put it aptly:

> A change of scale is not simply a linear extension of size. As Galileo once defined it in his square cube law, a change of *size* is a change in *form*, and consequently in institution. Most of our older discussions of rights and responsibilities are modeled on an organizational form whose size is of vastly smaller magnitude than our own. It is this change of scale, in all its dimensions, and for all its consequences, that still has to be explored.[12]

Present organizational systems, it has become increasingly clear, are neither suited to the needs we have nor the people who are members of them. Argyris, Bennis, Hummel, Vickers, Beer and others have repeatedly called our attention to the systemic misfit.[13] And yet, we continue to seek out remedies based upon a preoccupation with control.

This is an *idée fixe* which I believe is more fundamental to the individual—and more strongly defended—than the views held about religion, sex, nationality or even honor. These change, but the idea of an organizational system without conventional hierarchies is one that most people seem incapable of understanding, let along accepting.

The Individual and the System

We cannot, it seems to me, resolve our problem without examining our organizational systems for what they are and what those who are part of them do.

The term "organization" is, or course, an abstraction. It is the name we give to a collectivity of relationships between individuals. Actions are taken by individuals, never by organizations. These individuals are influenced not only by those within the system but also by those outside it. They are influenced, as we know, by persons "above" them in the hierarchy but also by peers and associates and even by those "below." And they are greatly influenced by the culture of which they are a part.

When we criticize, say, the Internal Revenue Service, we are actually criticizing the way we perceive individuals behaving who are involved in the business of collecting taxes. We may lump them together for purposes of generalizing but we are actually complaining about the way in which individual auditors or examiners have dealt with us. We fulminate against what we call bureaucracy but the object of our displeasure is always an individual, whether he or she can be identified or not. And— it needs also to be said—most of those in large organizations cannot be identified, let alone be held accountable for what they do. This is what is so frustrating about it all.

Individual behavior can, of course, be changed. It may not be easy but it can be done. The first step is the identification and modification of those behaviors within large organizations which we find so troubling.

During the past three years, I have been working with graduate students in an effort to determine specifically the major criticisms of large organizations. We began with a fairly long list, but have now reduced it to some 20 items. Although we have tried to make each item fully discrete, there is, as might be expected, some overlay between them.

In its present form, the list has been seen by over 1400 persons. The survey recognizes the contributions which large organizations have made and are making to our society but its purpose is to identify the *five most serious large organizational deficiencies*. After all, these are the foci of citizen and client complaints, and if these are to be lessened, they must be individually addressed.

An estimated 90 percent of those who thus far have completed this survey are from the Washington area, with a considerable number of them members of large organizations themselves. Some of these, incidentally, are among the most vehement critics of bureaucracy, and for quite understandable reasons.

The chief criticism which the survey revealed was that large organizations (this term was used rather than bureaucracies) are "incapable of taking immediate action save in crises; are slow, ponderous, wedded to old habits and processes." Nearly 46 percent of those surveyed included this on their list of five.

The second most frequently noted criticism was that "they are efficient only to a point, declining in efficiency as their size increases beyond it." This was selected by 36 percent. It is an important observation. Given the high percentage of respondents who work in large organizations, it undoubtedly suggests their own day-to-day experience.

Over 35 percent agreed that "individual responsibility for what is done is difficult to establish or determine." Another 32 percent said that "they are more concerned with rules, regulations, and procedures than with achievement or objectives." In fifth place was the comment (31 percent) that "individuals and units are not well coordinated" and are "poorly integrated."

A growing complaint, a point made by Hummel as well as Thompson, Presthus and others, is that large organizations are "destructive of those who work in them; they induce bureaupathic behavior." This was supported by 30 percent. A criticism with some of the same overtones (in seventh position) was that "they are cold, impersonal, without real feeling for people" (28 percent). This, however, seems directed to clients and public.

The next four ranking criticisms are as follows, supported by at least 25 percent of the respondents:

They are wasteful and profligate; they encourage repetitiveness and redundancy.   26%

They place their own values and goals ahead of societal goals.   26%

They make misleading statements; not fully to be
    believed or trusted.   25%

They do not respond easily or readily to guidance or
    direction.   25%

What was surprising was that so many selected among their five major criticisms of large organizations points which, while appearing in the literature of bureaucracy, are not popularly associated with it. These included the comment that they "make misleading statements; are not fully to be trusted" (25 percent); "are secretive, uncommunicative, zenophobic" (18 percent); "accountable to no one" (10 percent); and "undemocratic" (eight percent).

Such criticisms can provide a focus for our efforts to modify or change bureaucratic patterns. If critics of large organizations say that they are incapable of taking immediate action, that they are slow and ponderous, and that they are wedded to old habits and processes, these problems can be addressed. Systems analysis, in fact, can be directed to the specific problem.

Now an interesting point is that not all large organizations are slow and ponderous nor are most of them slow and ponderous in all respects. The U.S. Postal Service has, for example, done a better job than it has received credit for, in moving vast quantities of mail over large areas. Supermarkets and department stores likewise move huge volumes of merchandise, some of it perishable. The Internal Revenue Service, whatever our criticisms of it, has shown itself able to classify, record, relate and audit billions of dollars and millions of pieces of paper. These agencies are able to do as well as they do because professional analysts have understood the nature of the problems they face and have been able to do something about them.

This does not mean that those who criticize bureaucracy for its ponderousness are wrong. What has happened in the instances cited above—and in many others which could be supplied—is that there has been a positive effort to remedy situations which require remedying. Elements in the system have been explored and analyzed, new methods and equipments devised and used, employees trained to meet the new requirements, and controls instituted to monitor and measure achievement.

In general, of course, a process that requires extensive participation will take longer than one where only a few are involved. Those situations where multiple clearances are now required (often by custom rather than by need) ought to be examined and alternatives explored. When actions can be distinguished and isolated, there is usually a way of modifying them.

Changes can be instituted in the large organization as well as in the small one. A majority of the criticisms which have been leveled against the large organization can be addressed—and something done about them—if there is an inclination to do so. However cumbersome and xenophobic the system, individual actions within it can be modified, given the right incentives. This can be a productive first step even if it may not provide an ultimate solution to the problem. Changing the image which people hold of bureaucracy is another matter, but when it becomes clear that behavior has really been altered, views usually change also.

What Large Organizations Do Well—and What They Don't

The idea that businesses must expand and grow or else face decline and eventual demise is so well established in American industry that it has become accepted dogma. The fact that, numerically, we are still a country where small businesses outnumber by far the large ones does nothing to alter the axiom. As for the public sector, the urge to grow and develop is equally obvious. Old bureaus rarely die, and new ones are regularly being created and extended. There are reasons for these growth patterns.

It follows naturally that the entrepreneur, public or private, if highly achievement-oriented, will seek to enlarge the holdings of the company even to the point where he is likely to lose control of them. Public administrators, on their side, see themselves as increasing in stature as the institutions with which they are associated increase in size. We build big buildings, drive big cars (at least until recently), and harbor large aspirations. Traditionally, prestige is gauged not only by the kind of work one does but also by the size of the resources we manage and the number who "work for us." There is the added fillip that large organizations more often than small ones produce large, tangible rewards. There is probably a little of the empire builder in all of us.

These are not, of course, the only reasons or even the most important ones for largeness. There are, indeed, in a society such as ours, large needs to be met. Largeness provides large resources and usually greater stability. Large organizations will ordinarily have a more ample supply of capital than smaller ones. They will also have access to a greater variety of human resources, and a larger and more demanding market.

The availability of capital is greatly important where major investments are required in plant, tools and equipment. The automobile companies are a case in point. Smaller companies, less well financed, are unable to undertake the investment in machine tools that is required. There is need for largeness also where there are heavy advertising costs to be borne, but there is something of a reciprocal here. Large companies, in fact, require large advertising expenditures to support their existence. So one easily becomes involved with a self-perpetuating spiral.

Largeness may be needed to cope with largeness. Clausewitz made the point that in war mass could only be countered with mass.[14] This argument has considerable merit but it can be overemphasized as the Vietnamese War suggests. A visitor to Pope John XXII is supposed to have asked him about the size of the Curia, the Vatican's administrative arm: "How many do you have working for you there, Your Holiness?" His reply: "Oh, the majority, I suppose." The story may be apocryphal but there is a point to it.

Largeness may not be a handicap where the work to be performed is simple, repetitive and continuing, and the market a relatively stable one. This does not require sophisticated organizing skill, and its basic patterns, as in the taking of tolls on highways or bridges, can be repeated wherever they occur.

Large, structured organizations appear where the product is standardized. If the system is a national one, where there is little difference among areas, as in tax collecting, there will be a single, large organization to do the job. The actual work may be done on a decentralized basis, but it will be part of an umbrella-type system.

There are undoubtedly other functions which large organizations perform passably if not well, but the list is not a long one. The large organization, whatever its other merits and despite its appeal to the entrepreneur has significant limitations.

Its Disadvantages

A listing of those things the large organization does not do well is more impressive.

Large organizations ordinarily do not inspire individual initiative. The individual, in fact, is often lost in them. Nor are loyalties as strong as they are in smaller, more personalized institutions. Bureaucracies are basically impersonal. Members, or members and clients, ordinarily do not enjoy close relationships.

Large organizations do not offer the same opportunities for individual development as do smaller ones. True, there may be more and better paying promotional opportunities, but the competition is greater and the rewards often less satisfying.

Large organizations are, in fact, enormously self-serving. They must always be concerned with their own survival—which causes them to do things which may be against societal interest. Also, those within them increasingly find ways of putting their own interests and requirements ahead of organizational interests which leaves the community in a poor third place.

They cannot easily fix responsibility, and for some of the same reasons. ("Mass conceals complexity rather than exposes it."—William D. Carey.)[15]

They encourage neither innovation nor creativity as well as smaller organizations do. To acquire either, the large organization must establish separate semi-autonomous units or else purchase what it needs from others.

Large organizations are usually inflexible. They have difficulty adjusting to changing needs and situations. Witness the problems of the automobile industry or the Department of Defense.

Large organizations do not take risks readily. They are basically conservative by nature. They have much to lose if they are unsuccessful. They find it easier to serve well-established goals, using accepted methodologies, than to seek new ones. "He who is firmly seated in authority," James Russell Lowell has reminded us, "soon learns to think of security and not progress."

There is evidence also that largeness *per se* affects morality. Large organizations, whether public or private, tend to create their own moral and ethical standards and these are in turn imposed on members, including those who lead them; on the community where they are located; and also on the mores of the larger society. For more on this subject, see Chapter VI, "The Impact of Size on Morality."

Downs suggests in his Law of Imperfect Control that large organizations are virtually uncontrollable. "No one can fully control the behavior of a large organization."[16] The large organization, like an iceberg, steers uncertainly. Those who have accustomed themselves most readily to it, however, have found ways to live with the drift.

One final point needs to be made. There is little or no evidence, despite popular views to the contrary, to support the idea that large organizations are more efficient than smaller ones. They certainly are not more economical.

How Bureaucracy Adjusts

Whatever their merits or demerits, large, bureaucratic-type organizations will undoubtedly be with us for some time to come. As long as needs escalate, and bigness continues to appeal, there will continue to be large organizations. As long as we pretend there are no alternatives, we will continue to have to tolerate them.

This does not mean, however, that the large organizations of the future will be the same as the large organizations of the past. Indeed, there is growing evidence that the shape of our institutions is already changing.

I do not subscribe to the thesis so strongly put forward by Bennis a few years ago that bureaucracy's days are numbered, nor, indeed, does Bennis himself hold as fully to that theory as he once did.[17] Actually, the large organization is taking on increasingly the characteristics of an association or confederation with large pockets of group and individual autonomy within it. There is an analogy here to Mies van der Rohe's celebrated observation in architecture that "less is more," although, in this instance it might more appropriately be "more is less." The larger the bureau, the less likely it is to be a bureau in the traditional pattern. An examination of some of the things that are happening today will confirm this.

There are already, in fact, many areas of considerable independence in the midst of some of our more highly structured bureaucratic systems. These systems within systems exist for a number of reasons. They may be separated by distance from headquarters. They may historically (as in the case of the church) have always possessed a large measure of independence. Those who lead them may have earned this independence either because of their special characteristics or because of the acknowledged devotion of their followers. They have been freed, accordingly, in a *de facto* if not *de jure* fashion, from standard controls.

Others have found a measure of organizational freedom because of the nature of the work they perform: difficult, dangerous, and unpleasant tasks; assignments where needed manpower is hard to find; or tasks of a research, developmental and creative nature. There is a large degree of autonomy where special purposes are to be served in even the most tightly controlled systems.

Businesses, as previously noted, have turned to the profit center because this encourages individual initiative and responsibility. The same has occurred in large and territorially dispersed governmental undertakings. A ship at sea is itself a center for action, and its autonomy as an operating system has been traditionally accepted even when it is part of a task force or fleet.

The American Federal system is an example of dispersed and independent systems. We have long recognized the legal rights and prerogatives of the "state within the state" and, beyond that, such units as the county, the city, the town or the special district. This does not make them any less a member of the larger Federal system. It is, on the other hand, recognition of the value of decision making and decision implementation at the level of action where those officially involved are best able to address the problems which arise. The value of the initiatives which such arrangements encourage should not be overlooked. They are, organizationally speaking, an argument for the soundness of organizations within organizations.

These have their equivalents in the private sector. The many systems of licensing and franchising which business has evolved are worthy of attention. The fast food places, the various hotel and motel chains, and the car rental companies, combine local energy and initiative with product or service standardization. The conglomerate which continues in its own lines of business with its own executives in charge is a further case in point. It must meet certain standards or requirements, but it would have to do so anyway. These are some of business' answers to the problem of managing bigness.

Sayles and Chandler in their analysis of the accomplishments of the National Aeronautics and Space Administration have produced abundant evidence of the interrelationships of organizational units under a variety of "holding company" patterns in the development, manufacture, assembly and operation of space vehicles.[18] The Social Research Center at the University of Michigan is an example of an organization operating within a large system, yet largely untouched by the bureaucratic patterns of the University.[19] There are many other examples.

The more we explore the nature of systems, the more similar patterns are revealed. Because the system is so important as a performing agent, we are inclined to permit it a large measure of autonomy in operation. What may have occurred as a matter of chance and been barely tolerated is now being planned and implemented.

Alvin Toffler, in *Future Shock*, suggested that the future is more likely than the past to be marked by a need for flexibility of approach.[20] That there will be a larger amount of what he calls "adhocracy" within our organizations seems so obvious as to require little comment. Those who helped to set present managerial patterns—Fayol, Taylor, Gilbreth, Weber and others, to say nothing of the military planners and organizers—were seeking "best ways" (often *single* best ways) of performing certain tasks. They sought to avoid the casual, the indifferent, the "unscientific," the nepotistic, and the unprofessional which marked the systems then in vogue. This is not, however, the problem we face today and, because it is not, there is no reason to pursue the same highly structured arrangements which earlier theorists as well as practitioners have recommended. The shopping center with its individually owned shops and boutiques can be, for a variety of reasons, superior to the department store. We do not need a corporate-owned filling station to satisfy our needs for fuel and service. One that is independently owned and operated is often far more satisfactory. We require, as Schumacher has suggested, "two things simultaneously, which on the face of it, seem to be incompatible and to exclude one another:"

> We always need both freedom and order. We need the freedom of lots and lots of small autonomous units, and, at the same time, the orderliness of large scale, possibly global, unity and coordination.[21]

What all of this is suggesting is that we have reached in many areas a point of diminishing returns as far as organizational size is concerned. If we cannot, for a variety of reasons, make the institutions we now have smaller in size, we can at least encourage their modification so as to lessen the bureaucratic effects of bigness. Certainly, we do not need to opt with knee-jerk regularity for largeness and its accompanying dysfunctional behaviors.

Wherefore Bureaucracy?

The answer to some of the questions raised earlier in this paper should by now be obvious. Large organizations—bureaucracies—*in their present forms* are not adequate to the needs they are being asked to serve. The criticisms of them, whether public or private, by professionals, clients, and members of the public at large, should leave no doubt on this score.

There are alternatives.[22] The most promising of these is to reduce organizational size and to revise existing systems of control. This can occur in a variety of ways. Indeed, as previously noted, it is occurring already with the proliferation of smaller, autonomous units within the larger systems.

Thus far, this has occurred more often by happenstance than by design, but there is increasing evidence, as previously noted, that it is now being planned and programmed by thoughtful and far-sighted managers. More attention needs to be given to these efforts.

The modification of individual behaviors within large organizations needs to be given greater attention also. Emphasis should be placed on the development of individual responsibility for what is happening—or not happening, as the case may be.

I foresee no end to bureaucracy as such. Indeed, I cannot imagine a system that will not emphasize planned, rational patterns of operation. But I do believe that ways can be found to identify and lessen aberrant, dysfunctional and non-productive behavior. One of these, certainly, is to become more fully aware of the effect of size and complexity on our institutions. We must become more sensitive also to the needs of citizens and clients, and more alert to ways of relating on-going systems to each other.

Accordingly, a four-point program is suggested as a starting point for further examination and exploration of alternatives to present bureaucratic models.

1. Study of Organizational Systems

More attention should be given to the study of organizational size and form and their effect on performance. We have been quick to criticize bureaucracy, but much less so to criticize bigness which is a characteristic most bureaucracies have, and have spent even less time on the serious study of it, and the dysfunctionalism it creates. We need to look more carefully at the cause-effect relationships between what we do and what happens as a result.

We need, in fact, to examine more carefully our experience with organizations of all sizes and shapes. The idea that there is basically only a single type—one where major emphasis is placed on control—is to disregard what our own experience has taught us. In particular, we need to concern ourselves with the inter-relationships of systems, and how these can be managed. We need also to discover better ways of making citizens and clients part of the process.

2. Addressing Bureaucratic Performance

There is no doubt that much of the criticism of large organizations is well founded. Who is at fault is of little moment. The citizen and the client are not pleased with the way they are being served.

Much, I am convinced, can be done to identify and remedy these criticisms, but first they must be addressed. Not nearly enough is being done in this direction.

Many of the problems will undoubtedly continue to defy solution, given the variety of demands placed on the system, not all of which can be met, given the simplistic views which so many hold and given the habit patterns which have developed over the years. But the situation will surely worsen unless something is done about it. Large organizations *are* usually slow moving, but this can be improved. It is difficult where there are many participants in the decision making process to establish either full accountability or responsibility, but we can certainly do better than we are doing. Many achievements have been made in the reduction of waste, the elimination of redundancy, and the improvement of productivity. Certainly also, we can be more responsive to the needs of those we are expected to serve.

Four tools in particular have much to contribute to such an approach. One is systems analysis, a second is training, a third is evaluation, and the fourth is the computer. Experience with systems analysis indicates the value of the analytical approach. We need now to apply it to the specific criticisms of our organizations. Much has been done over the past decade to improve performance in such areas as merchandising, tax collection, mail delivery, record keeping, billing, the building of highways, and the performing of other essential services. There is much more, of course, to be done, but progress has been made. These serve as examples.

The potentials of training as a means of achieving satisfactory performance patterns are still to be realized, but much progress here has also been made. I believe the next ten years will continue to see increasing attention given to this approach to behavior modification.

A methodology of enormous importance, particularly in the public sector, is that of program evaluation. Despite a surface commitment, we have actually done little with it despite the attention in recent years to such approaches as program budgeting, project management, management by objectives, and, more recently, productivity improvement.

The farther removed a unit is from the top, the less likely those at the top will have any direct knowledge of its performance, or, what is worse, any real interest. This is a harsh but accurate judgment. There appears to be, however, an awakening of concern for oversight and accountability. It underlines the importance of the setting of objectives at all levels and the use of monitoring and auditing techniques to see that they are achieved. While it is not easy to predict what the outcome of the increased use of evaluative techniques will be, the periodic evaluation, done either by professionals from the outside or by a combination of internals and externals, is proving its worth. We can also encourage self-appraisal as is done in other areas, including the universities.

The computer, now that it has reached maturity, offers possibilities for both the decentralization of operations and new patterns of autonomy which could not have been considered even two decades ago. Many of these possibilities remain to be capitalized on. One of the more

important guarantees of effective administration is an understanding
and acceptance of organizational objectives at all levels. The computer
offers possibilities for goal-sharing not yet tapped. There is no reason,
given its availability and its potential, why it cannot be put to use as a
continuing source of information and guidance which is available to all
levels and all members of the organization on call.

3. Reduction of Client Expectations and Demands

A primary fact of life today is that we are overloading our systems.
We continue to demand more services from organizations than they are
capable of providing. Not only do we expect instantaneous compliance
from them, but we expect that whatever they do will be done with
equity, justice, and a smile.

The energy crisis should remind us that our demands are already
outstripping our ability to fill them. We are trying to find ways of
serving the escalating needs of the poor, the aged, the ill, the displaced,
and the unappreciated, while building more roads, more dams, and
more weapons systems. We cannot do or have everything we want.
Somewhere, sometime we will need to understand that the state of the
art is not sufficient for all of the things we would like to do. Nor have
we the resources to pay for them.

Many of the demands we place upon our administrators cannot
possibly be met. We must learn—and we must insist that our political
and economic leaders learn—that a statute which fails to take into
account the administrative problems of fulfilling it will surely fail.
There are clearly limits to administrative capability, and to exceed these
limits in areas where the welfare, security and "rights" of large numbers
of people are concerned is dangerous. For too long, we have tried to
live under a "can do" philosophy. It is time we accept the fact that
there are limits to performance.

Sir Geoffrey Vickers has made this point strongly.[23] He sees the
need for both a "winding down" of public demands on the system, and
also a lessening of individual rights which organizations are now being
asked to serve. But a society which is still unsatisfied with two cars and
two television sets per family is not likely to take seriously the idea that
there are things which, properly staffed and led, a government agency
cannot do. And yet it must.

We must acknowledge that administration is still a primitive art, and
that it is far easier to split the atom than it is to get the clerks behind
the window at the post office to smile and say "Thank you;" or that it

is easier to send a submarine submerged around the world than to get the member of a system to accept responsibility under present circumstances for what he or she does.

4. Revising Current Bureaucratic Patterns

The appearance of a new need or the demand for increased services is not a license for the enlargement of existing structures. Little that is good is to be gained by layering, and size, as we have noted, is hardly a guarantee of success. Big organizations, like big buildings, have problems.

Bureaucracy will continue to be, in some form or other, the only way out of our dilemma. Even revolutionary states will be run, as John Fischer has it, "not by violent romantics but by experts in marketing, sanitary engineering, and the management of bureaucracies."[24] That does not mean, however, that we need to feel committed to conventional organizational patterns or outmoded and costly systems. Should we choose to follow some of the directions we are now going, I see only greater frustration and malaise ahead.

I remain optimistic, however, that more can be done than is presently being done, and because of this optimism, the following suggestions are offered:

- That we accept the fact that bigness *per se* is neither to be desired or encouraged; that we try to keep organizational size always in check.

- That we consider ways of limiting the number of organizational levels by broadening the organization horizontally, or better still, by finding new arrangements by which individuals and units can be more realistically related to each other.

- That we try to encourage what a colleague of mine calls "centers of responsibility."[25] Relative autonomy within the system has great advantages.

- That we encourage the development of individual and group responsibility and accountability within the system. In the final analysis, there is no substitute for individual responsibility.

- That we constantly be on the alert for new organizational forms and arrangements. Darwin said that "there is more to man than the breath of his body." There is accordingly more to organizational theory than traditional forms suggest.

– That we seek to find ways by which clients or citizens can be involved in performing tasks or making contributions to the system.

– That we continue our efforts to develop new institutional models, leaving no area of human experience unobserved in our efforts to profit from it.

Finally, because I believe so strongly in the values of incrementalism, I would like to encourage those involved with the management of large systems to look to specific ways by which the weaknesses of existing sub-systems can be remedied. This should help to improve bureaucratic performance and might also at the same time bring home to its members the seriousness of the criticisms currently being levelled against them.

FOOTNOTES

[1]Max Weber, *Economy and Society*, NY: Bedminister Press, 1968.

[2]"Confidence in Government" as part of the "Image of the Bureaucracy Series" in *The Bureaucrat*, Spring 1979, pp. 26-27.

[3]*Ibid.*, p. 27.

[4]Javad Mojabi in *Notes of a Loquacious Person*, Tehran: 1970.

[5]Charles Frankel, *High on Foggy Bottom*, NY: Harper & Row, Publishers Inc., 1970.

[6]Henry Jacoby, *The Bureaucratization of the World*, Berkeley, CA: University of California Press, 1973.

[7]Cf. Charles Perrow, *Complex Organizations: A Critical Essay*, Glenview, IL: Scott Foresman & Co., 1979. See in particular Chapter I, "Why Bureaucracy?"

[8]Weber himself had serious misgivings about the system whose rationale he had earlier so highly praised:

> *It is horrible to think that the world could one day be filled with nothing but those little cogs, little men clinging to little jobs and striving towards bigger ones—a state of affairs which is to be seen once more, as in the Egyptian records, playing an ever increasing part in the spirit of our present administrative system, and especially of its offspring, the students. This passion for bureaucracy. . .is enough to drive one to despair. It is as if in politics. . .we were deliberately to become men who need "order" and nothing but order, who become nervous and cowardly if for one moment this order wavers, and helpless if they are torn away from their total incorporation in it. That the world should know no men but these: it is such an evolution that we are already caught up in, and the great question is therefore not how we can promote and hasten it, but what can we oppose to this machinery in order to keep a portion of mankind free from this parcelling-out of the soul, from this supreme mastery of the bureaucratic way of life.*

[9]Ph. G. Herbst, *Alternatives to Hierarchies*, Lieden, Netherlands: Martinus Nyhoff Social Sciences Division, 1976, p. 68.

[10]Duane S. Elgin and Robert A. Bushnell, "The Limits to Complexity: Are Bureaucracies Becoming Unmanageable?", *The Futurist*, December 1977, pp. 337-349.

[11]Chester I. Barnard, *The Functions of the Executive*, Cambridge, MA: Harvard University Press, 1956.

[12]Daniel Bell, *"Quo Warranto?* Notes on the Governance of the University in the 1970's," *The Public Interest*, No. 19, Spring 1970, p. 68.

[13]Chris Argyris, *Integrating the Organization and the Individual*, NY: John Wiley & Sons Inc., 1964; Chris Argyris, *Personality and Organization: The Conflict Between System and the Individual*, NY: Harper & Brothers, 1957; Warren Bennis, *Beyond Bureaucracy: Essays on the Development and Evolution of Human Organization*, NY: McGraw-Hill Book Company, Inc., 1973; Warren Bennis, "The Coming Death of Bureaucracy," *Concepts and Controversy in Organizational Behavior*, ed. by W. R. Nord, Santa Monica, CA: Goodyear Publishing Co., 1976; Ralph Hummel, *The Bureaucratic Experience*, NY: St. Martin's Press, 1977; Sir Geoffrey Vickers, *Making Institutions Work*, NY: John Wiley & Sons, Inc., 1973; Stafford Beer, *Platform for Change*, NY: John Wiley & Sons, Inc., 1975.

[14]Clausewitz, *On War*, London: Routledge & Kegan Paul, 1940.

[15]William D. Carey, "On Being Fed Up With Government," *The Bureaucrat*, Vol. 1, No. 1, Spring 1972, p. 44.

[16]Anthony Downs, *Inside Bureaucracy*, Boston, MA: Little, Brown & Co., 1967, p. 431.

[17]Warren Bennis, "A Funny Thing Happened on the Way To The Future," *American Psychologist*, Vol. 25, No. 7, July 1970, pp. 595-608.

[18]Leonard Sayles and Margaret K. Chandler, *Managing Large Systems: Organizations of the Future*, NY: Harper & Row, 1971.

[19]"Interview: Rensis Likert," *GAO Review*, Fall 1978, pp. 79-90.

[20]Alvin Toffler, *Future Shock*, NY: Random House Inc., 1970.

[21]E.F. Schumacher, *Small is Beautiful: Economics as if People Mattered*, NY: Harper & Row, Publishers Inc., 1973.

[22]An experienced observer, Neely Gardiner, a long time California state executive and now a professor at the University of Southern California, has this to say:

> *It does not tax one to build a case which condemns bureaucratic organizational structures. Finding alternative solutions, however, becomes speculative and difficult. It is not clear that anyone knows how to organize for the present, let alone the future. Thus, attempting to develop an alternative becomes an exercise of art which at best reflects the understanding of the individual "artist."*

"The Non-Hierarchical Organization of the Future: Theory vs Reality," *Public Administration Review*, Sept.-Oct. 1976, p. 591.

[23]Comments made in a recorded lecture at George Washington University, Nov. 18, 1974.

[24]As quoted by George Will in *The Washington Post*, April 19, 1979, p. A27.

[25]David O Porter, "Adapting the Responsibility Center Concept to Government Administration." International Institute of Management Paper 77.1, West Berlin, 1977.

PART III

ORGANIZING AND ORGANIZATIONS

CHAPTER IX
ORGANIZATIONAL SYSTEMS: SOME VARIABLES*

There is nothing really mysterious about the word "organizing." It is simply the relating of one person to another towards the achievement of objectives.[1] This can happen in a variety of ways: from the almost casual association of two people with each other in a one-time-only undertaking to the large formal organizations which mark governments and corporations. The family is also, of course, an example of an organization.

Each of us is a member of many organizations, and for the most part has no difficulty in keeping separate our differing roles. From the cradle to the grave, we relate to each other. We could not do what we are doing without organizing.

The purpose of this chapter, accordingly, is to examine some of the factors which bear upon the shape, size, nature, and behavior of organizations. Of these, there are none more important than those within the viewer's mind—the concepts one holds of organization and the manner in which it functions.

The Conceptual Barriers

The Simplistic Approach. Perhaps the most formidable of the conceptual barriers is the simplistic approach so many have of organizations. None of us has ever seen one, and never will. We have seen the buildings in which people work, we have seen these people (or at least part of them), we are familiar with organizational tools, and the like. But an organization, being a system of relationships, is neither seeable nor touchable. That does not keep us from constructing something called "organization" within our mind, and giving it material and

---

*The author is indebted to Miller B. McDonald, formerly of the training staff of the Department of Commerce, for his encouragement, support and assistance in the preparation of this chapter.

even human properties. There is a name for this—reification—but it is an idea indulged by most of us despite the fallacy it contains.

A Fixation on Formal Structure. Those involved with organizational design have always been preoccupied with its formal aspects, the "paper" organization. It is always more intelligible—and certainly a great deal easier—to contemplate than the flesh and blood reality. It also gives the manager a sense of power in playing with boxes and lines, as if with toy soldiers.

Concern for the "Here and Now." A failing of many organizational designs is the lack of thought given to the requirements of changing times and circumstances. The static organization is, of course, a failing organization. Organizations as well as people must be able to adjust to new circumstances and new demands.

Tradition and Habit. This is the century of change. We accept, without much thought, communicating with vehicles in space or humans traveling at orbital speeds of over 17,500 miles an hour. Yet there are few areas of human activity that cling as strongly to the traditional as those relating to organizations. Until those who hold these theories are willing to think beyond them, this conceptual obstacle will continue to limit human achievement.

Each Man an Expert. There is the tendency also for all of us to consider ourselves organizational experts. We *feel*, therefore, we *know*. We know that the organization of which we are a part is not working as intended, and, being aware of its shortcomings, each of us has our own remedies to suggest. Because organizational behavior often baffles the amateurs does not mean that the professionals have the answers either, no matter how insightful some of their observations may be. Perhaps what is needed is a little of both.

The Search for "Principles." Organizational problems lead us to a search for solutions, and the search for solutions invariably suggests "principles." However, belief that the knowledge necessary to the development of human institutions can be usefully reduced to a list of ten, twelve, or even twenty "principles"—or for that matter contained in a single volume—is patently absurd. Guidelines and suggestions there may be; principles, no.

And yet such lists do exist and are widely cited. Most of them, however, are so general as to have little real value, resulting in what one writer has called "a hardening of the categories" and another "the parables of administration." What they fail to take into account are the great differences in organizations and their functions—in people, objectives, tasks, methods, values, and time.

Organizational Reality

Given an understanding of some of the conceptual problems—the self-imposed barriers within the individual—one needs to explore what the organization really is. In fact, organizations have a little bit of "Wonderland" about them. They "are," and yet they "aren't." A useful starting point is the realization that there are many organizations in one, depending upon what one wants to see.

The Formal Organization. There is, first of all, the formal organization. This is the planned organization, the one which appears in the organization chart. At the top of the chart ordinarily one will find the head man. Beneath him, connected by unbroken lines like an electrical system, are names of other offices and persons in descending order of importance.

The formal organization emphasizes power, status, and, in part, authority. In a way it defines work assignments, but is only partially successful in doing so. Its major contribution—other than the sense of assurance it gives to those who occupy its command posts—is its orderliness. Its major deficiency is that so many take the formal organization to be the real organization, which it most emphatically is not.

Informal (or Real) Organizations. In the fifty years since Chester Barnard first identified the informal organization by name, there has been increasing attention given to it not only by students of administration but by practitioners as well.[2] It has become, in fact a commonplace term.

But like many other commonplace ideas, informal organizations are still not fully understood. Barnard may even have done us a disservice by referring to *the* informal organization, as if there were only one. There are, of course, many.

The term "informal" may be misleading as well. The organization is hardly informal in the usual meaning of the term. It is merely "nonprescribed." Perhaps a better word than informal would be "real."

The "real" organization does many things. The most important of these to organizational life is that of getting the organization's work done. Without the real organization, performance would be virtually impossible. No organization can survive by following rigorously either the organization chart or the procedural manual. Short-cuts, communicational by-ways, work patterns, and person-to-person relationships so vital to the achievement of objectives are molded by convenience, friendship, good sense, and a sound American predilection for what works. Some of the most important of these work systems are indicated below.

Communicational Systems. People within the organization relate to each other in a variety of ways and patterns, each of which has its own meaning. The network required to pass the word with respect to policy is quite different from that concerned with social matters or with supply. Individuals and small groups work seriously to develop ways and means of getting information from whatever sources have it. The network which gets information *from* the top is usually quite a different one from that which seeks to get information *to* the top. In neither case does the formal organization suffice.

Member-Client Systems. There are also the member-client relationships which serve a wide variety of functions. Sometimes the client is within the organization, sometimes outside. The manner in which the two relate has large bearing upon the success of the enterprise. By cultivating those who actually provide the goods or services, clients find their needs most likely to be met. Higher level negotiations may be an important part of the process but they are only a part.

Work Systems. The work system is the way people work together to achieve objectives. Few elements are complete in themselves, the organization chart to the contrary. Others are needed, as partners, suppliers, trouble-shooters, sources of information and support, and also as clients. Organizational products are the result of an intricate system of integration of effort. The failure to achieve their integration results in a failure to achieve organizational goals. Indeed, the supervisor who can mobilize needed resources most effectively as a means of keeping one's own workers busy is clearly one of the more effective supervisors.[3]
The "work system" organization is basically a lateral system, involving those at peer levels more frequently than those higher up. This is why peer group relationships are so important to the life of the organization.

The Power Systems. There are power people and power systems in all organizations—and these are not necessarily those at the top. The power system (some think of it as the "decision system" although there are significant differences between the two) varies according to the issue. Those who "own" the company have power, but often not as much as their ownership would suggest. They share it with those who have knowledge and expertness ("know-how"), those with long experience, and those of proven loyalty. Power also accrues because individuals are strong minded, and do not hesitate to use sanctions to enforce their will; because they have high status; because they have been there a long time; because they know what is needed; because they command the loyalty of others; or because they control important resources. Each of these sources of influence has its own exponents who, under the right circumstances, will have a major voice in what takes place. Thus, a power structure comes into being.

The Social Systems. Each organization has its internal social systems. Those of various professions tend to stick together (lawyers, chemists, salespeople, stenographers, etc.) and in doing so support each other. So also do those who are "process related," who combine to produce a given product or service.

Another aspect of the internal social system is the friendship-based alliance. Such friendships arise from similarities of experience and interests, from job associations, geographic proximity, and the like. They provide sources of information, assistance, and influence which go well beyond the capabilities of other relationships and certainly well beyond those of the formal organization.

The Search for Form and Structure

Thus, the organization may be viewed as a community of interrelated systems. This may be quite natural, but it also imposes a burden on those who would hold the structure together. As the organization becomes larger, this burden increases. In fact, the integration of internal systems which sometimes have little in common beyond a nominal one is one of the more pressing problems facing present-day management.

To deny the existence of such systems and sub-systems—to pretend, by hiding behind the formal organization chart, that they do not really exist—is of little help. Architects of organization, insofar as they can do so, must understand what behavioral patterns exist, what they mean, whom they influence, and how. They should know how they contribute to, as well as the manner in which they detract from, organizational objectives.

Those who design organizations—and in particular those who "direct" them—are usually concerned with a number of organizational issues which, over time, have been associated with "good management." Some of the more prominent of these are: (1) the source and nature of authority; (2) the unity of command; (3) the problem of span of control; (4) patterns of departmentation; (5) staff and line concepts; (6) hierarchy and status; (7) patterns of centralization and decentralization. These will be examined briefly in the following pages. It is not the purpose here to suggest what the answers ought to be so much as it is to question traditional ways of approaching them and to suggest emerging points of view.

1. *The Source and Nature of Authority.* In government, both laws and constitutions provide a source of authority for what is done. The authorization for a private venture is similar. "Ownership" is established by law and covenant.

Unhappily, the simple solution is sometimes also the simplistic one. As organizations have become larger and more complex, there has been increasing realization that there is more than one kind of authority and that authorities are sometimes in conflict with each other. Those who direct or own the enterprise are not the only persons who can speak authoritatively. This has been treated in greater detail earlier and will not be repeated here. It is sufficient to remark that organizations are not monoliths.

2. *Unity of Command.* What Simon calls "the folklore of management"[4] places a great deal of emphasis on unity of command. The belief is that no organization can survive without it. If what is sought is harmony and integration, then the effort is probably worthwhile. Unfortunately, too often what is meant by unity is "one-ness" or the single executive. The traditionalist view is that a single man, and only a single man, is capable of giving organizational direction. The arguments in support of singleness are too old and hoary to need repetition here. They cite kings, presidents, captains of ships, generals, and even poets in support of their theory. ("Who ever heard of a poem written by a committee?") What they fail to cite is common experience with which, certainly, they must also be familiar.

The family—one of the most successful of all human institutions—rests not upon the singleness of command theory but upon a sharing of responsibility by husband and wife along basically functional lines. Observation of on-going relationships in governmental and industrial as well as educational, social and cultural organizations supports a similar theory—that leadership is more often shared than exercised unilaterally. This is not an argument in semantics. It is a point of fact.

Galbraith brings his persuasive genius to bear on this point in *The New Industrial State*.[5] His disclosures are hardly new but they are strongly and well said:

> The modern business organization, or that part which has to do with guidance and direction, consists of numerous individuals who are engaged, at any given time, in obtaining, digesting or exchanging and testing information. . . .*One can do worse than think of a business organization as a hierarchy of committees.* Coordination, in turn, consists in assigning the appropriate talent to committees, intervening on occasion to force a decision, and, as the case may be, announcing the decision or carrying it as information for a yet further decision by a yet higher committee.
>
> Nor should it be supposed that this is an inefficient procedure. On the contrary it is, normally, the only efficient procedure. [Emphasis added.]

What we ought to be thinking about when we talk of unity of command is agreement on purposes and objectives. This has nothing to do with the way power is distributed which, as any reader of *The Wall Street Journal* or *Business Week* will testify, can be managed in an infinite variety of ways.

3. *The Problem of Span of Control.* Conventional organizational planning reinforces the single man concept by placing him above the organization and, in effect, out of reach of the majority of those in it. It does so by the simple expedient of limiting the span of control or the number of persons one will supervise directly. How can a position be made more imposing than to deny others access to it?

Although, as Golembiewski points out, there is not a single shred of empirical evidence to support conventional limitations on span of control,[6] there are a great many theories concerning it. Graicunas, a Polish management expert, suggested that industrial usage be limited to five or six under the theory that more than this required more of the supervisor than he could possibly give.[7] Whether because of his suggestion or for some other reason, this figure is the one usually cited. There is no divinity attached to it, however, and little logic.

The number a given person can supervise will depend on a variety of factors: one's own talent and predilections; the nature of the work to be done; the type of persons being supervised and the kind of equipment they use; their relationships with client groups; and the history of the organization. Some people and some missions require very little direct supervision; others, more. Historic methods of thinking about span of control (the theory X mentality) have dictated closer supervision (and therefore smaller spans) than are really needed.

A small span of control, of course, is not without costs. It means more supervisors—and the duplication this entails—and greater distance of those who actually do the productive work of the organization from those occupying leadership (or "policy") positions. Direct costs, as well as indirect ones, increase. The latter includes the costs of lengthy and peripatetic communicational systems, lack of feeling for organizational purposes and objectives, increased need for control systems, and the growth of impersonality and dysfunctionalism throughout the organization. Some consider management's decisions with respect to span of control the most significant ones it makes.

I have actually witnessed organizational arrangements where one person supervised as many as 60, and appeared to have no problems doing so. Golembiewski reports instances of over 100. There are many situations, as I indicated in an earlier chapter, where little or no supervision is needed.

4. *Patterns of Departmentation.* Over the years this has been an area of primary managerial focus. Indeed, more time and attention have probably been given it than to any other organizational problem, and still there are problems. Of the twelve patterns described below, the first five are most commonly used.

Functional. The organization is divided by function under the theory that a commonality of experience is thus achieved. Major divisions will ordinarily include: manufacturing, sales, legal, controllership, and the like. Staff divisions are usually functional divisions.

Purpose and Objective. Emphasis is upon identifiable purposes or objectives. The organization's purpose may be to educate schoolchildren—or more specifically, children in certain grades; it may seek to provide assistance to business; to set standards; or to achieve a specified purpose. This is a more meaningful type of departmentation.

Product. Product is another form of purpose and objective and one particularly suited to industrial organizations. General Motors, for example, has its Chevrolet and its Cadillac divisions, with emphasis upon an identifiable finished product. The product division is a favorite with industry.

Geography. All organizations of any size must sooner or later determine how they are to deal with the problem of territory. Those with far-flung responsibilities as in the case of many government agencies and the larger corporations, establish regional or area offices in order to meet local needs. Most organizations, in fact, require some kind of regional system.

Clientele. It is often important to indicate the clientele being served, such as veterans (the Veterans Administration); old people (geriatrics); or those needing maternity aid. By identifying with the client, assurance is given that their needs are addressed.

Profession. An organization will sometimes divide its various professionals into divisions which reflect their professionalism. (This might also provide functional departmentation.) Its advantage is that it brings them closely together, usually with their approval.

Time Phasing. Experience with Program Evaluation Review Technique (PERT) and similar systems underlines the importance of the time factor. Under arrangements such as this, units are given responsiblity for the development of segments of the whole. These segments usually work together in sequential fashion.

Equipment. Some units are designated by the type of equipment used. An example is data processing which develops around the computer.

Alpha-Numerical. Where the organization must provide a similar service to large numbers of people, divisions are often created on the basis of alphabet or, as in the instance of Social Security, by numbers.

The Matrix. The matrix type of organization is centered around a particular product which then negotiates with other units for the performance of services needed to build, assemble, or repair it. It is found more frequently in industry than in government.

Member-Oriented. All organizations are at times member-oriented. Who does not know of the company or agency which redefines its divisional structure to take into account the ability (or lack of ability) of some older hand, or the organization which makes allowance for the special capability or inclination of this or that group:

researchers, part-time employees, drivers, etc. Such practices are often disapproved in principle but work well in practice. More recently, however, organizational architects, at the urging of behavioral scientists, are giving attention to ways and means of organizing which consciously take into account the characteristics of those who make them up. It is an interesting new development.

Mixed. Organizations of any size cannot follow a single pattern of departmentation. Most organizations accordingly use several.

Such patterns of departmentation, however useful they have been, have by no means solved management's problems. Indeed, the tendency to turn hopefully from one to another underlines the difficulties which any selected type of structure presents. By selecting one form of departmentation over another, management, of course, prejudices its case. In so doing, it raises new, albeit different, types of problems. A division identified with a particular product, for example, will often commit itself so fully to that product that the total organization will suffer. A division concerned with a single geographic area may find itself in conflict with a national program. One identified with the interests of a particular group may do a disservice to other groups or to a broader interest. Still, the choice of departmentation is an important choice and its pros and cons should be weighed carefully.

5. *Staff and Line.* Present day ideas of staff and line derive historically from the military. The initial distinction was made between those who served as eyes, ears, and legs of the commander, and those with responsibility for doing the actual fighting. A staff man might be a messenger or an *aide de camp*. It was his function to carry messages between his chief and subordinate commanders. He could not command them. Later the specialization that this entailed was enlarged to include a variety of auxiliary functions: medical, supply, plans, intelligence, recruitment, training, and the like.

Similar ideas have attended the development of staff in civilian (industrial or governmental) operations. The staff man was there to perform a variety of specialized functions:

- To advise a superior in specialized areas.

- To perform certain functions of an auxiliary nature.

- To advise others also in the chain of command.

- To perform specialized functions for them.

- To act in place of superiors or for them.

- In large organizations, to act for someone or some agency on the outside or above. (That is, a controller might also speak for a higher corporate authority.)

As in the military, conventional doctrines hold that the staff officer is not entitled to command. In fact such persons often are ineligible for line assignment. This helps to encourage the dichotomy between staff and line which is one of the more serious defects of many organizations.

An examination of who staff officers are and what they do, as well as the influence they have in organizations, belies the judgments once made of them. That they perform vital functions is now well established: no organization can survive without them. A listing will produce no fewer than fifty well-accepted staff types of activity (budget officer, chaplain, attorney, librarian, etc.) and perhaps more. If staff people and staff organizations are not there to perform these functions, they must be done by someone else. Nor is there any longer any doubt that staff officers do give directions and sometimes command in general as well as in functional areas. The question therefore arises: Are the purposes of management really being served by the schism that the staff-line division suggests? Should not some less divisive way be found for doing what needs to be done?

6. *Hierarchy and Status.* The narrower the span of control the deeper the hierarchy. To put it another way: the fewer persons reporting to a given supervisor, the more levels will be needed in the organization.

Hierarchical levels underline the distinctions between people and units at a time when management theory is attempting to lessen them. They make communication downwards more difficult and render communication upwards through channels virtually impossible. They require new and more complex procedures for dealing with organizational problems. They emphasize duplication of effort and pointless rivalry. At best, good supervision is difficult to come by. The more levels, the more of it is required. The greater the number of levels, the greater the need also for controls and control systems. More will be said about this in the next chapter.

7. *Centralization and Decentralization.* A major question in the life of every large organization is the degree to which it will permit decisions affecting it to be made elsewhere than at headquarters—or if at

headquarters, elsewhere than in the office of the chief. A related question is the manner in which decentralization should be administered. There is no single best way.

The greater the extent to which decisions are made outside of headquarters, the less the degree of leadership control over them. This may or may not be the problem it once appeared to be because of the use of new and sophisticated communications systems. A decentralized staff, properly prepared and trained and clear as to organizational objectives, will, for example, ordinarily be closer to leadership than an ill-trained, imperceptive one close by. There is much evidence to support the need for decentralization. In the first place, it is closer to the clients who will ordinarily have more faith in it. It is more sensitive to on-the-spot conditions. It provides for the growth and development of employees. It requires clearer thinking from headquarters as to organizational objectives. And because no one person today can do everything, it requires that thought be given to ways by which staff is made more sensitive to and appreciative of what needs to be done.

There are many forms and degrees of decentralization. Managers are free to make a number of choices. They may decide to retain close control of one type of activity while permitting a large degree of discretion in another. If resources are limited, they may choose to watch tightly over these. They may select from any of a large number of informational and reporting systems. In fact, with the computer making the contributions it is now making, a larger degree of discretion may be permitted than ever before at field level.

The Organization in Flux

The art of organizing, albeit an old art, is still an evolving one and, as purposes and institutions become more complex and knowledge of how people relate to one another increases, greater burdens are placed upon it. There are many ways by which this can be done. No one need be committed to ideas which have outlived their usefulness.

What of the organization of the future? What will be its shape, its characteristics? Will organizations continue to become larger and more diverse? Will bureaucracies take over? Or, as some have already suggested, is their death already in progress? No one can say for sure what the answers to those and other questions may be, but there are certainly signs of what may be in store. Whatever its ultimate form, the organization of the future must be able to meet the demands placed upon it. These will include:

The Organization as a System. It is probably more useful to think of what has traditionally been regarded as the organization as a *system*. This provides a more realistic overview of the multiple relationships which have evolved. It enables us to observe and understand what is really happening and to take the action which seems most appropriate.

Those in the top positions become more like negotiators and less like directors. They accept the fact that a large proportion of their time must be spent with governors, competitors, related organizations, suppliers, the media, the courts, professional organizations, unions, and the community. This calls for a different approach than the textbooks have traditionally suggested. Whatever the future holds, the systems it suggests will have many ramifications and those who guide them must be prepared to deal with them.

A Variety of Objectives. The future organization must also be able to serve a number of objectives and serve them well. The emphasis of the present generation has been upon specialization, and our organizations reflect this. Expertness will still be necessary. Indeed, the requirements of expertness are increasing. But there are signs that versatility and variety will also be required, not only of individuals but of organizations and institutions. With new and unknown demands constantly arising, those organizations which survive will be the ones best qualified to cope with these demands.

Community Purposes. The business organization which sought only to make a profit is also a thing of the past. While profit—or at least fiscal viability—is essential, this is far from the total requirement. Organizations, business and government, today are being asked increasingly to become members of their communities with all that this implies. The community depends on them, and they on the community.

The organization, whether business, governmental, or eleemosynary in nature, should be able to perform in a variety of ways not contemplated fifty or even twenty years ago. Social legislation has seen to that. Along with it, a change has taken place in the organizational executive. This role, and that of the institution the executive heads, is vastly different from what it once was.

Individual Needs. Future organizations must take into account the behavioral characteristics of those who make them up. Not only must the informal organization be recognized for what it is but insofar as possible, the formal organization must reflect also the behavioral patterns and social needs of those who serve it. This is a point which has only recently been understood. To optimize their performance, organizations must come to understand the characteristics, abilities, needs, and goals of their members. It is not enough to think departmentally in functional or regional terms: organizations must shape themselves to reflect those who are a part of them.

In America, this calls, as we have seen, for an understanding of American characteristics. Organizational systems can reflect these characteristics and many of them, to their own advantage, already have. They are usually leaders in their field.

A recent national advertisement complained that many "college kids" who ought to be interested in careers in business were growing indifferent to it. It explained why: "Because they think business is dull, money-grubbing, conformist, self-centered—you name it." The new organization cannot survive unless good people come to it and also find it worthwhile to stay and to contribute.

Form and Structure. Organizations must make sense to those who work with them. They must have face validity. The complexities of many modern systems, including interlocking corporate relationships, leave much to be desired. They suggest either clumsiness or duplicity. Many others are seen as being primarily self-serving.

The criticisms of bureaucracy underline many of these same points. Not only do they burden performance but they also discourage many of those who, if they became a part of the organization, might be able to do something about it. Bureaucracy, in its present forms, will not do.

Organizations must involve both their members and their clients to a greater degree than in the past. This is important for a number of reasons. It makes no sense to make the sharp distinctions we now do between the "insider" and the "outsider" when the two have so much in common—in fact, depend upon each other. Ways will have to be found to bring them closer together.

Economy of Resources. Future organization must also make better use of their resources than their predecessors. If these, human and material, are as limited as evidence increasingly has shown, new organizations must use them more sensibly than they have in the past. They can no longer afford to waste time, facilities, goods, or people, as if they would always be available.

FOOTNOTES

[1]As Schein has put it, "organization is the rational coordination of the activities of a number of people for the achievement of some explicit purpose or goal, through division of labor and function and through a hierarchy of authority and responsibility." (Edgar H. Schein, *Organizational Psychology*, Englewood Cliffs, NJ: Prentice-Hall Inc., 1965, p. 8.)

[2]See Chester I. Barnard, *The Functions of the Executive*, Cambridge, MA: Harvard University Press, 1956, pp. 114-126.

[3]This point is strongly made by Leonard Sayles in *Managerial Behavior*, NY: McGraw-Hill Book Company, Inc., 1964, pp. 58-82.

[4]See: Herbert Simon, *Administrative Behavior: A Study of Decision-Making in Administrative Organizations*, NY: Macmillan, Inc., 1947.

[5]J. Kenneth Galbraith, *The New Industrial State*, Boston: Houghton Mifflin Co., 1967, pp. 63-64.

[6]Robert P. Golembiewski, *Men, Management, and Morality: Toward A New Organizational Ethic*, NY: McGraw-Hill Book Company, Inc., 1965, p. 172.

[7]V.A. Graicunas, "Relationship in Organization," in *Papers on the Science of Administration*, ed. by Luther Gulick and Lyndal F. Urwick, NY: Institute of Public Administration, Columbia University Press, 1937, pp. 183-187.

CHAPTER X
THE HIGH COST OF HIERARCHY

Organizations of any size have hierarchy. Like the pyramids of Egypt, which in its classic form it resembles, hierarchy has been around a long, long time. The Bible speaks of "rulers of thousands. . .rulers of hundreds, rulers of fifties, and rulers of tens." The Romans recognized its importance in the administrative system which perpetuated the empire long after the capital was dead. Frederick the Great incorporated it into his revolutionary new army system.[1] It is the "scalar principle" which Henri Fayol, the great French student of management, identified and proclaimed near the end of the 19th century.

Hierarchy is so common and well accepted a phenomenon in organizations today that most of us take it for granted, even in its most bizarre and extravagant forms. What is, in fact, a hierarchical explosion is taking place around us without our being aware that anything out of the ordinary is happening.

No one would deny that scalar distinctions are both necessary and desirable. People vary in skills, ability, drive, power, and status. Organizations have differing needs. Hierarchy helps to accommodate both.

A good thing, however, can be and often is overdone. As organizations have increased in size, hierarchies have gotten larger, deeper, and much more complex. Distinctions between levels have become more precise in theory and yet less so in fact. Sometimes they have worked as the designers planned, more often not. Predictably, there have been side effects. The architects of organization are accordingly taking a new look at hierarchy and what it is doing. This time they are not neglecting its costs.

The results of this new look are some startling facts and conclusions. One of these is the view held by an increasing number, including this observer, that hierarchy is being misused and overused in today's government and business. It has, in short, shown every evidence of getting out of hand.

Hierarchical Effect

That hierarchy has an effect on the behavior of those touched by it, no one denies. Heretofore, however, the assumption was that such an effect was functional—that those in a specific unit at a particular level functioned more or less as operating instructions required. We are now beginning to discover, however, that this is only partially so. Those far removed from the boss, for example, are less likely to perform as indicated than those directly beneath.

We are also beginning to discover that large organizations with many layers and levels are producing particular kinds of behavior that, for want of a better term, must be regarded as pathological. Victor Thompson, for example, has identified in his insightful study, *Modern Organization*, a variety of bureaupathic behaviors ("bureausis") many of which he indicates, and others agree, have their origins in hierarchy.[2] These include nonidentification with the goals of the organization, exaggerated aloofness, insistence on the rights of office, resistance to change, overcompliance, and the like. Robert Presthus in his *Organizational Society* points out that we are breeding a generation of indifferents, ambivalents, and upward mobiles, none of whom really answers our organizational needs.[3]

The term "dysfunctional" is being increasingly used in the literature of administration to describe what is happening. It points up the side effects or byproducts of organizational action. The dysfunctions of large organizations include, in addition to those already noted, impersonality, lack of commitment, dependency, infantilism, Zombie-ism, overidealization of superiors (often followed by underestimation and depreciation), territory-guarding, feuding, absenteeism, job hopping, red tape, and the like. The number of such phenomena is increasing. A relatively new field of research is developing—organizational mental health.

Increasingly, the members of the organization are becoming aware of what is happening to others—and also to themselves. They find themselves disturbed and disheartened by it. As a teacher of administration and instructor in executive programs, I hear frequent comments on the subject. It helps to account, I am convinced, for the high turnover at the lower professional grades. Later on, the incumbent will have to put up with it, but while still young and uncommitted, can look elsewhere for escape—and does. Alas, if the new organization is a large one, it may be much the same as the one just left.

Some Specifics

There is, of course, no single cause of what is taking place. Those who expect to find one are deluding only themselves. But there can be no doubt that the ever-expanding systems of hierarchy and subhierarchy which most large organizations seem intent on establishing are major offenders.

The following are examples of hierarchical effect. They have been chosen because they illustrate vividly what layering has done and is doing to organizational behavior.

Communications Downward. The greater the number of levels through which communications must pass, the greater the likelihood of distortion, diffusion, and error. This is so obvious as to require no further elaboration. The use of modern communication methods may lessen the miscommunication but only in part.

The rationale for each organizational level is that it has some special (and unique) function to perform. Each message it receives is accordingly scrutinized before being amplified or passed on. This takes time and manpower and is all too often redundant.

Communications Upward. Communicating downward is simple compared with that of communicating upward. As Thompson has pointed out: "Hierarchical relations overemphasize the veto and underemphasize approval of innovation. Since there is no appeal from the superior's decision, a veto usually ends the matter. However, an approval will often have to go to the next higher level where it is again subject to a veto. A hierarchical system, therefore, always favors the *status quo.*"[4]

Employees at lower levels are often greatly frustrated by their inability to get either information or ideas upward despite frequent appeals by management for suggestions. This, of course, accounts for the suggestion box. It is a way, albeit only moderately successful, to get around hierarchical blocks in the communication systems.

Relationship Problems. The greater the number of hierarchical levels, the greater the problems of individual and group relationship. Dwaine Marvick, for example, in his study of bureaucracy, found that those occupying hierarchical roles in a Federal bureaucracy were considerably more concerned with prestige, influence, security, and career achievement than their specialist colleagues.[5]

A result of such tendencies on the part of employees is the development of rules, frequently in great detail, governing their conduct. These may even go so far as to specify who shall talk with whom and under what circumstances, the nature of the business to be conducted, the "chain of command," and when exceptions can be safely taken and when not. There must also be provision for policing the rules, penalties for violating them, appeals procedures, and the like. The larger the organization, the more formal these become.

The greater the number of levels, of course, the greater the problems posed by delegation and decentralization. These are difficult enough concepts to begin with, but when anywhere from three to 15 echelons are involved, as is often the case, a wholly new range of problems is encountered. How and under what circumstances, for example, should top executives communicate with those at lower levels? What is the real role of the middle manager? What can be done to preserve operating freedom, yet keep others fully informed? Management is constantly wrestling with such problems—ones, incidentally, it has had a large hand in creating.

Individual Creativity and Commitment. Individual creativity is always lessened by ignorance of what is wanted, by lack of knowledge of organizational needs and problems, by the feeling that there is little understanding or appreciation by superiors of the contribution the individual is making, and by lack of status. Studies indicate that the individual's morale is lowered and frustration increased by the feeling of little or no control over matters of great concern to one. Frustration, ennui, lack of initiative, and outright hostility are commonly observed phenomena of highly structured organizations.

The greater the distance of the individual from sources of organizational leadership, the less serious its problems are likely to be and the less committed one is to them. Correspondingly, the claim on one's energies and loyalties by clientele groups, peer professionals, employee betterment associations, and personal interests is greater. Hierarchy thus helps to draw an employee away from organizational purposes while appearing to be involving him more closely in them.

The Dispersion of Decision Making. Decision making in the highly structured, deeply tiered organization is ordinarily both fractionalized and dispersed despite the appearance of unity it conveys. Moreover, top management is often blissfully unaware not only of how decisions are actually made but of what has been decided. The same bureaucratic processes camouflage both. Whether or not aware of what is happening, management is committed by it.

The Use of Control Systems. Management's response to patterns such as the above (when it is aware of them) is to search for ways of "tightening" the organization. The management journals describe the uses of such varied approaches as suggestion systems, statistical sampling, internal audit staffs, computers, synectics, management programming (such as PERT), and the like.

These have their uses but are also costly. In fact, they produce dysfunctional effects of their own. Some examples of these effects are a concern for procedures rather than for objectives, a preoccupation with what Simon refers to as "satisficing" rather than optimal solutions, the choice of the "safest" rather than the most constructive course of action, lack of faith in immediate superiors, and hostility toward those in the control unit—and also in top management. Instead of solving the problems of hierarchy, control systems may indeed create new ones.

The High Costs

As the above suggests, the costs of hierarchy come high. They are paid for by management, whether directly or indirectly, in terms of the time it must spend in undoing their effects. They are paid for also in terms of loss of employee loyalty and creativity. While such costs may never show in the agency budget or on its balance sheet, they are inescapably there. They must be included in the final cost of the product.

Large organizations, for example, move more ponderously than small ones because more people at more levels are involved. Where orders as well as ideas must move from level to level, much time is required. The time thus spent translates easily into money.

Large organizations with complex hierarchies and status systems require, as we have seen, carefully developed rules and procedures. The growth of such professions as administrative analyst, coordinator, expediter, liaison officer, and systems engineer testifies to the extent to which such efforts have gone. Like all overhead, these place a substantial burden upon the organization. Someone has to pay for them.

There is the cost also of the control systems which hierarchies require—not an inconsiderable item in itself. It includes the salaries of control personnel, such as the internal auditors, inspectors, and security people. To these must be added the indirect costs which arise from installing the system—its own dysfunctional elements. Might not managements have been better advised to address themselves to the hierarchical problems which caused the breakdown in the first place, rather than seeking ways around them?

The real cost of hierarchy, however, is its cost in people. This is the price of what it does to those in the organization, and ultimately, of course, to the organization itself. Such a cost must be measured in terms of duplication of effort, wasted motion, discouragement of initiative, atrophy, disinterest and non-commitment, lack of creativity, and irresponsibility.

The signs of such phenomena are everywhere. They are being increasingly revealed by the study of employees deep in the recesses of the organization. Industrial waste is not only the garbage dumped into America's rivers and bays. It is also the cumulative effect of burdensome and stulifying organizational systems on the human beings who attempt to serve them. As Drucker has repeatedly emphasized, "the human resource is of all economic resources the one least efficiently used." Abundant evidence supports him.

Alternatives to Hierarchy

Hierarchy can no more be done away with than sin, but it can be managed better than it is. If its use is excessive, it can be curbed. There is no sense to the continued piling of level upon level and no need for it. Several courses suggest themselves:

- Broadening spans of supervision or control.
- Increased delegation and decentralization.
- The use of new and imaginative patterns of organization.
- A deemphasis on status.
- New patterns of leadership.
- More open systems of managing.

These are not brand new approaches, of course, but more attention should be paid to them.

Broadening the Span of Supervision or Control. For much too long a time organizations have been patterned on archaic beliefs concerning the number of people who can be supervised properly. Not only have such ideas encumbered operations, but they have also failed to take into account the breakthroughs in knowledge of the past 35 years.

A proper span of control might be six, 16, or even 60. This will depend on the job to be done, the type of leadership or guidance provided, the kind of people supervised, and the nature of the controls available. A major league baseball manager directs 30 or more; the second baseman reports to him neither through the first baseman nor a coach. A sales manager may oversee any number and so may an army commander.

Robert Golembiewski reports a British firm with one superior for every 250 production workers with good results. As he points out, "no convincing demonstration of the efficiency of a narrow span of control exists, nor has one been attempted."[6] This is strong language. Organizers should take heed.

Much of our organizational *errata* can be laid to amateurs but much also is the work of professionals. Parochialism, unfortunately, applies as often to organizational architects as it does to other people. What is required is greater sensitivity to organizational behavior and less to symmetry. By a broadening and flattening of the organizational structure, those at the top and those at the bottom can be brought more closely together. In doing so, communication lines are shortened, objectives are harmonized, and a greater sense of immediacy and participation are provided. These are all important values.

Increased Delegation and Decentralization. Few ideas have received so much lip service in both government and industry as those relating to delegation. Yet few are so difficult to put in practice. Much more has been achieved by decentralization, which is really a form of delegation.

This suggests that a useful approach to the problem of hierarchy may be through managing space. The physical distance between two persons or two organizational units may indeed contain a key to their relationship to each other. Even modest distances—another building or another part of the same city, for example—produce different behavioral responses than, say co-existence on the same floor.

For both the delegator and delegatee, spatial separations *and their attendant delegations* suggest different standards of performance, greater flexibility in fulfilling work assignments, different leadership patterns, and different responses. On the whole, they make for more satisfactory relationships than those where there is a layering of echelons in close physical proximity to each other.

New Patterns of Organization. We have learned important lessons during the past 25 years from our observation of a variety of organizational arrangements. Foremost among these lessons are those concerning the real (or informal) organization. Work proceeds in most organizations because goal-committed individuals make it possible via systems of individual and group relationships *outside* formal channels.

Trailblazers in both government and industry have demonstrated the advantages of project teams, matrix organizations, contract service units, ad hoc groups, licensing and franchise arrangements, and similar patterns. In other instances, individuals have been given freedom from traditional organizational restraints on condition that they apply their talents to needed problems. The results of such variations in hierarchical norms have been sufficiently rewarding both to the individuals and the organization to bring about substantial commitments in this direction.

Department stores have done much to encourage individual entrepreneurship, in effect leasing to departments floor space for their operations. The franchise system which permits individual ownership (and risk) is being used widely by an increasing number of businesses. The profit center is now widely used. Doctors who have strongly opposed governmental health systems have learned the advantage of associating themselves voluntarily with insurance and medical care plans under varying types of fee arrangement. Other types of organizations emphasize the importance of the team (as in research) and the face-to-face group.

Such arrangements emphasize the possibilities open to us. The traditional pyramidal organization is neither the only system nor even the best. In fact, as our observation of the informal organization shows, it is consistently violated. Only in this way does work get done.

Deemphasizing Status. The fact that status and status systems exist even in the so-called classless societies is no argument for emphasizing or elaborating them. In fact, the lessening of the status extremes which the conventional organization chart has encouraged is of considerable merit.

There is clearly a cause-effect relationship between hierarchy and status. The chart which reduces the appearance of hierarchy will, accordingly, have its effect on status feeling.

Any serious attempt to deemphasize status and hierarchy will include the following:

- Study of the functioning organization—literally, how work gets done.

- Greater understanding and use of voluntary contributions both from inside and outside the organization.

- The elimination of anachronistic and vestigial units and arrangements.

- Greater opportunities for the exchange of ideas via study groups, training programs, and policy-considering committees.

–   Improved management visibility: top management, specifically, being seen and heard by those at all levels of the organization.

–   Greater recognition of the contribution of individuals at all levels to both operational and policy decisions.

New Patterns of Leadership. The large bureaucratic organization should not be confused with the small one any more than an elephant should be confused with a mouse. That there is a similarity in basic cell structure does not mean that the similarity extends to other things. The two, in fact, require different patterns of leadership.

In the small organization, face-to-face leadership will suffice. There is, of course, need for it at specific levels in the large organization. But in a large organization a different kind of leadership is also needed. Instead of addressing themselves to limited goals and specific subordinates, persons with top managerial responsibilities within the many-layered organization must concern themselves with ways of reaching all levels of the organization. The leaders's role must take into account not only the level and type of activity involved but also the behavioral patterns of those addressed.

Leaders are, and should be, many things: goal setters, planners, resource providers, encouragers, persuaders, developers of people and of ideas, organizers, trainers, and gadflies. They should, as Barnard, Selznick and others have suggested, direct themselves to the institution-building requirements of the job. It is too little and too late to think only—or primarily—of controlling and directing. If these were all that were required, hierarchical patterns would suffice, and there would be no need for chapters of this nature.

More Open Systems of Managing. Ours is a democratic society but our organizations are hardly examples of democratic behavior. We are being asked, in fact, to forego the patterns we have lived under the moment we step into our office or factory. This is an idea well worth contemplating.

An open society requires a greater degree of openness in its institutions than a closed one. This is why it is important that managements look to ways by which native characteristics and habit patterns can be built upon.

The Japanese have in recent years shown us some approaches that encourage the individual workman to contribute more fully to the system than has been possible in the past.[7] There are examples from American enterprise as well. The point here is that we should not become so fully wedded to traditional ways of doing things that we overlook others which, long-range, have greater merit.

What Price Hierarchy?

Present organizational patterns with their emphasis on hierarchy are likely to be with us for some time to come. Tradition, habit, lack of appreciation of what they are costing us, lack of knowledge of alternatives, and fear of change itself, are among the reasons why they will remain. Executives wedded to well-established ways of doing things will have no trouble finding acceptable reasons for leaving things as they are.

Organizational patterns do not, however, need to be as massive or as imposing as they now are. An organization of 20 or more levels—and they do exist—is not only anachronistic but nonfunctional as well. It is a monument to absurdity.

The real contest between East and West is to make our organizations do what we want them to do. The future belongs to those who first master their bureaucracies.

If this estimate is correct, we need to give more attention to what we have previously taken for granted. We need to understand what is happening and why, how much it is costing us, and what we can do about it. Persons sensitive to the changing requirements of people *and* organizations will need to find more productive arrangements than we now have.

There is nothing sacrosanct about hierarchy in its present patterns. It has expanded beyond reason in costly and profligate ways. It is high time we remedied it. In fact, as the insightful Pogo of Walt Kelly's comic strip has reminded us, "We has met the enemy and they is US."

FOOTNOTES

[1]While it is generally accepted in military circles that Frederick the Great was father to the modern army organization, and in particular the originator of the general staff system now present in nearly all armies, he has yet to receive the credit these innovations deserve from management historians. In fact, his name does not appear in most histories of management even though there is substantial evidence that organizational arrangements successfully used by the military were later replicated in industry and civilian government.

[2]Victor Thompson, *Modern Organization*, NY: Alfred A. Knopf, Inc., 1961, pp. 152-177.

[3]Robert Presthus, *The Organizational Society*, NY: St. Martin's Press, Inc., 1975. See in particular Chapters 7 and 8, pp. 184-251.

[4]Thompson, *op. cit.*, p. 61.

[5]Dwaine Marvick, *Career Perspectives in a Bureaucratic Setting*, Ann Arbor, MI: University of Michigan Press, 1954. See Chapters 2 and 9.

[6]Robert T. Golembiewski, *Men, Management and Morality: Toward a New Organizational Ethic*, NY: McGraw-Hill Book Company, Inc., 1965, pp. 169-179.

[7]Japanese experience with Quality-Control circles has received considerable attention in this country, much of it from the popular as well as professional press. Two such examples are Robert E. Cole, "Made in Japan—Quality Control Circles," in *Across the Board*, Nov. 1979, pp. 72-78; and Ed Yager, "Examining the Quality Control Circle," *Personnel Journal*, Oct. 1979, pp. 682-684 *et seq.*

CHAPTER XI
THE CHAIN OF COMMAND—AND WHAT IS HAPPENING TO IT

As we have seen, there are few ideas as strongly held or as vigorously defended as those involving chains of command. Many in fact will contend that if they have not been ordained by God, they should have been. Yet "going through channels" is among the most frequently violated of the so-called "principles" of management. No sooner has the superstructure been set than those caught in it must face the fact that if it is to function successfully they must find ways of circumventing the chain of command. This applies to those higher up as well as those down below. In fact, this is an example of dysfunctionalism at work that is present in nearly all large organizations.

When a "principle" is violated often enough, it is, of course, no longer a "principle" or even a proverb. This is what is happening to chain of command despite protestations to the contrary, as this chapter should make abundantly clear.

I have for many years observed top executives reaching down to lower levels under a variety of pretexts to find out what was going on there, and taking steps to set it right if in their judgment this was needed. If they had waited to have the information they sought come to them via the hierarchical line, it would often have arrived too little and much too late. If they had failed to act in situations they have learned (usually outside of channels) that were developing in counterproductive ways, they would not have been fulfilling their responsibilities. If they had limited their instructions to the chain of command, they would needlessly have penalized both themselves and their organization. They have learned to go through channels when it serves their purposes but they deal directly when it does not.

Likewise, those at lesser levels with strong feelings of responsibility for what happens and a desire to see that it goes well will usually find ways of getting around the roadblocks and the way stations between them and those up above when they believe this needs to be done. No one feels guilty about it either.

Down and Around

It is always easier for the high level executive to go out of channels *downward* than it is for a lower or middle level one to do so upward.

No leaders worth their salt will let their cause be betrayed because someone in the hierarchy fails to pass the word or take the action needed. In fact, the more enterprising among leaders and managers have often taken a special delight in violating the administrative arrangements on which so much time and effort have been spent. If you haven't perceived this, you haven't been observing.

Napoleon had no hesitation whatsoever in getting to the nub of the problem by whatever means were available to him. The by-passing of either a commander or an echelon of commanders troubled him not at all. He practiced the same policy in affairs of state. Surely no one would doubt that he did so effectively.

Lincoln's willingness to violate chains of command as it served his purposes produced a number of significant achievements which management traditionalists would as soon not be reminded of. We titter a bit at some of the homespun practices of the prairie lawyer, but he was clearly one of the most effective U.S. presidents. Surely, this had something to do with it.

Franklin Roosevelt and John Kennedy provide other examples of high level executives reaching far down into the organization, well past their key surrogates, to find out what was happening and on occasion to suggest what should be done. Kennedy insisted during the Cuban missile crisis on talking direct to the captain of the ship which intercepted the Russian freighter bringing in more missiles. His argument was that, as commander-in-chief, he carried a heavy responsibility for making sure that he knew what was happening and also for having his own instructions clearly understood by those who would be carrying them out. The Navy didn't like it, of course, but in view of the precedent set by some of its own leaders, from Nelson on down, did not make anything of it.

Both Kennedy and Robert McNamara, his Defense secretary, often made their own telephone calls to subordinates well down the line. If their staffs tried to keep them prisoners, they did not always succeed. General of the Armies Douglas MacArthur is another example. He made a career, in fact, of by-passing superiors as well as subordinates whenever he felt it appropriate. "It's the orders you disobey," he has been quoted as saying, "that make you famous." He is not the only one who has discovered that this is often so.

The invention of new electronic equipment makes the by-passing of individual levels simple and quick. But before that there was the bullhorn and the loud-speaker system which enabled a commander to speak direct to troops at whatever level and wherever they were.

The examples given above are from government and the military.

Others could as easily have been cited from private business. High level executives, in fact, find it's simpler and more effective to visit operating levels than do their opposite numbers in the public sector. (After all, they do represent ownership.) If you doubt this, read what many of them have to say in *Fortune, Business Week, Nation's Business* and the *Wall Street Journal* about their management styles and methods.

The Japanese have even institutionalized the process, which makes a great deal of sense. Their executives will often sit in open spaces in plants and factories, in effect inviting whoever wishes to pay them a visit. The paper curtain is often a rice paper one.

Few things have, of course, contributed more to the violation of the chains of command than the telephone. It provides one of the simpler means of going around subordinates. Ma Bell does not advertise this fact but she doesn't need to. Subscribers can usually manage to think of it on their own.

Up and Over

Those farther down the chain of command have similar reasons for violating it. If they are to do their jobs properly, there will be times, perhaps many times, when they will need to get around the fellow immediately above them and perhaps the fellow above him as well. Consider this:

- There is an emergency. Those at the top have to know about it—and quickly. Going through channels won't do. Three Mile Island was a case in point.

- Someone at lower or mid-levels has something important to say. It's not an emergency, but if left to the chain of command it might well become one. So, doesn't it make sense to speak up and go around?

- Organizational middle-levels are notoriously myopic. (Microscopic may be a better word.) Someone well down the line has an idea, an observation, or some information that is macroscopic in its nature. How can one be sure it will get to the proper persons Up Above without it being stopped along the way?

- A higher-up invites suggestions from all levels. He or she says that they are personally welcome—and actions indicate this is so. In fact, there is a real "open door" policy.

- A lesser employee conversant with stated organizational policy discovers that an immediate supervisor, if not directly violating it, is not really following it either. The subordinate is eager to see that matters are set right.

These are, of course, good *organizational* reasons for communicating upwards *outside* the chain of command. There are others of a more personal nature. The communicator may see this as an opportunity to ingratiate himself or herself with higher-ups, which is certainly an old American custom. It may provide a chance to get around, or get back at, someone holding him down. The end-runner may also enjoy the role of the non-conformist. By advertising one's self, one is in effect indulging in self-development. Whatever the reasons, organizational or personal, there are arguments as well as opportunities for going out of channels.

Now for some of the risks.

Are the Risks Real?

Conventional wisdom holds that the person who goes outside of channels is courting disaster. Sometimes this is made to seem so frightening that information which ought to be quickly put into the hands of those at higher levels is kept from them because subordinates are too timid to do what good sense would seem to require. Sometimes action which ought to be taken is stalled while subordinates debate what to do. The dangers of going outside of channels, however, are more fancied than real.

Actually, the chances are that nothing really bad will happen to the end-runner. If the message is accepted—and acted upon—by higher ups, the message bearer will usually be rewarded. One's immediate superiors may grumble a bit, and may even threaten in indirect ways, but this will probably come to nothing. The violator of the chain will be seen by those in the executive suite as someone whose development is worthy of being watched. They will probably give credit for initiative as well as judgment. If the idea or information put forward is not accepted, there may even be apologies for its not being used.

Pick a dozen persons you know who have become successful in your company or agency and you will find plenty of examples of their going around others who were frustrating either their desires or their professions. Many of them will boast about it later. Some will claim it was a turning point in their careers.

Much of the time they will have done it in ways that either cannot be fully identified with them, or are so obvious that those who feel bypassed will prefer not to make an issue of it. About the worst that can happen is that the person to whom information is passed will choose not to do anything with it, in which case contact with an even higher level may be in order. The fellow circumvented may fuss and fume a bit—but it's bad manners today to be vindictive. Almost every organization manual provides the right of appeal. Explain that you are merely exercising an honest difference of opinion. As for the substantive issue, the person circumvented may even change his or her mind and go along with whoever went around him.

A woman, or someone having minority status (race, ethnic origin, age, etc.) is in an even stronger position. The person gone around may even end up on the defensive. It has happened.

There may even be admiration, albeit sometimes a bit grudging, on the part of the person circumvented for the fellow who did it. Who has not secretly admired those with courage, tenacity, and ingenuity? What organization does not value initiative?

Management in practice, if not in theory, encourages circumvention. The appearance in force of such recent managerial innovations as the ombudsman, the special investigator, the internal auditor and the employee counsellor, to say nothing of those older mainstays, the adjutant and the chaplain, underlines this point.

A few organizations even provide for what one calls an "action hot line" for those who know something they feel the top people ought to know. A supervisor at whatever level is entitled to reach the top managers within an hour merely by filling out a form detailing the problem. (The immediate superior also gets a copy but cannot stop the message from going forward.) The military has over the years worked out systems by which subordinates can send their views upward with the guarantee that they will reach the top, if necessary, without delay. Those in between can add their comment if the message goes through channels but must see that it goes on anyway.

If the boss has an "open door policy" you are provided the opportunity for at least one visit. (Sometimes restrictions are placed on repeaters.) The top dog in the private sector is often easier to reach than a public service counterpart. Those who make the rules feel less reluctant in violating them.

Some Ways of Doing It

This does not mean, of course, that one should go out of one's way to remind a touchy superior that he or she is about to be circumvented. (No one likes to be threatened and those in the hierarchy no better than anyone else.) There are much more effective—and sophisticated—ways of getting around this.

Sometimes this can be done by the chance remark. A lesser level person in a meeting, attended also by those in higher echelons makes a report on a matter of mutual interest. Woven into it is a comment which it is "assumed" the people upstairs already know. Their show of interest will indicate whether they do or not. The remark-maker acts innocently enough. One is merely doing one's job.

Report-writers can put what they want to into reports that bear their name. If it's critical *to* the program, or *of* the program, only someone truly stupid will try to bury it or edit it out. If either is done, and it's discovered later, it's usually the neck of those who tried to cover up. They know that. So they will let a lot that they really don't like go through for higher ups to read.

The task force or the fact-finding committee is of enormous importance in circumventing traditional lines of command. In fact, it is an *ad hoc* substitute for the on-going organization and is thus licensed to go around or through it. Members have great freedom of suggestion, but so also do those who contribute information and ideas to it. The same is true of internal advisory committees. Internal auditors always have an ear cocked for whatever they are told *sub rosa*. Like newspaper reporters, they will usually protect individual sources.

Occasionally an organization will invite its employees to make known information covering organization integrity (honesty) and other similar matters via the unsigned letter to the appropriate persons. Most, however, prefer not to suggest openly such an approach even though they will usually pay careful attention to what is said, and if important enough, will look into it.

The "old boy" (and now the "old girl") network is something else. It is used regularly, and with a relatively high degree of approval, as a means of passing information informally around the organization. A suggestion system is another device for reaching the higher echelons. The car-pool has uses other than transportation. Although limited by its size, it is a guaranteed method of disseminating information about the organization as well as the best place to go for a brake job. Finally, there is the matter of who sleeps with whom, and its effect upon what goes on.

People outside the organization serve some of the same purposes. Like bumble bees, they help to fertilize the system. There are many instances where the in-house operator goes to clients, supporters and fellow professionals so as to get around organizational roadblocks. A friendly reporter, looking for scoops, can also help out although higher-ups sometimes resent having to learn about their own organizations from the columns of the morning *Gazette*. The advice to those who leak information to the press is to be discreet about it. More of this goes on in government than in private circles but it still takes place.

The union can sometimes be useful as well. Not infrequently, wives of those within the system lend a hand in receiving and conveying information. They have their own ways of passing the word.

As a last resort, if all else fails, there is "whistle-blowing." Most members of Congress welcome the whistle-blower, whether business or government. If the charges are dramatic enough, they will make the front pages. The price one is asked to pay, however, despite new legislation passed to provide protection is likely to be great. Whistle-blowing should probably be used only as a last resort, but ordinarily it won't be necessary. As the above suggests, there are so many alternatives.

Organizational Accommodation

The point that is being made here is that most organizational systems work with only limited success when confined to channels. So, pragmatists that we are, we have found ways of going around the chains of command we have so laboriously developed.

It is time, therefore, that we recognized and accepted this fact and encouraged it to occur as naturally as possible. It is time indeed for the theory to catch up with the practice.

Employees are urged at all levels to contribute their ideas, their suggestions, and their support to organizational objectives. Yet few legitimate ways other than through the chain of command are provided by which they can get these ideas to the attention of those with need of them, higher up or lower down. The larger the organization, the farther removed is the majority of its members from the planning and policy-making levels. The farther removed also are those in policy places from those who are needed to make this policy effective. The brash, the bold, the gamesmen and the upward mobiles, have already found ways around the system. Others need help.

Some of the devices which are needed are:

- Suggestion systems that are more than "tool improvement" systems—systems that come to grips with organizational policies, goals, and also operational methods.

- Internal advisory committees on which selected lower- and middle-level employees serve for fixed periods.

- Devices by which higher level executives can address those at other levels on matters of concern to both.

- Devices (and possibly equipment) by which employees at all levels can learn of agency policy by mechanical means and can make contributions to it.

- Greater use of task forces and other *ad hoc* groups.

- Shorter, and less rigid, hierarchies.

- "Open door" policies that are open in more than name.

- Study, and perhaps adaptation, of what the Japanese have done with Quality Control Circles.

More important than all of these is a change in conventional management thinking. Instead of pretending that the chain of command is to be violated only under exceptional circumstances, organizational leaders should assume that intercourse between interested and dedicated people is a normal and intelligent way of doing things, and that in fact no other course is really possible if one is to obtain the commitment and contribution of those who are members of the system.

The rank a person holds should certainly be recognized as having been justly earned through qualification for the job; it should be respected for what it stands for. But it does not entitle its holder to block or sidetrack whatever another regards as important to the common objective. The idea that the modern, fast-moving organization should be compartmentalized into rigidly controlled principalities and enclaves, presided over by petty functionaries, each jealous of his or her own turf, is repugnant to the cooperative ideal. Those in leadership roles should make it clear by both word and action that they mean to have a more open system, and then see that this occurs.

We must divest ourselves of some of the habits and customs of other, less sophisticated times. The chain of command has its merit but is hardly sacrosanct. Good judgment requires that we recognize in theory as well as practice that, in an increasing number of instances, it will need to be violated.

CHAPTER XII
ORGANIZATIONAL MANTRAP: THE DEPUTY CHIEF

A characteristic of today's large organizations, both private and public, is the proliferation of the position of deputy or assistant chief. Indeed, a sufficient number of *deputy* directors, administrators, managers, superintendents, chiefs, and department or division heads is already on hand to form a new professional association concerned with the problems and preservation of the species.

Many deputies are badly needed, but many others are not. What is worse, they are getting in the way of effective performance by confusing the leadership role while at the same time adding another hierarchical level to the organization. Consider the following cases:

• The head of Staff Service Division A, consisting of only four branches, has a deputy. The boss explained that it was needed to "man the fort" when the former was away from his desk.

• A field division of five elements has a chief and deputy although both readily admit that they are not overburdened with work. Reason: field offices in this agency follow a standard organizational pattern regardless of workload.

• A leader of five units (a total of 15 people) saw himself as the policymaker and his deputy as the person in charge of operations. Both, of course, became involved with policy *and* operations, and things sometimes became badly tangled.

These illustrations are by no means unusual. There are many instances of organizations with three, four, or five divisional units, or people, which have both chiefs and assistant chiefs. Occasionally, there will even be cases of a deputy for organizations with as few as two divisions.

On the face of it, of course, there seems much to recommend the single deputy arrangement. It has historic roots, as military experience suggests. It is a device for sharing the leadership load as that load multiplies in volume and complexity. It provides a "spare tire" for security coverage when the boss is absent, as our own form of government with its President and Vice President exemplifies. It brings additional expertise to the top levels. It is a "proving ground" for executive training. Indeed, one of its illusions is because its rationale is so easy to support.

Problems with Deputies

A closer look, however, at the manner in which the chief and deputy actually work together will often show another and less convincing side of the picture, as the following criticisms suggest:

-- Division-of-labor problems are created between chief and deputy which are always difficult, sometimes impossible, to resolve.

- A new, and often unneeded, hierarchical level is added to the organization.

- The span of control is reduced at a time when organizational theory is seeking to expand it.

- Duplication of effort and overlap of duties frequently result.

- Uncertainty and confusion take place among those at the lower working levels.

- Disagreement, and sometimes open conflict, is encouraged between the boss and the deputy.

These are serious charges. Not only do they place large requirements on the individuals who are called upon to fill the principal and deputy roles, but they also place burdens on the organization as a whole. Let us examine each in greater detail.

Division of Labor. For the principal and the deputy to function properly, there must be some kind of workable division of labor between them. This means that there must be some way of dividing up the tasks so that others will know with whom to deal on specific matters. One hears occasionally of two-man teams which have worked together over a period of time without such an arrangement—that is, with no discernible pattern regulating what each is to do—but my own observation is that this happens infrequently.

Sometimes the workload is split between "inside" and "outside" activities, between "policy" and "operations," between "big" issues and "lesser" ones, or between divisions. The last sometimes occurs because one man (often the chief) prefers, or thinks he or she is better at, one type of work than another. The deputy gets what is left.

The likelihood of conflict between chief and deputy is increased when any of a number of circumstances prevail. When the leadership workload is light, there is a tendency to compete for what is left. Differences can also arise over policy and methods, or when, as is sometimes the case, the deputy stands higher in the views of either superiors or subordinates than does the chief. If the deputy is given operations—which is usually thought of as the least desirable share of the assignment—he or she may, in fact, turn out to be more influential than the boss.

A New Hierarchical Level. The existence of a deputy with real authority inevitably introduces another hierarchical level into the organization. The work performed must be reviewed in some way or other by the chief, who, of course, can reverse whatever has been done. Some chiefs actually encourage appeal from their subordinate's judgments without really seeming to do so, to show their fairness or their power.

For whatever reason, one more step has been put into the communicational and decision-making processes; one more filter has been inserted.

Those who have tried to visualize these relationships on the organization chart are quite aware of the problem. Should the chief and the deputy both be in the same "box," or should there be a separate "box" for each? Should one overlay the other? General practice is to box them together but this does not mean this is the way things actually work out. Whether a new level, or only half a one, has been added, there is always an additional person in the pecking order.

Shortening the Span of Control or Supervision. Having a single deputy shortens the span of control and lessens the delegation which would ordinarily be extended to the operating levels. This can have repercussions in a number of ways. The deputy is seen as a bottleneck by those whose authority has been lessened by his or her presence, and perhaps as a usurper by the boss. It is easy for both to be resentful.

Duplication of Effort. The principal-deputy relationship often produces costly duplication of effort. Consider, for example, the need for informing each of what is going on in the organization, as well as what the other is doing. Much paper must be seen by two people. Both must be briefed. Many times both must attend meetings. Such practices occur frequently and routinely. Over a period of time, they can become very costly.

"Deputy Problems." The existence of an assistant chief creates special types of problem relationships between the assistant and subordinates which may be identified as "deputy problems." These may appear in a variety of forms, but whatever their base, they detract from the deputy's usefulness as well as status.

If he is seen as an "heir apparent," as some assistants are, one becomes the object of the familiar "testing" phenomenon. What are the areas of weakness, of uncertainty? How well does he or she really stand with the boss? Jealous subordinates know many ways of making life unhappy for fledgling executives.

If there are difficulties between the two principals, no matter how slight, these will be picked up by those below them and almost certainly amplified just as differences between parents are seen and used by children. An interesting side effect is that subordinates are given the opportunity under bifurcated leadership to select the superior to be reported to on a given issue. Naturally, the one picked is the one most likely to agree with what is being asked. This is a characteristic by-product of the system.

Conflicts Between Chief and Deputy. The situation is built to order for conflict between chief and deputy. Consider the following:

- The boss gives the deputy the unpleasant jobs—the ones fraught with "danger," or the ones the boss doesn't want to do.

- The boss takes the credit, or seems to, for successes, but blames the deputy for the failures. Although the two are expected to complement each other, they really disagree on some rather basic issues.

- The deputy is considerably more successful in dealing with people (key people?) than the boss, so jealousy develops.

- Or, if you like, the boss is more successful in outside relationships, so the deputy is the failure.

- The deputy is seen as a rival for the boss's job. So the boss tends to play it cozy.

Such situations do not invariably occur, but they appear frequently enough to raise major questions concerning the use of the single deputy.

Why So Many Deputies?

If the single deputy role has so many defects, why are there so many of them today? Some of the reasons are good ones, but others are more likely to be rationalizations and well after the fact at that.

A proliferation of single deputies is usually a characteristic of the large rather than the small or medium-sized organization. There are probably more of them in government than the private sector for obvious reasons but there are really no statistics on the matter.

An honest explanation for their presence in a great many cases will be, "Why, we've always had an assistant chief, or at least as long as I can remember." In one government bureau, the regional office's explanation was that national office instructions called for one. Those in the position—both chief *and* deputy, incidentally—admitted they were not happy with the arrangement, but SOP called for it. They would not think of questioning Washington—at least, not in this matter.

Others probably see the position as a way of rewarding someone or getting a position level not otherwise possible. There can be many reasons, whether or not they make good sense.

The Case For a Single Deputy

A good case for a deputy is often made because of the volume of the work to be done. The Forest Service, after a major study of its field installations, concluded that this was the case. The boss cannot be expected to be everywhere at once. So an assistant chief was created to help share the load. Sometimes also the case is made for an "inside" man and an "outside" man, which is, of course, another variation of the work volume idea. The deputy may be a "spare tire" or "stand-in" when the boss is away. Considerations such as these may have a great deal of merit, but each needs to be examined carefully to see whether or not some other arrangement might not be more satisfactory.

There are other reasons for having a deputy, some of them hidden ones. Take, for example, the matter of status. "I'll have my assistant take care of that," a division director may say, implying that his role is of a loftier nature. The principal may feel insecure in certain areas, or not want to do certain things, such as provide supervisory leadership. There are the cases also where the chief is given a deputy by those higher up. They no longer trust him or her and want their own person in the organization.

These are some of the reasons why it is so easy to add an assistant or deputy to one's organizational directory.

Situations where the use of the deputy may be warranted will include the following:

1. Where there is a large amount of work to be done in the leadership of a *large* organization. The top man may be concerned with outside (or clientele) affairs, while the deputy will spend most of the time with internal operations. Thus, opportunities for conflict or overlap are minimized.

2. Where the work of the organization readily divides itself into major, logical groupings. Each can then provide leadership to an appropriate segment of it, although the primacy of one of the two is usually recognized.

3. Where the organization (or division) is new or expanding and a premium is placed on getting things under way.

4. Where geographical considerations apply. The deputy may be head of a major field installation, or responsible for certain area activities.

5. Where the single deputy is being trained, although not necessarily for the job the principal holds.

6. Where there is a record of two persons having worked well together before in a team relationship, and where the volume or priority of work calls for more than one.

Whatever the arrangement, its terms must be understood and accepted by all of those concerned, including those subordinate to both principal and deputy.

Some Alternatives

The alternative to the use of the single deputy is really quite simple. Get rid of the position. The leadership role belongs clearly to the chief. Operational responsibility lies with the heads of the next-level units below.

The deputy is no substitute for an ineffective chief. Neither should the deputy be asked to do the work of the unit heads.

If the chief needs assistance in being informed, in informing others, or in performing particular services, special assistants can be added. These, however, are not the same as a deputy, even though, unhappily, many deputies seem to have become personal assistants to their superiors.

The rewards of a campaign to reduce the number of assistant chiefs in an organization may not be seen immediately but they are sure to be felt over a period of time. Not only does a saving in manpower result in a saving in dollars, but a reduction in the number of hierarchical levels and a broadening of spans of control will almost certainly help to develop personnel at all levels of the organization.

It is easy to remark in this day and age on the vestigial characteristics of the locomotive fireman, the hand-set printer, or the elevator operator. It is far more painful to find that other kinds of featherbedding may be taking place on one's own premises, and that we as either chiefs of deputies may be personally involved.

Of all the mantraps in large organizations, the single deputy is one of the most insidious.

CHAPTER XIII

STAFF PEOPLE AND THEIR PROBLEMS

A great deal has been said and written during the past 40 years about the staff functions. In addition to the many articles and books, many universities offer graudate level courses on such subjects as personnel administration, budgeting, management analysis, and planning. Each year, hundreds of young men and women enter careers in the staff areas in government alone, in addition to many thousands more in private business.

This attention is well deserved. The more we know of large organizations, the clearer it becomes that staff people have a vital part to play in the work to be done. It is inconceivable that we are going to be able to get along without them in the foreseeable future.

Yet, one cannot get very deeply into organizational theory without realizing that relationships between staff and line people are still far from what they should be, and that, among the areas of management, this is one where a great deal of friction, and sometimes outright controversy, is still likely to be found.

At least a part of the reason for this unhealthy state of affairs can be attributed to our failure to understand the real nature of the staff role. Much of what has been written about it is by way of sweeping generalization—so sweeping, in fact, that the sophisticated ways by which the staff often inserts itself into the control (or policy) processes are glossed over or overlooked entirely. Much more of the literature is an attempt to describe the procedures or techniques which the specialist must use, or to outline, as in job description sheets, the specific functions one is asked to perform. All of this is useful but it is far from telling the whole story. Indeed, the generalization of the duties to be performed, or the techniques for performing them, often misleads rather than enlightens. What we need to know is what staff people really do, how they work with others, how they are seen by them, and how they feel about it all. We need to know, also, how staff and line relate to each other; how, as the organization grows more complex, staff serves the leader; and what, in short, the staff man's contribution is to the organization.

Interviews with Staff People

In an effort to obtain insight into this problem, the writer sent some 125 graduate students into government agencies over a five year period, armed with questions which sought to probe beyond the conventional approaches.

Interviewers were encouraged to talk with staff officers in selected agencies, using the guided interview technique, and to report back their findings. Their reports revealed something of a consensus. In all, staff officers of more than 30 government bureaus or agencies, ranging from grade 11 (in a handful of instances) through grade 18, were visited with the mean falling between GS 14 and 15. Staff areas visited included budgeting, comptrollership, personnel, legal, information and public relations, security, internal audit, organization and methods, and administrative services. In all, approximately 400 interviews took place.

The questions that were asked varied. Those most frequently used included the following:

- What do you consider your particular role to be? (That is, how do you view your duties and responsibilities in the organization?)

- How do you feel you are seen by others? (Do they agree with your interpretation of role?)

- What are the major problems you face in getting your job done?

- What ways have you found for approaching (solving) these problems?

- What are your chief satisfactions?

- What are your chief dissatisfactions (frustrations)?

- How is your performance measured by your superiors?

- Do you prefer a career in staff or one in line?

- How do you apportion your time? (Here, an effort was made to obtain a breakdown of time spent on the job, using a suggested classification pattern.)

On the whole, the interviewers were very well received. In only a few instances was an interview refused. After gaining admission to the staff office, however, much depended upon the facility of the interviewer, or the pressure of time on the interviewee.

Most interviews lasted approximately an hour. A few of the interviewers reported that they talked with their principal for two or more hours. Several had even taken the trouble to bring together pertinent materials for the occasion. Sometimes other staff members were invited in. A few took so favorably to the exercise that the interviewer felt he or she was "getting a life story." Most interviewers were of the opinion that, generally speaking, they had been given straight and honest answers. Several were outspoken in criticism of their superiors. More were critical of line people. There were few failures to obtain answers to specific questions.

While no statistical tabulation of responses could be made, useful general conclusions are possible. These are summarized in the following pages.

Nature of the Staff Role

Considerable difference of opinion existed on the nature of the role of the staff officer. This difference was not so much difference in kind as difference in the degree to which the staff man felt that the role could be practiced. There was a tendency in answering this question to resort to generalities, but when the interviewer probed more deeply, most staff people recognized the multiple nature of their assignment.

Most interviewees agreed that the staff officer's first responsibility was to the administrator or the head of the agency or unit. Staff was seen as being primarily responsible for giving advice, for providing resources, and for assisting the executive in carrying out the mission of the organization. But these were also understood to be only parts of the staff role.

The staff officer has a wide variety of relationships with line people also. They must be advised, assisted and serviced. Most of those interviewed acknowledged the importance of having good relationships with line people and took particular pride in reporting theirs. Several, however, noted conflicts between themselves and the line and a few between the boss and the line. Some noted the differences between what the line wanted to do and sound management practices. Such situations, it was clear, made their own staff role more difficult.

That the staff officer is not limited to the service, advice, and assistance noted above, but is also involved in policy making and operations, was brought out by a number of those interviewed. One may also be involved with actual control, although generally there was hesitation in stating it in these terms. Sometimes this is done indirectly, in the name of the administrator; sometimes it is done directly, with custom and practice playing a major role; often it occurs in the name of "good management." The staffer's part in a policy might be one of representing the director's point of view. ("After all, I am fairly close to him.") Or, it might be based on delegated authority in a specific area (such as the budget) or in areas in which the staff man possessed acknowledged expertise (such as the law). Sometimes the staff officer exercises control because it needs to be done. "The requests I have for service," one man was reported as saying, "are always greater than my ability to supply them. So I have to make decisions as to who gets what. Who else should make them?" Another commented, "My boss doesn't like problems; he likes solutions. So I give him solutions. He generally goes along with them."

Most staff officers, however, shied away from admitting that they actually made policy, or even had a major hand in shaping it, by taking refuge behind such phrases as "I'm only a technician" or "I only recommend—I don't control." On the other hand, several (particularly in the fiscal and legal areas) acknowledged quite frankly that they had considerable influence on agency decisions. Several lawyers generalized their own functions along the line of Charles Evans Hughes who said, "the law is what the judges say it is." A budget officer commented, "The Secretary thinks the budget job is one of the most important in the department." He agreed that, as a result of his knowledge of it, he probably had a great deal of influence on agency policy.

How Others See Them

Wide variation was noted in the way in which staff officers perceive themselves as being seen by others, particularly by those in the line. On the whole, they seemed to believe that those in operations felt their status to be superior to staff's, although, in the final analysis, this might depend upon the staff function performed. A lawyer, for example, sees himself or herself as having relatively high status, but an administrative services officer, on the other hand, holds quite a different view.

Most budget officers feel that they have high standing also. They know their jobs are vital to the agency and, based on the time they spend with the administrator, they have come to regard themselves as close to being indispensable. One confided: "I think that the budget officer, after all these years, has finally arrived."

This kind of optimism, however, is not really shared by the majority of those in staff roles. While views vary, depending on the function and the agency, staff people know that, however vital their roles, they are seen by many as "necessary evils." Still the feeling exists that the situation today is considerably better than it was ten years ago, and still improving.

The low man on the totem pole is undoubtedly the administrative services officer, although pressed for this distinction by a number of other very useful professionals, including the accountant, the administrative auditor, the librarian, and sometimes, the public information officer. Some idea of what those in administrative services feel their image may be is provided by the following comments from five interviews. Four of these reflect a negative feeling.

- "My job is thought of as a necessary evil."

- "I think most people think of me as a person to help them."

- "Most people wouldn't want my job."

- "People I deal with don't remember the jobs I do—only the mistakes I make."

- "Others don't envy me."

The internal auditors, in recognition of the views which many have of them as "intruders," "snoopers," and even "hatchet men," are now embarked upon a campaign to change this image. Their comments are distinctly on the cheerful side, reflecting in part at least the efforts of the Institute of Internal Auditors to make them understood and accepted by all of management. In most Federal agencies, the head internal auditor now reports directly to the administrator. Many internal auditors take an active part in management training activities and have earnestly tried in a variety of ways to gain the "cooperation" of those whom they audit. As one man commented: "We are no longer looked on as outcasts or lepers."

The case of the "P.R." people is an interesting one. In general, they see themselves as the "fall guys" for others over whom they really have no control and with whom they sometimes have very little influence. As one of them stated, meaningfully if somewhat ungrammatically, "P.R. is now a dirty word." Of all of those interviewed, the information people seemed to show the greatest reluctance to talk, which may be an indication of the way they view their position. Or, it may be, as others have suggested, an indication of their distrust of what may happen to the spoken word.

Satisfactions in One's Work

The kind of satisfactions staff people find in their jobs, as might be expected, varied with the jobs themselves. Still, there was substantial agreement on several major points which were mentioned repeatedly during the interviews.

A Job Well Done

The personal knowledge that the assignment the staff man has been given has been done well was probably the satisfaction most often mentioned. While the praise of others is welcomed, no one knows better than the individual who has done it whether it is deserved. One training officer stated, "I get a good feeling out of seeing change in people's outlook and development." A lawyer added that he takes pride in "seeing results of things I believe in." An administrative services officer took great pride in a 50 percent reduction in accident rates in his department over the five years he had been on the job. He also mentioned a reduction in operating costs of motor vehicles two cents per mile below the government average. In a sense, the point of view that performance was its own reward was summed up by one man who said, "You just can't be rewarded by money for the job you do in government. The reward is the appreciation of what you are doing for the good of the country, both by yourself and others."

Varied and Interesting Assignments

There was frequent mention of varied, interesting, and important assignments as one of the major staff job satisfactions. Sometimes, even, the interviewee described in detail the varietal nature of the work done. One man, citing his years of service and wealth of background, said that he thought of each new telephone call as a challenge to this knowledge. "It isn't often I get a call," he said, "about something I haven't already had experience in." Several spoke of a liking for problem-solving and an opportunity to be creative or to do original work. One man described in detail a proposal he had a major hand in developing, which will shortly be placed before Congress. If adopted, it could save the government millions of dollars over the course of the next 25 years.

Personal Recognition of Accomplishments

This satisfaction appeared in a variety of forms. It might be either the approval of the boss or of someone outside the agency. As frequently, however, staff people spoke of the fact that those in operational areas called them personally as problems arose. When this occurs, staff men feel that they "have arrived."

Indications of the boss's approval might range anywhere from the "no comment," which one special assistant reported as a good sign in his principal, to "a kind word from upstairs." Several remarked that thier superiors had not only assured them of their backing but had given it to them in fact. Two or three were able to point to agency citations.

A lawyer said that operating people always called him personally with their problems. A personnel officer spoke of her close relationships with those in the line and mentioned how she was regularly consulted in organizational matters before commitments were made. An information officer stated, "People trust me and call me personally." An internal auditor reported with a sense of achievement that people in operations did not hesitate to call him for advice—often on "how to get around the regulations."

Working with People

Staffers seemed to indicate a preference for those jobs which bring them into frequent contact with a variety of people to those which require little or no daily contact. "I know everybody," one man said with obvious pride. Personnel and training officers in particular felt this way about their work, but, interestingly enough, so did some of the internal auditors.

The Status of Their Roles

Whether or not the status factor was noted usually depended on the closeness of the staff function to the seat of power. Those most likely to mention it were the "assistants to," the budget officers, the lawyers, and, occasionally, the information people.

Sometimes they spoke of it directly. More often, it was remarked upon obliquely: "I like to know what is going to happen before it happens." A number of interviewees provided interesting insight into the part they played in the process—the lawyer writing budget messages and handling legislative relationships, or the budget man "keeping people from selling the Secretary 'a bill of goods'."

Other Satisfactions

As one might expect, a number of satisfactions fitted none of these categories. Several mentioned salary or "my pay check," but, more

often than not, the interviewers felt this a negative response (when not
a humorous one), indicating a lack of other satisfactions. One cited the
satisfaction of getting to testify before Congress—which is certainly not
the way many feel about it. Several commented on being with an
agency with "humane objectives," or at least, goals with which they
strongly agreed. There was also favorable comment on the loyalty and
support of subordinates. Another took pride in "fighting the business"
and still another said his greatest happiness came from "seeing people in
plush offices sweat." These, however, were in the minority.

Frustrations and Dissatisfactions

Staff people clearly have their frustrations and dissatisfactions in
greater number, and also in greater variety, than their satisfactions.
Those most frequently mentioned are indicated below.

Bureaucratic Restrictions

One of the major annoyances felt by staff people was in the restrictions which bureaucracy imposes on them. This was constantly remarked upon. Not only was it mentioned as applying to procedures,
standards, and types of equipment, but also was seen as being involved
in "excessive regulation," "endless paperwork," "reports for reports'
sake," and the like.

Lack of Real Leadership

In one form or another, the failure of executives to take the action
which their subordinates felt they ought to take was reported by
persons in all of the staff areas. In the case of internal audit, this took
the form of a complaint that the boss would not act when deficiencies
were disclosed—a very sensitive subject as far as this type of staff officer
is concerned. Information people spoke of bosses who fail to keep them
informed; training and personnel officers or those who do not recognize
the importance of their programs; and others of "poor planning" at the
top, "crash programs," and "too many bosses." Several spoke of
"people who don't know what they want, or don't tell you what they
have in mind." One budget officer objected because his director usually
turned to him to answer specific Congressional complaints at legislative
hearings, clearly implying that he thought the "buck" was being passed.
One said, deprecatingly, he gets only the work the boss doesn't want.

Lack of Resources to Do the Job

A lack of resources to do the kind of a job that was wanted and needed ranked high among the frustrations of staff service. Sometimes this took the form of complaints over budget, sometimes over the kind and type of personnel available. The comment was frequently made that grades and salaries were too low to attract the right kind of people, that those available were neither well qualified nor properly motivated.

Problems of Working with Others

Staff people noted the difficulties of working with people generally, and, in one form or another, cited this as one of their major problem areas. Some (as in training) mentioned those who would not respond to what they did for them. Others reported difficulties in getting persons in operating areas to "buy" the recommendations that were being made. A budget man said quite bluntly, "We are just not understood by others."

Trivia

The constant trivia of bureaucratic life was seen as a continuing source of irritation and frustration. An administrative services officer complained of having frequently to go to the Secretary with small matters, such as "mice in the building or a flat tire on his car." Others noted time pressures, frequent distractions, and doing jobs they felt were not important.

Problems of Communication and Coordination

There is no question that problems of communication provide a major distraction in the staff areas. Staff people noted that frequently they did not know what was going on elsewhere or even what was really wanted of them. Mention was made of "people reducing budgets without giving reasons," of requests for "rejustification of funds," of "not being understood (or appreciated) by others," and of delays in coordinating matters or resolving disputes between units.

Other Dissatisfactions

Several mentioned the size of the work loads they had and doubted the ability of ever mastering them. The difficulties of measuring work achievement were mentioned by a number.

Interestingly enough, salary was mentioned only occasionally as a specific dissatisfaction. One man complained over his title, which he felt degraded him; one or two noted the "lack of future" in their jobs; and some of the information officers, in a moment of candor, talked about their own lack of status vis a vis the practicing journalists from whose ranks they had sprung. Complaint was also heard of the lack of "P.R." sensitivity of most bureaucrats. One man (administrative services) confessed his fear of the on-coming data processing. A number objected to agency criticism of them before Congress or in the press. On the other hand, there were several who said they had no frustrations or dissatisfactions at all.

Measurement of Performance

The question, "how is your performance measured?" elicited a wider variety of responses than any other question. Most interviewers felt that for some this was the first time they had ever really faced up to the matter of evaluation other than as a part of an annual rating system.

There was overwhelming evidence, however, that, as far as most of the staff functions are concerned, no reliable system of measurement is currently in use. Interviewees fell back upon such concepts as "boss" or "client" satisfaction. A few tried to shrug off the matter by saying they were measured on "results" without precisely explaining how.

Many gave evidence, in support of this gauge, that they had no problems as long as things were going smoothly. Frequently, an interviewee spoke of pleasant "day-to-day" relationships with the top people in the agency and the appreciation they voiced. A lawyer said that the administrator had expressed satisfaction with his work and noted he had kept the agency out of trouble.

That negative criticisms have an impact was pointed out by several. One (in administrative services) said he had a half-inch "complaint file" but that this was more than counter-balanced by an inch-and-a-half "commendation file." Most staff people made it clear that they are sensitive to criticism and take steps where possible to set affairs to rights. Yet, they admitted that in carrying out unpopular orders or rationing scarce items, this is not always possible.

There has been some effort, however, to apply work measurement, if only in a general and preliminary way. Personnel people keep records of the number of actions they handle, although it is easier to record what is done than it is to set qualitative or quantitative standards with respect to it. Training people know the number of persons for whom they have arranged training programs. Budget officers know the success of their programs. One reported a "1.000 batting average," based on the fact Congress had not cut a penny from his agency estimates in six years, certainly an unusual record. Another said he had doubled the volume of work handled but gave no indication of whether his staff had been increased meanwhile. An information officer knew the number of press releases he had put out, where they had been published, the requests for speakers supplied, and similar data.

Still, one is left with the impression that such quantitative information has little bearing on the esteem in which a given staff man is held.

Staff or Line?

At the time the interviews were planned, the hypothesis was advanced that many, perhaps most, staff people would prefer to be associated with a line activity. A majority of those interviewed did show such a preference. However, a substantial number, particularly in accounting and administrative services, appeared well satisfied with their staff roles. For them, present assignments met personal objectives; where they did not, work in another agency might.

Among those who preferred a line assignment, the reasons given were the desire to be more closely associated with the agency's end product; to be in the chain of command; to avoid existing ceilings on advancement; and to be in areas where one's own contribution could be more readily identified.

The Changed Image

The interviews clearly provided a great deal of useful insight into the role, functions, opinions, and feelings of staff officers. Among other things, they revealed the commonly held concepts of the staff officer's role—that the chief functions are service and advice—have undergone considerable change in today's administrative patterns. In most large government agencies the staff officer is concerned, directly as well as indirectly, with policy matters.

Unfortunately, this view is not held by everyone in public administration. There are many, particularly those in the line operations, who still see the staff person as someone with only a limited contribution to make, and often one of a negative rather than a positive nature. As long as such opinions prevail, the staff role is likely to be hedged in frustration and the organization will be deprived of the full utilization of some of its most important professional people. It is unlikely also that it will be able to recruit the bright young men and women so much needed. More needs to be done, therefore, to make the staff role a more fully accepted part of the organization.

CHAPTER XIV
THE MYTH OF REORGANIZING

A generation ago, Clarence B. Randall, a former president of Inland Steel and later a public executive, wrote a thoughtful little book entitled *The Folklore of Management*. In it he described a number of the "myths of management." He might have included also the "myth of reorganizing." It is one of the more pervasive.

This particular myth holds that if things are going badly, a reorganization will set them right. If a company is losing money, if a government bureau is mired in its own procedures, or if someone at headquarters is not doing his job, a reorganization is obviously needed. Jimmy Carter won the presidency in part because he promised the American people that as soon as he got to Washington, he would reorganize things.

That reorganizing means reform is, of course, a myth and a most dangerous one at that. It is a myth also that reorganization will result in either changed behavior or improved results. Sometimes it is useful and there are times when it may even be necessary. But it is only one among many approaches open to the executive to resolve what is usually a complex and often a chronic problem and in no way the cure-all that so many take it to be.

There is also a side to reorganizing which is very rarely talked about—its costs. Not only does the conventional reorganization often fail to achieve the objectives set out for it, but associated with it are costs, direct as well as indirect, which are of sufficient magnitude that one should think seriously about them before undertaking it at all. They may or may not be temporary in nature. Sometimes, in fact, the reorganized agency never recovers from the surgery.

Yet we continue to press with knee-jerk regularity and simplistic fervor for reorganizing. Dr. Harold Seidman, formerly a high level staff member of the President's Office of Management and Budget and now a professor at the University of Connecticut, speaks of the recurring Federal reorganization proposals as a religion. "Reorganization," he points out, "is deemed synonymous with reform and reform with progress. Periodic reorganizations are prescribed if for no other reason than to purify bureaucratic blood and to prevent stagnation. Opposition to reorganization is evil. . ."[1]

What is true of Washington is probably equally true of a lot of corporate headquarters whether in New York, Philadelphia, Chicago or elsewhere. The business press speaks regularly of company reorganizations across the country as if they were solutions to whatever was wrong. What they do not report is how well they succeed or what they cost.

Reorganization Objectives and Achievements

On the surface, the word *reorganization* seems simple enough. In conventional usage, it suggests the rearrangement or regrouping of organizational units so as to produce new, different and more effective work patterns. Unit A is split with part of it remaining in Division X and another part going to Division Y. Or it may mean that functions performed previously in a variety of agencies are now to be consolidated in one. In either event, new systems are created. People are moved from one office to another although physically they may stay in the same place. A function may even disappear entirely.

The word "reorganization" can refer to a detailed redoing of basic procedural arrangements, as in a *financial* reorganization. President Carter repeatedly referred to the changes he instituted in the Federal personnel management system as a reorganization. In fact, *any* change in a company's or bureau's ways of doing things often is spoken of as a reorganization.

In this chapter, however, "reorganization" will mean a major rearrangement of organizational units, a shifting of functions and systems, a redistribution of power, and the accompanying changes in personnel which these will require. A change in leadership, whether of the whole or merely a division or two, would not be seen as a legitimate reorganization even though its consequences might be substantial.

The announced purpose of most reorganizations is to enable the organization to deal more effectively or efficiently with the problems it is either facing or expecting to face. There are changes in objectives, in clients, in technology, and geography which older patterns have not been meeting satisfactorily. The new system, their proponents claim, will clear away the organizational debris which may have been accumulating for years, will institute new and simpler ways of doing things, will get rid of unneeded units, and eliminate waste, duplication and what is euphemistically called "deadwood." It will also provide a fresh look at a company or bureau, often by new people with new ideas.

There may, however, be other more sinister reasons. Reorganizations frequently occur when new people take over. They may, as some feel, want to show their muscle and choose this way to do it. Or it may be a smoke screen to hide some other action they expect to take. In the confusion which surrounds the reorganization, people who have held positions of influence suddenly find themselves out in the cold with little or no possibility of recovery.

That reorganizations do rearrange, no one will deny. But whether the organization actually works better because of the changes which have been made, is, of course, something else. What of performance? Is the improvement a temporary one? If there *is* improvement, will it last? There will certainly be new problems. How serious will they be?

Those who have instigated the change can usually be counted on to claim success for their efforts, but interviews with those farther down the line in operations often tell a different story. The work habits of those at operational levels are, in fact, influenced little by most reorganizations.

What is clear is that there is virtually no evidence available that reorganizations actually achieve the goals set for them. A search of major management publications over ten years reveals little that has been written about it.

In one of the very few books on the subject, Professor Frederick C. Mosher of the University of Virginia in his *Governmental Reorganizations: Cases and Commentary* underlines the lack of hard data. He concludes that "the majority of reorganization efforts are unsuccessful or only partially successful in reducing the tensions underlying them." He sees a "reorganization effort," if it is to be undertaken, not as a single episode with a beginning and end but merely a step or stage in the life of an organization.[2]

Whether or not reorganizations achieve the purposes announced for them, they do have their costs. The gains of reorganization should be weighed against these possible disadvantages:

- The disruption of on-going operations.

- Lowered morale.

- Loss of confidence in organizational leadership.

- The possibility of new internal power struggles.

- The departure of key personnel.

- Increased union activity.

- Involvement in the organization of people from the outside.

- A general reduction in both efficiency and effectiveness.

- Further reorganization.

One of the reasons there has not been greater study of reorganization is that its effects are difficult to measure. Most of the failures that come from it relate to the uncertainties felt by those at lesser levels as to how the new arrangements will affect them personally. It is usually next to impossible to keep the proposed reorganization a secret. People suspect even when they do not know, and even innocent questions will lead to shattered morale, counter-measures, or both. Reorganization, if it produces nothing else, produces dysfunction. In today's marketplace, this is expensive.

A recent calculation showed that an organization of 500 employees paid at a minimum wage would lose $56,000 per year if those employees spent five minutes each per day doing something other than their assigned tasks. Expand this by a substantially higher average salary and many more than five minutes per employee per day and the calculable losses attributable to reorganization go "out the top."

In the cynical nature of the times, people expect the worst of reorganization and seem to be disappointed when it does not occur. It is difficult to measure the effect of this upon work performance but it has to be substantial. In the public sector, even the most moderate of reorganization proposals are likely to come under major attack. In a private company, unions are involved routinely, but so are professionals and occasionally even professional associations.

No matter what the criticisms of the existing arrangement have been, there will be those who find the new remedy inappropriate, inadequate, and perhaps perfidious as well. No cause is so small as to be without its adherents. Reorganization proposals can usually be counted on to arouse instant and dogged opposition. Each citizen is his or her own expert in sex, politics, and organizational matters. Reorganizations provide endless opportunities for individual theorizing and lobbying. Where government agencies are involved, legislatures and the press will also be involved.

There is a law of organizational behavior which holds that every action produces an equal and usually opposite reaction. The reaction to reorganization proposals—even before they are definitively known—is often massive, continuing, and debilitative. The results can be equated in terms of time lost while the new proposals are being discussed and debated, of lowered morale, and a building of defense mechanisms by those who see themselves being injured by the changes. There is also the matter of the development in a hostile climate of new work systems, the resignation or replacement of key employees, and the recruitment and training of others.

Anthony Downs, a former staff member of the RAND Corporation and an acute observer of organizational behavior, suggests in *Inside Bureaucracy* that the long-range effect of reorganization is to obliterate the short run gains which may accrue. He holds that reorganization leads inevitably to further reorganizations.[3] The more controversial the program, the more likely it is to be reorganized frequently. The U.S. foreign aid program, for example, has been reorganized regularly since its inception in 1953 with no apparent improvement and probably a considerable loss in effectiveness. A Housing and Urban Development employee was quoted recently by *The Washington Post* to the effect that that agency is in its twentieth reorganization since 1960. "The gloom is so thick," he reports, "you can almost see it, and people are walking around like zombies." Much the same can probably be said for many private companies which have faced marketing or manufacturing crises of their own.

The Alternatives

Alternatives to reorganizing do exist. There are, in fact, many of them. They are available not only to those directing private organizations but to those responsible for public ones as well. They can be applied at all organizational levels and include:

- The incremental approach.

- Understanding and addressing the system.

- A focus on the individual.

- New faces and new leadership.

- Training and re-training.

- New equipments and facilities.

- Innovation.

A Commitment to Incrementalism. The most important of the change processes is an incremental one. This is of enormous importance where organizations are large, diverse, complex and geographically dispersed.

Recently I have had the opportunity to explore a remarkable about-face in the performance of the Documents Function at the U.S. Government Printing Office. This is a customer service organization which is one of the half-dozen largest mail order operations in the country. A huge backlog of unfilled orders has now been eliminated. The volume of business has greatly increased, service has been enormously improved, "through-put" time heavily reduced, over-time severely cut back, and complaints substantially curtailed. The organization no longer operates in the red.

"We have made many changes," reports the Superintendent of Documents, Carl LaBarre, a veteran government official, who takes a personal day-to-day interest in what is happening. "Some of these changes were large ones, some not, but there has been no major reorganization nor has anyone anticipated any. We did not try, despite the pressures, to do everything at once. We divided our work up into programs and pieces, so that something could be done about each of them. That is how we proceeded."

"In fact," he went on to say, "I don't believe in reorganization as such or at least what usually goes under that name. I don't think there is ever an occasion when a mass reorganization is required."

There are those, of course, who would disagree with him, but his record stands for itself. Reorganization is not necessarily reform, and it is reform we are usually after.

Understanding the System. The most important element in organizational change is an understanding of the nature of the systems which produce the needed goods and services.

This leads to approaches best described as "systems analysis" or "systems thinking." A system is a set of interrelated elements or parts which as a whole produces a given effect. As we have come to understand systems, we have come also to appreciate what can be done with and about them. There are many ways by which changes in the system can be brought about easily and naturally.

The manager should seek to understand the nature of the system, its components, and how they relate to each other. By so doing, one is able to address those elements of it which are not producing what is needed.

A Focus Upon the Individual. In our attachment to the authority structure, we often overlook the increasingly professional nature of most organizations.

Social science research and organizational practice have revealed many ways in which the individual employee has become a more positive participant in the affairs of the company or agency. Individuals have shown a willingness to make substantial changes in their work methods, thereby becoming a willing partner in the change process. The logic of circumstances is always more convincing than a fiat from above.

Each of us has come to the organization voluntarily. We want it to succeed but we also want to succeed with it. The systems approach emphasizes the importance of the individual contribution. This is why it is important that it be used.

New Faces, New Leadership. One does not have to reorganize to change an old face for a new one. Many reorganizations have undoubtedly been inspired because those at the top wanted someone out of a particular role but were unwilling to make the change openly. So, they resorted to other tactics to pull it off, shifting functions and responsibilities and disrupting an ongoing system in the process. There is little excuse for this kind of approach. The bureau or company would be better served by simply shifting the person in question. Replacing people is an improvement over organizational surgery.

Training and Retraining. Much can be done to modify behavior through training and education. More and more, those with responsibility for the work of others are learning that such conventionally accepted ideas as "command," "direction," and "control" are not producing the results claimed for them, and are turning to other, more effective approaches. Training improves a person's capability for dealing with a problem; it benefits both the individual and the organization.

A football team will spend 95 percent of its time in training, but most organizations feel they have over-taxed themselves if as much as five percent of their budget goes to these purposes. Training, in all its many applications, is one of the more important tools of organizational change.

New Equipments, New Facilities. Among the better friends of management are the equipment manufacturers and their representatives. Most managers are unaware of what some of the new equipments can do for them. When made aware, they discover they can resolve some of their more pressing problems.

New ways of using space will often have similar results. People can
be moved closer together, or farther apart, to achieve new and different
relationships. Space makes a difference, and the management of space
will often resolve other problems as well.

Innovation and Creativity. Most organizations fail to avail themselves of the creativity they contain. The knee-jerk response seems to be
preferred to the innovative one. It does not need to be that way. New
products, new services, new tools, and new methods, as well as new
organizational arrangements, hold great promise for the future.

Nowhere is this of greater importance than in dealing with organizational problems. As these approaches become better understood, a
change in relationships between individuals or units becomes more of
an adjustment and less of a restructuring. If "form follows function,"
the organization will gradually restructure itself.

A preoccupation with reorganizing causes us to overlook new and
innovative ways of doing things. The last two decades, for example,
have seen the emergence of the service contract as an organizational
form. We are also involving the client in new and useful ways. The line
between what is public and what is private has also become increasingly
blurred. What we seek are new systems that are more synergistic.

Repudiating the Myth

Reorganizing sometimes has merit. It symbolizes action, and there
are times when this is important. It also shows where the power is.
Under certain circumstances, either or both of these objectives are
worthwhile.

It is, of course, a myth that reorganizing by itself will produce
either real or lasting change. There is little evidence that it will, and a
great deal that casts doubt on it. Reorganizing is threatening to those
who are part of the system, it is at times destructive, and it is always
costly. Costly in terms of the disruption it creates. Costly in terms of
human and financial resources.

If it were the only way of resolving the many and difficult problems
which managements face, it might be acceptable, but it is not. It is a sad
fact of organizational life that each new management is so often
doomed to repeat the errors of its predecessors. Those approaches
which seem so easy and so simplistic continue to entice us. As H.L.
Mencken has remarked: "There's always an easy solution to every
human problem—neat, plausible and wrong." Too often it is the promise of bringing about the constructive change we need by reorganizing.

FOOTNOTES

[1] Harold Seidman, *Politics, Position and Power*, NY: Oxford University Press Inc., 1970, p. 3.

[2] Frederick C. Mosher, *Governmental Reorganization: Cases and Commentary*, NY: Bobbs-Merrill Company, Inc., 1967, pp. 500-502.

[3] Anthony Downs, *Inside Bureaucracy*, Boston: Little Brown & Co., 1967, pp. 165-166.

PART IV

THE INDIVIDUAL: THE BASIC BUILDING BLOCK

CHAPTER XV

WHY SUBORDINATES DON'T DO WHAT THEY ARE ASKED TO DO—AND WHY THEY DO

It often comes as a surprise to the new manager or supervisor when a subordinate fails to do what is asked of him or her, or, more often, fails to do it in the fashion or time required. It is particularly frustrating when the request is one that falls clearly within the duties of the job, and badly needs doing.

An older or more experienced manager would probably share the frustration but not the surprise. The older hand might not always understand the reasons why—they are often complex and sometimes deeply hidden—but has probably long since come to understand that only in theory are instructions carried out as they are given, and sometimes not even then.

There are, of course, many explanations for "non-compliance." The simplest, and the one most frequently advanced once one's blood pressure has lessened, is that there has been a failure in communications—and perhaps there has. Most of us do not communicate either well or clearly, and with the increasing complexity of life and labor, the likelihood that a message will be received in the fashion intended decreases proportionately.

The message can, of course, be distorted in any number of ways: by the choice of words or symbols, by the gestures or expressions which accompany it, by the medium used, by background noises, by competing messages, by the inattention of the receiver, by failure to listen, by unfamiliarity with the terms which are used, and the like. A communication is not really a communication until it is received, understood in roughly the fashion sent, and receipted for. This is why communications are so often a part of supervisory and managerial training programs. Most of us need all the help we can get.

While failure to understand what is wanted—when, how, how well, and why—is clearly one of the reasons why the subordinate does not act in the fashion wanted, it is only one among several and even if our systems of communication were perfected well beyond their present state, there would still be non-compliance. Improving communications is a worthwhile objective but no one should be led to believe it will resolve management's problems. Indeed, as previously noted, there are many reasons why orders or instructions are not carried out as wanted, and one should reflect upon what some of these are before making a final judgment in the matter.

What Some of These Are

The first of these has to do with the aptitude or capability of the individual addressed. No one expects another to carry out an instruction he or she is incapable of performing. This may sound simple enough but the problem is that most of us try hard to avoid revealing our weaknesses to others. We know we ought to be able to do what is asked. It makes better sense to pretend we haven't heard than to expose our deficiencies, particularly to superiors. Perhaps the request will be forgotten, or, better still, made of someone else. So we do nothing and wait to see what happens. This is often a successful tactic.

We may fail to do what is asked because we do not understand the reason for it or, if we do, because we feel it does not make good sense. One of the first things the child learns to ask of the parent is "why?"— in fact, is encouraged to do so. We expect an explanation and will often not act until we get one. We feel it is due us.

If the request that is made is one that, on its surface, does not appear to conform to organizational policy, law, prevailing codes of morality or good sense, this is usually reason enough also for failure to act. A request made is not necessarily an imperative, and unless it is a routine one (about which, more later) is likely to be critically examined before action is taken. We encourage our subordinates to think for themselves. It is, in fact, essential that they do so. We should not be surprised to find that when they do, they sometimes reach conclusions not fully in agreement with their instructions.

There may also be personal as well as professional reasons why subordinates do not do as instructed. A member of the union may, for example, feel that the request violates the union contract, or is not covered by the description of duties previously agreed upon. One may feel that he or she is being asked to do something which ought to be done by someone else, or is in some other way being taken advantage of.

The subordinate may be confused by the priorities of several requests. He or she may object to the manner in which asked, or may not like the person who is doing the asking. The request may also conflict with the receiver's view of self. Under emergency circumstances, we may be willing to do certain things but find them repugnant at other times. We may volunteer for difficult, dangerous, and unpleasant tasks but will not accept their being assigned to us.

There is another category of non-compliance which has been called to our attention by Mary Parker Follett, writing many years ago, whose understanding of the worker and the workplace deserves far greater attention than it has gotten. Follett observed that there were occasions when non-compliance occurred *even though people understood the assignment they were being given and*, what is more, *agreed with it*. Their inability to do what was wanted, she suggested, resulted from habit patterns which had developed over the years and which, for a variety of reasons, they had great difficulty in revising. This is probably more common than most of us realize. Even where we make an effort to comply, we do not do so well or happily, if at all, and then revert to previous practice.

To understand this, we need only to reflect on some of our own practices. We dislike intensely certain foods and even though we know they are good for us, we simply cannot swallow them. We are revolted by certain things which others do. We have acquired habits over the years but now have great difficulty in changing them. We cannot easily change smoking, eating, or drinking habits, although we know we should. There is an important truth here, and it must be understood. The individual cannot do what is wanted because habit and value patterns prevent it. The manager is well advised to expect this to happen from time to time, often enough to cause problems.

Why They Do What They Do

This leads us to a more basic—and profound—question: Instead of asking why subordinates *don't* do what is asked of them, let us explore *why they do what they do*. The answer may be more simple—and reasonable—than it at first appears.

Consider for a moment, with one's self as an example, what one's feelings and intentions were as we took on a new job. If it was one that had been seriously sought, it was probably entered upon with high expectations and a very positive desire to make good. Translated into functional terms, this meant an acceptance of organizational objectives, a desire to do what the duties of the job required, and a strong motivation to please the people who did the hiring and with whom one was prepared to work. Most people, on undertaking either a new assignment or a new career, share such hopes.

The will to succeed, as this suggests, is already there. Its fulfillment, however, depends upon a number of things. One of these is the nature of the work to be done and the existing system of which it was a part. Another is one's own, already formed personal values and work habits.

The difficulty with intentions, of course, is that of applying them to unknown and perhaps eccentric circumstances. Application will probably occur, given the will for it, but slowly and perhaps experimentally. What seems at first to make good sense is often revised by unknown (at the time) and often unpredictable competing forces.

Take the duties of a policeman, for example. When someone joins the force, the duties to be performed and the objectives to be achieved are seen in a much more precise and simplistic way than after a couple of months of boot training. The alternatives this experience exposes will themselves be revised by what happens when the new officer takes on a working role as a member of the force. As the case of Serpico has reminded us, the new man (or woman) is subjected to a variety of pressures, each of which may make sense by itself but which en masse reduces one's ability to pursue the initial objectives one accepted in joining the force.

There may still be the desire to do, for example, what higher-ups have indicated they want, but there is now one's immediate superior, whose point of view may not be consistent with theirs, to contend with. (Who speaks for the group the cop is now a member of—the police commissioner, the chief, the captain, the sergeant?) What does the new police officer do when there is inconsistency among them?

In addition to those in the chain of command, there are one's associates to be satisfied. This was a problem Serpico faced. One works on a daily basis not with the chief or even the sergeant but with others of equal or relatively equal rank and much greater experience—one's peer group—and discovers in the process that on most matters their views are likely to hold. They have, in fact, special ways of enforcing them. If these coincide with what higher ups are asking, well and good. When they do not, very often the case, the new officer faces difficult choices. We know what the work force does to rate-breakers. We have heard, if we have not experienced, "putting people in Coventry." These are two among many ways by which the group forces the individual to conform.

If the new man or woman is a supervisor, he or she must also take into account what subordinates will accept. There are coffee breaks and "schmooze time" to be observed. There is an unofficial reporting time and a time for knocking off which are not always the same as those prescribed. The supervisor is often the "man in the middle"—whether male or female—who is neither a real part of management nor an accepted part of the work force.

There is also the matter of the pressures generated by clients and client systems. Sales people are often closer to those who buy from them than they are to their own company. We say of department store clerks that "the customer is always right," and while, as most customers now know, this is very much of an overstatement, the sales clerk who does not satisfy a majority of customers will not be long in the job. Perhaps a better example is the case of the prison guards who must be rotated in their assignments because *their* clients, the inmates, often bring strong pressures against them.

These are merely some of the forces which act upon the individual to prevent the fulfillment of the hopes and intentions which they felt on initially entering the organization. But there are others also, *within* the individual.

The Importance of Habit

Over the years, each of us has developed habits of hand and habits of mind. We may not be precisely aware of them, but they are now a part of us. As a result, we are moved to take or not to take action by such factors as:

- Our own ideas of propriety.

- Our own feelings for excellence.

- What we feel we are good at doing.

- What we like to do.

- What we don't like to do.

- What produces positive responses from others.

- What produces negative ones; and, finally,

- What we do without thinking about it.

Some of these—perhaps many of them—may, of course, coincide with what we have been hired, or are expected, to do, but often they do not. When they do not, the individual has choices to make, and since decision-making is a time-consuming as well as an onerous task, we find it useful to adopt patterns which, repeated over time, become habits.

We may not be clear precisely how (or why) choices are made, but made they are. If the results "get one by" without substantial negative response, they become what Herbert Simon has called "satisficing" behavior, and will surely be repeated.

What is being suggested here is the organizational equivalent of water seeking its own level. Whatever the reason for the initial choice being made, habits are soon established both in the individual and the system (the collection of individuals) and if they are tolerated will soon be perpetuated.

Man, on the job or off, is a creature of habit. Ask yourself how much of what you do in a day, from the time you awake in the morning until you fall asleep at night, proceeds from habit. I have asked this question of many people in management training programs. The average of the answers varies from 85 to 95 percent. Perhaps because I have examined my own ways of behavior over a longer period of time, I put the figure higher than this.

We are not, of course, talking of either good habits or bad habits. We are talking of habits, and essentially how some of them have developed. As one grows from infant to child and from child to adult, the practices we have been trained to follow—or have learned to follow—become a part of us. They become not only habits of mind but ones that involve the nervous and muscular systems as well. The paraplegic survives because of patterns that have developed in the physiological system. Those who comb their hair day after day in the same fashion will find that over the years it will virtually arrange itself. We brush our teeth and make our toilet in much the same way we first did years ago. And, of course, our work habits develop—and set—in much the same way.

This is no new discovery. It was noted in the first book on psychology, in the 1880s, by William James. But somehow, somewhere, we have overlooked the importance of habit and habit formation in our desire to understand and manipulate individual behavior. Perhaps if we had spent more time in trying to understand what habits are and how they develop we would have been more successful in dealing with them. Here is what James has to say about them:

> Habit is thus the enormous fly-wheel of society, its most precious conservative agent. It alone is what keeps us all within the bound of ordinance. . . .It is well for the world that in most of us, by the age of thirty, the character has set like plaster and will never soften again. If the period between twenty and thirty is the critical one in the formation of intellectual and professional habits, the period below twenty is more important still for the fixing of *personal* habits, properly so

called, such as vocalization and pronounciation, gesture, motion, and address. . . .There is no more miserable human being than one in whom nothing is habitual but indecision, and for whom the lighting of every cigar, the drinking of every cup, the time of rising and going to bed every day, and the beginning of every bit of work, are subject of express volitional deliberation. Full half of the time of such a man goes to the deciding, or regretting, of matters which ought to be so ingrained in him as practically not to exist for his consciousness at all.[1] [Emphasis his.]

What Can Be Done?

If all of this is so, what does one do about it? Can habits firmly established be changed? The answer, of course, is neither a clear-cut Yes nor a positive No. It depends.

The first and most important point is to recognize that we cannot control the behavior of others, and sometimes not even our own. This is a sobering thought, but a useful one nonetheless. And, to carry the idea a bit further, if we cannot control the action of an individual, we certainly cannot control a collection of individuals (which in the final analysis is what the organization is), no matter how imposing our title or authoritative our manner.

That does not mean, however, that we are without influence or resources. Both of these are of consequence provided that we use them wisely.

If we cannot control the behavior of others, we can at least observe it. We can generalize it and, what is more, learn from it.

Patterns of individual thinking and behavior are not, as James reminds us, established overnight. They develop as they do because they have been permitted—and sometimes encouraged—to develop that way. We harvest what we have suffered to grow. The field which has become weeds could easily have been grain if we had taken the trouble to plant the right seeds and cultivate them.

There are a number of ways in which individual and group behavior can be influenced, but, first, they must be understood and worked at. We can mold the organization, as Chester Barnard has reminded us, by bringing in new and able people and seeing that they are supported. Acceptable behavior can be encouraged and reinforced. Unacceptable behavior can be denounced and corrected. Training is an important tool for change. The manager's job is one that must be worked at. The tools to be used are well known: discussion, consultation, persuasion, fact-finding, the granting or withholding of favors, support, encouragement, criticism, and, in some instances, coercion.

In the case of the individual, James recommended that we "make our nervous system our ally instead of our enemy." He suggested that "we must make automatic and habitual, as early as possible, as many useful actions as we can, and guard against their growing into ways that are likely to be disadvantageous to us." The same holds true for organizations. What the manager should seek to do is to make sure that individual performance fits with the purposes of the organization, and, insofar as possible, made habitual to it. We owe much of our achievement in groups to habit patterns that serve the general purpose of the organization and become part of its ethos. Certain organizations are noted for the industry of those who are members of them. Their courtesy and helpfulness are well known, and their responsiveness to clientele and public needs among the more important reasons for their success. Such behaviors rarely occur by chance. They are encouraged by those who have understood their importance. On the other hand, those that have developed in negative ways have done so because of lack of leader interest or its ineffectuality.

It is the manager's job to see that the proper tone is set, and then to insure its permanence. James again reminds us (in the individual instance):

> Never suffer an exception to occur till the new habit is securely rooted in your life. Each lapse is like letting fall of a ball of string which one is carefully winding up; a single slip undoes more than a great many turns will wind again. Continuity of training is the great means of making the nervous system act infallibly right.[2]

This is, of course, a more difficult assignment where a number of people are involved and where there is a history of accepting less than optimum performance. It is by no means, however, out of reach. The functioning of highly productive systems is proof that it can be achieved. But for this to happen, both managers and members must commit themselves to these ends.

Thus, habit in the individual and standard patterns of practice within the group are part of the successful system. They must, of course, be the right kind of habits and to insure that they are, must be constantly re-examined. As the Japanese are beginning to show us, this can become both an individual and a group goal—in fact, a habit itself.

One begins with the felt needs of the individual. There is first and foremost the desire of the individual to make good, to be part of a successful team effort, to develop himself or herself and to be respected for it. With goals such as these, one will not be long in discovering that the work ethic is not yet dead.

One must involve those who are most affected by the system one is trying to support. The ability to work together is historically a part of the American ethos. We have achieved what we have because of it. That so many of our work systems have overlooked this point does not mean that it is no longer there. The perceptive manager will search it out, and will build on it.

The leader's behavior, whatever the title, should be consistent with what is asked of others. Such terms as director, commander, administrator and boss mislead the holder of them as often as they repel one's associates. The *functional* role is one of producing group effort, even though organizational systems are traditionally autocratic. Understanding this, those in managerial positions should proceed slowly with change no matter what the need for speed. Within their own spheres of influence, they should focus upon objectives. The daily task is to build support for these objectives.

The essence of the task is to change habits. We know the price of trying to change our own—of trying to replace old and well-established ones with new ones—but we conveniently forget how difficult the process is when we are dealing with others. This is why we usually have no better luck than we do—and why we deserve some of the results that we usually get.

FOOTNOTES

[1]William James, *Psychology: The Briefer Course*, NY: Harper and Row, 1961 ed., edited by Gordon Allport, pp. 10-11.

[2]*Ibid.*, p. 12.

CHAPTER XVI
CONSTRUCTIVE USES OF CONFLICT

All people have preferences. Some prefer vanilla ice cream and some chocolate. Some have long hair and some short. Some people are orderly, some not. Some believe in saving their money, some in spending as they go.

These preferences, which are really values, often get us into trouble with others. When they do, we call it "conflict." Persons with one set of values disagree with others with dissimilar ones.

When the differences have to do only with the flavor of ice cream, the problem is usually easily resolved. Not always, as any father of four children will probably be willing to testify, but usually. Hair style, however, can be a more serious matter. Its significance lies in what it symbolizes.

Differences having to do with basic values, needs or expectations lead easily to disagreement. Disagreements lead to antagonism and antagonism to open conflict. Say the right words, flash the right symbols and we are off to war with grim lips and deep commitment to our own intrinsic purposes.

Conflict—which is where our differences so often lead us—is very much a part of our everyday lives. It is often a costly part. Problems with family, neighbors, friends and associates occupy a substantial portion of our day. Much of our energy is devoted to dealing with these conflicts—to talking about them, thinking about them, and plotting ways of coping with them.

There will always be a certain amount of conflict between people just as there are differences among them. The amount, of course, will vary. It is more prevalent in certain societies than in others, in certain places as against other ones, and in certain organizations over others.

Our concern here is with business organizations. A survey, for example, of 258 company executives made with the help of the American Management Association revealed that an average of 20 percent—one fifth—of their time was spent in dealing with conflict.[1] Middle management contributed the most—26 percent. The study revealed further that the ability to "manage conflict" has become increasingly important in executive eyes over the past ten years.

The primary sources of conflict, these executives reported, were communication failures, personality clashes, value and goal differences, performance failures, differences over methods, differences over responsibilities, authority issues, frustration, irritability, competition for limited resources, and non-compliance with rules and policies. There are other differences, of course, but these, organizationally, are usually among the most important ones.

The costs of conflict are measurable not only in the dollars and cents of lost time, missed opportunities, and misused resources, but in the more disturbing area of human costs. These include perturbation, frustration, unrest, and the negative effect of people who ought to be working together pitting their energies against each other and the company.

Types of Conflict

There are several types of conflict which affect the organization. There is, first, conflict within the individual. This is followed by conflict between individuals, conflict between the individual and the system, conflict between organizational groups, and, finally, conflict between the organization and the outside.

Conflict Within the Individual

Much of the conflict within organizations stems from conflict within the individual. Each of us is a party to many loyalties—to ourselves, to our families and friends, to peers and community groups, to our work organizations, and to values and principles with which we associate ourselves. The demands which these loyalties place upon us are often in conflict with each other. These dilemmas, in turn, raise major behavioral problems. Toffler, for example, makes much of this in *Future Shock*.[2]

The individual, as a problem-solving system, tries to resolve these internal conflicts. The need for consistency, or at least harmony, among one's own views requires this. But in the process, one is often faced with uncertainty and doubts, and as a result, is not clear about what factors are actually in collision. In given situations, one's reactions may include fighting, taking flight (or withdrawal), denying the conflict, ventilating frustration in a variety of ways, and the like.

In particular, we should be aware of "role conflict." This is the conflict the individual must resolve between role requirements (such as one's supervisory responsibilities), and one's feelings as a person. As a representative of management, one may be expected to discipline others. As a person who likes others, one may find this distasteful. So there is conflict within. Some people are able to cope with substantial role conflict; others are not.

Conflict Between Individuals

Interpersonal conflict occurs between individuals in every social setting. It arises from many sources. Competition for position or attention is one. Today, greatly increased tensions exist because of feelings about race, sex, and age as well as personality styles.

Conflict may arise because of the treatment (or fancied treatment) one receives at the hands of another. An example is the relationship between subordinate and superior. The subordinate may believe that he or she is being asked to take on assignments beneath his or her dignity; that the work being done is not appreciated; that the superior has little feeling for the problems of others. The superior, on the other hand, may regard the subordinate as not being sufficiently competent to do the job which needs to be done and is unwilling to accept coaching or direction. Feelings are expressed in behavior. The superior regards the subordinate as a troublemaker and the subordinate in turn regards the boss as an autocrat. Both confirm their views by the way they act. A self-fulfilling prophecy is at work.

There are also, of course, conflicts between peers. Mary cannot abide John and John, in turn, detests George. At the executive level, two of the top division heads, to put it bluntly, hate each other's guts. Animosities such as these are expressed in many ways: remarks by one about the other, undercutting, open flareups, solicitation of support from other persons, withdrawal, elaborate systems of avoidance, and even physical conflict. "If," one observer noted, "we could only reduce by one-half the energies that go into fighting each other, we would be well ahead of where we are now."

Conflict Between the Individual and the System

Our society encourages the development of the individual, but there is always a time when the individual is expected to abide by the mores of the group. Yet, increasingly today—in families, in social groups, in work organizations, in voluntary groups, and, in fact, in society as a whole—we see examples of lone-wolf or rebel behavior.

Some people congenitally cannot accept, for one reason or another, the standards of the group—even though they may be members of it. There are also the anti-authoritarian personalities which are overly sensitive to efforts of others to influence or control their actions. Every manager, if it has not already happened, will someday have to face those individuals who are fighting the system. As its representative, the person "in charge" will inevitably be drawn into the conflict. This may even produce role conflict in the manager as well.

Conflict Between Organizational Units

Management consultants often speak of the built-in potentials for conflict between various organizational units. There is an odds-on likelihood that controversy will erupt in specified areas and between certain divisions. There are, for example, the traditional differences between headquarters and field, between plans and operations, between manufacturing and sales, between procurement and R&D, between inspection and whomsoever may be under surveillance, and, in general, between line and staff. Such differences may originate in part from conflicts or overlays in assignments or responsibilities, but they are triggered and undoubtedly aggravated by inadequate communication, by tensions elsewhere in the organization, by different attitudes and values, and by differences in the styles of the people involved. Such factors explain why personnel and budget officers, planners, researchers, lawyers, and controllers are sometimes seen as the enemies of operations, rather than as fellow team members providing supportive services in a complex organization.

Some of these conflicts may require restructuring of the organization. But many of them can be resolved in less traumatic ways.

Conflict Between the Organization and Those Outside It

The most obvious is conflict between businesses seeking the same market but in no worse than second place is the conflict between the company and any number of governmental agencies.

Conflict with those in the same business is accepted under the rubric of competition. There are fairly well defined ways in which it is expected to operate. Sometimes the rules are followed, sometimes not. But there is invariably the feeling of "them" and "us."

Conflict with governments—local, state, and national—is quite another matter, made more acerbic by what is commonly accepted as an adversary relationship. The shrewder of those in business place major emphasis on compliance, or at least on the appearance of compliance, but beneath the surface there is often deep-seated resentment of the regulatory role of the state. The promise of the Reagan administration to reduce regulation has been hailed by the business community. Given the nature of the problem, it is doubtful, however, that it will be fully satisfied.

There is also the conflict between the company and the union. That the two must work in some kind of harmony, if the best interests of each is to be achieved, is beside the point. Members of management feel that their intentions are maligned. Members of the union feel that the company is taking advantage of them. And, of course, there are many with mixed feelings.

The company is increasingly in conflict these days with the community, in addition to its government. This conflict has to do with such matters as the quality of life but often extends to other areas as well. And so the lines are drawn, with employees in conflict with both parties.

The Positive Contributions

Much of what has been discussed above are the negatives of conflict. There are, however, positive contributions which come from conflict and these need to be understood also.

Differences, genetically speaking, are the source of enrichment and development. We cross plants with each other to produce a superior line. We breed animals of differing qualities to achieve excellence. Differences—and also conflict—can produce important positive results which we probably would not have had without it. As Lewis Coser has noted:

> Far from being only a "negative" factor which tears apart, social conflict may fulfill a number of determinate functions in groups and other interpersonal relations; it may, for example, contribute to the maintenance of group boundaries and prevent the withdrawal of members from a group.[3]

The reader of history will recognize the debt we owe the social rebel who refused to accept the mandates of the group. By persevering in this conflict, the deviant was able to convince others of wiser courses of action which themselves later became the norm. Lewis Mumford, in *The Culture of Cities*, speaks of the great value of controversy. As he points out, it is not the periods of harmony but rather those of *lack of harmony* which will be longest remembered for their contributions to civilization.[4]

Let us then give the credit their contentiousness deserves to the non-conformist, the malcontent, the dissenter, the reformer and the revolutionary. Even the eccentric and the crackpot come in for a share.

They may not have been easy to live with, and it may be difficult to sort out the good from the bad, but they have left their mark on our society. It is an important one.

"Conflict," wrote the philosopher John Dewey, "is the gadfly of thought. It stirs us to observation and memory. It instigates to invention. It shocks us out of sheep-like passivity, and sets us at noting and contributing. . . . .Conflict is a *sine qua non* of reflection and ingenuity."

Nor is this applicable only to ideas. The rebel within the organization has, in fact, helped all of us. Harlan Cleveland, in *The Future Executive*, speaks of "the fruitful friction of administration." Out of travail comes progress, if the travail has not exhausted us in the process.

The problem, then, is one of recognizing the contributions which *difference* has to make, but avoiding the high costs which open conflict so often brings. We do not want anarchy, but we do not wish a regimented organization either.

Can Conflict Be "Managed?"

A great deal has been said and written during the last few years about the management of conflict. I am not sure that it can be "managed" in the conventional meaning of the term. In fact, it may even be dangerous to try. But there are a number of things that can be done, given a desire to do so, and it may be helpful to discuss some of them.

The action for dealing with conflict should begin with a "non-action." I recommend, first of all, a healthy dose of introspection.

It is always more satisfactory for most of us, being American, to be doing something rather than merely thinking about it. Thinking is hard work, and when the subject is an unpleasant one that demands some habit-breaking (or at least adjusting), it becomes even more difficult. But the action-oriented American is also a pragmatist, and what I am suggesting is surely pragmatic.

The thinking that I urge on the manager will involve an examination not only of the situation but of the people involved in it—and one's self. It should, of course, get at the facts, but it should take into account that how people see the "facts" and feel about them are as important as the facts themselves.

As for one's own part in the process, the manager should approach his assignment with a tolerance for both difference and dissent. If real and deeply felt, it will be one of the most valuable talents a person can have.

There is nothing in the literature of management to suggest that managers must control the minds of those being managed. They know, if they stop to think about it, that they cannot do it anyway. But there is something in the managerial *ethos* which tempts many of them to try. There will be pressure, for example, real or fancied, from higher-ups, to "show authority." It is a dangerous approach.

Now if managers will understand that differences between themselves and others do not challenge this authority, nor even the unity of the organization, they will by this decision alone have done much to keep differences from developing into hostility and hostility into conflict. One does not lead by intimidating or dominating others.

The second requirement of those who are managers is a "non-action" also, but one which clearly leads to action. The resolution of differences, they must understand, is a shared responsibility. It is not theirs alone but one which they hold jointly with their associates. It is not enough for managers to be tolerant of differences: *those they work with must be tolerant also.*

Their focus, therefore, must be broader than the deviant. It must be upon those others who make up the group and the organization. This is a tougher assignment because its implications are greater.

It is never easy to persuade those with hardened points of view that they may be wrong. It is even more difficult when they are part of a strident majority. It may help, however, to talk about their responsibilities—to the community, to the company, to their fellows, and to themselves.

With this as a starting point, the manager can give attention to the conflict itself. There are several ways to approach it. Some of these will occur almost as a reflex: head-knocking, trade-offs, bribery, promises, etc. They may have had their uses, but the thoughtful manager is urged to look farther. K.W. Thomas[5] has listed what he calls "conflict handling modes," which deserve greater attention. He speaks specifically of:

- Competing
- Accommodating
- Avoiding
- Compromising
- Collaborating.

Each has its applications.

Competing is opposing. We compete with each other for acceptance of ideas, suggestions, or programs, knowing that in most competition there is a winner and also a loser. But unlike sports in which the loser returns to play again, one cannot really be sure in the organizational world that this will happen. So people hedge their bets. This leads to some interesting forms of dysfunctional behavior. Alliances are formed, the rules are studied to discover loop-holes, and efforts are made to influence the decision-maker. The win-lose exercise may produce acrimonious and protracted results. Still, it has its uses.

If competition can be regularized, legitimized, and conducted in a friendly and non-threatening way, it has very real possibilities. But it must be clearly established that it is friendly, and that those who finish second or third, or even farther down the line, will not be taken advantage of. Often this is hard to do, particularly where there is a great deal of pressure as well as individual intensity, but it is a possibility nevertheless.

Accommodation. One cannot have lived to maturity without having learned to accommodate. Some people do it more graciously than others, some more often, but it is increasingly a requirement of a crowded society. By being willing to accommodate, we are recognizing that the preserving of a relationship is more important than the winning of a particular point.

Avoidance. There are many occasions when it is better to avoid a conflict than to accept one. Who has not sought to escape an unpleasant encounter by going out of the way? Who has not broken off a meeting because there seemed so little point, given the heat already engendered, to continuing it? The most belligerent is not necessarily the wisest or the bravest. Better under certain circumstances to avoid an action than to face it. This is one of the first rules of war, and also of administration.

Compromising is the settling for less than one asks for because, given the dynamics of the situation, it is better to do this than risk the greater loss. It does not deserve the bad name it has sometimes been given. It is a sensible approach to problems which cannot easily be settled other ways. One does not compromise one's principles by accepting compromise as an important tool of administering and managing.

Collaborating is mutual problem solving. It is a joined effort to resolve the issues being faced. It has much to offer. If people who have once opposed each other can be helped to seek a solution collaboratively, all are likely to benefit. But, for obvious reasons, it is probably the most difficult of the "conflict handling modes" to follow.

Communications and Conflict

No tool is more important in the resolution of conflict than communication. If the parties to the conflict can be brought together to talk about their differences, if these can be gotten into the open, something may be done to help resolve them.

There are exceptions, of course. But it is usually a safe rule that those who have worked closely together, who have talked openly with each other, have also acquired a mutual respect and sometimes an affection for each other. This has long been a rule of statecraft but also one of arbitration. It applies to business organizations as well.

Meetings with those holding other points of view, if they can be managed in the right way, will usually help to develop an appreciation of the other fellow and his or her values. Even where the adversary nature of the situation is pronounced, as in labor-management meetings or international negotiations, it is likely to hold true. "I don't really agree with what he is saying," I once heard a negotiator remark, "but I know be believes it strongly and I respect his point of view." Thus has a basis been established for conflict resolution.[6]

There are other advantages to "talking it out." If one side does not convince the other, at least there is a temporary cessation of the fighting while the talking takes place. For different reasons, each may want it this way. "If you're not a part of the solution," Eldridge Cleaver has reminded us, "you're part of the problem." Without the talking, people tend to keep on shooting.

The Manager Needs Help

It is a primary responsibility of managers to try to get the opposing parties together, but others should lend a hand also. It is not so important that managers be the ones to do it: what is important is that it be done. Skillful managers are able to sense at an early stage which differences are most likely to lead to open conflict and try to do something about them.

They should not try to submerge these differences, to overpower them, or to avoid them. They should, in fact, for a variety of reasons solicit them. Creativity, as we have seen, feasts upon varietal points of view. They are as important in determining policies, plans and procedures as in developing new products. The division or department, with its intermixture of disciplines, skills, and experience, can be an important source of organizational judgment. The manager must see to it that they are put forward in an orderly way.

In recent years, much has been made of confrontation as a conflict-resolving approach. It has its merits, of course. Those whose habit it is to speak openly and frankly, and who act accordingly, will be thoughtfully heard by their associates. Confrontation, however, sometimes has an accusatory ring to it which excites more than it helps. It should therefore be used with care.[7]

Third parties are sometimes greatly helpful in conflict resolution. They are particularly useful when affairs have gotten to a crisis stage. Some people have great skill as conciliators. Lawyers, when they are not acting as advocates, are in this category. They act as a moderating force when the choler of the participants rises. The manager should appreciate their possibilities.

Sometimes, of course, there is no alternative except for one, or both, of those in conflict to withdraw. They may be helped to do so with the understanding that to continue would be neither in their own best interests nor the interests of the organization. A skillful negotiator can help the "loser" to avoid losing face. (Losing is not necessarily losing face.) There will always be other opportunities, as one seeks to find more agreeable status within the organization.

Sometimes, however, the conflict can become so acrimonious that the manager must leave. If one threatens to do so, one must be prepared to carry out the threat. This is one of the occupational hazards of managing. It doesn't happen often but it's a possibility.

Because a dispute has ended does not mean that it is over. Wishful thinking might have it so but life is not wishful thinking. Strong feelings run deeply; they may be nursed for years. Like smoldering volcanoes, they are capable of further eruptions. The manager should take care that feelings are not unnecessarily exacerbated. One should be solicitous of those who feel rebuffed. The winning of a battle or the disarmament of a foe does not mean the end of hostility. Nor is "an agreement to agree" necessarily the end of the affair. The manager who is truly concerned with the long-time health of the organization will be alert to what may follow.

The manager should not be considered a failure because, despite every effort, differences still remain. Nevertheless, the addressing of conflict is one of the basic managerial requirements and this is particularly needed in large organizations where infections, unless treated, may spread widely. Selznick rightly regards the "ordering of internal conflict" as one of the major functions of organizational leadership.[8]

There is more controversy in the world, of course, than all the statesmen or clergymen can heal. The manager will have served well, however, if conflict is held in moderate proportions in his or her domain. It is not all bad as pointed out in the introduction to this chapter but it can get out of hand.

FOOTNOTES

[1]K.W. Thomas and W.H. Schmidt, "A Survey of Managerial Interests with Respect to Conflict," *Academy of Management Journal*, Vol. 19, No. 2, June 1976, pp. 315-318.

[2]Alvin Toffler, *Future Shock*, NY: Random House, Inc., 1970.

[3]Lewis Coser, *The Functions of Social Conflict*, Glencoe, IL: The Free Press, 1956, p. 8.

[4]Lewis Mumford, *The Culture of Cities*, p. 485.

[5]K.W. Thomas, as cited by W.H. Schmidt in "Conflict: A Powerful Process for (Good or Bad) Change," *Management Review*, Dec. 1974.

[6]*New Ways of Managing Conflict* by Rensis and Jane Gibson Likert presents a scholarly analysis of the application of the celebrated "System 4" style of organization in its application to internal conflict. It advocates group problem-solving combined with supportive leadership. NY: McGraw-Hill Book Company, Inc., 1976.

[7]For further discussion of confrontation, and third party intervention, see Richard Walton, *Interpersonal Peacemaking: Confrontations and Third-Party Consultations*, Reading, MA: Addison-Wesley Publishing Company, Inc., 1969; and William G. Scott, *The Management of Conflict: Appeal Systems in Organizations*, Homewood, IL: Irwin, 1965.

[8]Philip Selznick, *Leadership in Administration: A Sociological Interpretation*, Evanston, IL: Row, Peterson & Co., 1957, pp. 63-64.

CHAPTER XVII

WHEN NOTHING SUCCEEDS LIKE EXCESS

Note: Since this chapter was originally published, Dr. Laurence J. Peter has come forward with the Peter Principle. His point is that "people rise to the level of their incompetence." This is an interesting observation, and judging from the wide acceptance, it has tickled the national fancy. What the "Principle" overlooks is that many rise much higher than this—their incompetence was revealed several levels earlier—and continue to be tolerated by the organization of which they are a part. This chapter provides a number of such examples, and suggests how such situations can be avoided.

The history of warfare speaks often of the "walking wounded"—men who are still with the army but are not really capable of bearing their share of the battle. The histories of organizations, if they were equally frank, could talk of the "promoted ineffectives." These are people, most of them unfortunately in their forties and fifties and occupying medium high or higher level positions, who fail to carry their weight and yet always seem to move onward and upward in the process.

How many there are who fall into this category cannot be determined statistically. Suffice it to note, almost every organizational unit of any size has several who are seen by their fellow workers as burdens. Not only do such persons provide little or no real leadership, but their occupancy of key, coveted positions belies policies which management has spent so much effort and money to support. Chief among these policies is the one which holds that superior performance will be recognized and rewarded and, conversely, that poor performance will be penalized.

A certain amount of the criticism of these "promoted ineffectives" is undoubtedly personal. Some of it may have its roots in jealousy. Even so, this still leaves a substantial share to be accounted for. More often than not, the men or women who have gained the disrespect of their fellows richly deserve it. Promoting or otherwise rewarding them is likely to have far-reaching repercussions throughout the organization.

There are, of course, bound to be instances through no one's fault where someone will get into a position for which he or she is not qualified. Most subordinates understand this. They know that getting that person out often calls for face-saving finesse as well as time. They make exceptions also for taking care of those with a great deal of seniority, whether competent or not; and those to whom the organization has an obligation—perhaps members of the boss's family, if a private business, or an infrequent political hanger-on, if the public. They are tolerant as well of the occasional administrative need for "kicking someone upstairs." After all, it is better for all concerned if an ineffective is put into a relatively unimportant staff job, even if overpaid in the process, than to have him obstruct the production processes at a lesser level. These are the exceptions.

Effect on Rank and File

However, the rank and file employees do not accept the continuing promotion of certain employees from one inferior performance to another. Nor do they accept the pattern—frequent in many organizations and with many highly-placed executives—of bringing in new employees from the outside who will eventually either be forced to leave or be put into sinecure positions. This may happen only a few times a year, but for those concerned it has major consequences.

The following case histories drawn from actual experience are illustrative.

John Ogg (not his real name) is the first example. Although he was well-liked as a person and possessed a fair degree of technical knowledge, Ogg had a talent for "keeping things in an uproar." For over 30 years he moved from one hectic and essentially disorderly experience to another. His leadership was marked by its lack of system, its disputatiousness, and the uncertainty and hostility of his subordinates. The personnel problems he has faced have been explained as the natural effects of many of the crash programs he was called upon to mount. But why were they crash programs? Why was it necessary to so arouse his associates?

Other managers seemed to be able to function in a more orderly way. Others planned and executed their plans with a minimum of fuss. Why not Ogg? The answer seemed to lie in the fact that the kind of tempo he practiced was the only one he knew. Yet his career is an excellent example of nothing really succeeding like excess, for he was promoted successively from one position to another. His final assignment, before age charitably retired him, was in one of the top spots his organization had to offer. Like the officer in the old British Army, "he progressed triumphantly from one debacle to another."

Luther Bigelow, on the other hand, lived in many respects a thoroughly mild and self-effacing kind of existence. Those who worked most closely with him knew him to have very few new ideas, to be afraid not only of the ideas of others, but sometimes of his own; and, above all, to fear making decisions. When a major problem faced him, he became nervous and distraught, debated its various aspects endlessly, was short with his associates, and was often moved to act only because of pressures from others upon him. His subordinates said little about him. They had little real respect for him or faith in him, although they did not actively dislike him. Yet a person looking at his career from the outside would note steady if unspectacular progress. His present job is head of an important division. One of his superiors said of him: "Don't forget that we have grown greatly while Bigelow has been with us." He did not say whether the organization had grown because of him, or despite him. His associates are sure they know the correct answer.

The third instance of a man who continues to move ahead despite less-than-adequate performance is that of an outsider who was brought into the organization to take over an important executive post. Call him George Blanding. In the six years he was with the organization, he managed to alienate not only his superiors but the most influential of his associates and subordinates as well. This is not to say there were no achievements under him—there were several—but these were out-weighed by continuing failure to do what the situation seemed to call for. He left to take a better position elsewhere at more money. A check of his previous employers indicated that he had done no better there. They, in fact, had been relieved to see him go, as were his present employers.

The fourth and final example is Paul Goodkin. He was bright enough, and also well related. A brother was a VIP high up in government, although there never was any evidence that the latter had any role in his hiring or for that matter interceded in what occurred there-after. Goodkin's problem was alcoholism—and lack of initiative which a three-martini lunch did little to alleviate. His job had little substance but the one before that, and the one before that, had little either. Perhaps no one had been able to reach the real Paul, but his promotional record looked as if they had—and had been impressed by what they found. Ultimately his alcoholism provided him an opportunity to indulge a disability retirement with its attendant benefits. The real mistake was letting him in in the first place.

Why Ineffective Executives?

How often such illustrations as the above occur is not so important as the fact that they happen at all. After all, management today is not the same as it was in the 1920s. Today, we know the importance of capable and respected executives. We have the tools to find out about a person's past and current performances. There can be no real excuse for perpetrating inefficiency by promoting it.

Why, then, are such situations permitted to exist? Is top management really aware that they do? Does it understand the depth of feeling on the part of the associates and subordinates who have to live with these situations? Does it underestimate the cost of such mistakes to the organization? Or is it really inured to them and indifferent to their implications? While questions such as these intrigue the researcher and teacher, they should do much more than this to those whose money is involved. At the very least, they should incite them to find why things like this occur—and also what may be done to prevent them.

A study of ineffective executive behavior confirms the suspicion that situations of this kind are likely to be more prevalent than those in positions of organizational responsibility believe. Subjects reported a wide variety of aberrant behavior by superiors, resulting in a list of 30 general groupings of items. While this contained many of the usual complaints (failure to delegate, indecisiveness, failure to communicate, alcoholism, etc.) it also included a number of charges such as crudity, boorishness, lewdness, deceitfulness, cruelty, and flagrant disregard of individual rights. There were reports also of unlawful and dishonest actions such as kangaroo courts, false affidavits, and phony expense accounts.[1]

One of the questions asked was "why, in the opinion of the subordinate, had superiors of the bad bosses failed to take remedial action?" A wide variety of answers was given. Because these have bearing on the problem, they are included here. One hundred and three persons were queried. Some of them gave more than one reason which explains the total of 177 responses below:

Why Superiors Fail to Act

	Number
Superiors were uninformed of what was taking place.	36
The ineffective supervisor had offsetting abilities, often of a technical nature.	21
Lack of effective supervisory ability (at executive level).	16
Outside influence or a high ranking sponsor.	11

Lack of interest by superior in the situation; inertia; desire to avoid unpleasant incidents.	11
The person guilty of the action was able to make a convincing explanation for it or had a cover-up.	9
Those with knowledge of the situation were unable (or feared) to get it "up the line."	9
Lack of courage by superiors to take necessary remedial action	8
Office politics; friendships within the organization.	8
Superiors guilty of some of the same things.	7
Superiors would not believe situation or accept information from below.	7
No readily available replacement; difficulty in making changes.	6
Protectiveness of the system.	4
While the supervisor was incompetent, his staff did an excellent job "covering" for him.	4
Lack of authority of superiors to take action.	3
Recognition of the deficiencies would have required taking serious action and this was not believed desirable.	3
Double standards—one for officers, one for subordinates.	3
Seniority of person concerned.	2
Reprimands were given.	1
No answer or did not know.	8
Total	177

The explanations this survey contains are helpful even if they are not fully definitive. They indicate, for example, that the most frequent cause of failure of those in higher positions to take action against an errant subordinate supervisor is ignorance of what is really taking place. Thirty-six responses (20 percent) were in this category. If, however, several other categories which suggest much the same thing are combined with it, the percentage is considerably higher. Nine responses spoke of the failure of those with knowledge of the situation to get it to actionable levels. Seven said that those at the executive level would not believe what was reported. There were 11 instances of "disinterest" and "inertia," indicating that over one-third of all instances of failure to act can be attributed to failure to possess information. If one adds to this such other executive deficiencies as "lack of effective supervisory ability" at the top, nearly half of the explanations given are accounted for.

How Ineffectives are Appointed

If those higher up in the organization are unaware of much that is going on beneath them, they cannot be expected to act with intelligent judgment. Nor can they be expected to know, except in a most elemental way, the merit (or demerit) of a subordinate. Vacancies, however, must be filled. Selections of persons to fill them are made, if not on the basis of fact, on other criteria which undoubtedly seem believable enough to the decision makers. Often this turns out to be a variety of personal assumptions, sometime observations, miscellaneous testimonials, and, not unexpectedly, half-truths.

Personal Knowledge

Some of the gravest errors in evaluation are made from limited personal knowledge. Because someone is known to the appointing officer who finds that person attractive as a personality, no inquiry is made, except in the most casual way, concerning previous performance or others' views. The autocratic executive whose judgment has played so important a part in building an organization is one of the most frequent victims of this error. At one time he was close to all his subordinates and had a better chance to see them in action. This is no longer the case, but he is not aware of it. He persists, however, in his belief in the infallibility of his own judgments.

The Upward Mobiles

People are often taken in by the appearance someone makes or by what he or she professes to believe, rather than by what they can do. Organizational sociology has made much of the "upward mobile" who smiles brightly and easily to those in power positions but has never learned to work well with associates and subordinates. Thus, personal knowledge, while valuable as an executive attribute, can suffer from its incompleteness.

The Old School Tie

Assumptions, of course, lie at the root of the "old school tie" or "member of the club" system. The belief is held that because a person has such-and-such a background, there is a better chance of success than someone of a different background. Recently a British banking institution admitted it was still following its old, old policy of recruiting young executives only from Eton. This type of approach may or may not explain Britain's current economic problems. Most companies or agencies do not go this far, but each is likely to have its own "establishment," and individuals within it are likely to show preference to this or that kind of background. Having such credentials is often a substitute for more discriminating ones.

Professional Standing

Another common explanation for selecting square pegs is the tendency to equate excellence in a particular professional area as indicative of the administrative skill which the position really calls for. If a man is a first-rate engineer, lawyer, or economist, it is often assumed that he is the man for the job, irrespective of its duties. Many times reference checks ask more precise questions about technical skills than managerial skills, even though the job being filled is basically managerial.

The professionalization of the personnel function has sometimes contributed, albeit unintentionally, to a similar result. Because it is not easy to identify individual contributions to organizational productivity, there is a tendency to focus on components—personality, ability to express one's self, etc. This can have the unhappy effect of singling out individual characteristics, but overlooking the whole person. Thus, a rating is had not on what the individual produces, but on other factors only partially related to performance.

False and Misleading Information

There are, of course, also instances where the appointing organization is given false or misleading information by those who want to get the incompetent in question out of their own hair. There are ways of avoiding this, and they should be used.

The "Safe" Appointment

Much more frequent, in all probability, is the decision by the appointing authority to appoint someone who will not cause trouble to those currently in command. The real reason sometimes for selecting someone is that the person is known to be loyal, or safe, or "middle-of-the-road." There may be other even more personal reasons. The comment of the political leader when told that so-and-so is an incompetent is a classic: "I know," he admits ruefully, "but he is *our* incompetent."

How much easier to put someone into a new or higher position who always does what is asked than to take a chance on another who is known as an independent thinker and may also be ambitious to boot? A higher premium is placed on loyalty than on creativity in most organizations. This, of course, has resulted in the cult of the so-called "organization man."

A cartoon during the McCarthy days pointed out how a certain ungifted bureaucrat had risen to the top. "I've always been terribly, terribly loyal," he explained modestly. The way to the top for many is by polishing not only the handle of the big brass door, but their superiors as well.

How to Prevent Mistakes

There is little that can be done by way of developing either a procedure or a system that will keep people of little talent from key positions if those at higher levels continue with their "see no evil" policies, or, even as is sometimes the case, insist on having them. Fortunately, there are executives in every organization who want competence in their subordinates and will take advice on how to get it even though it means a change in thinking and policy.

The Manager's Role

Basic to all else is the manager's willingness to give time and attention to the important business of personnel evaluation and recruitment. It is one's business to know what is going on in the organization and, within limits, who is responsible for doing what.

This point cannot be overstressed. The theory of delegation does not require a "keep-out" policy. The good manager will visit subordinates frequently, will observe their work product (and work environment) first-hand, and will talk from time to time with those in echelons twice or more levels removed. This is not for the purpose of handing out accolades or soliciting complaints. Rather, it is a means of knowing what is going on. If conscientiously and unobtrusively done, it is inconceivable that the examples of executive incompetence, such as described earlier, could exist.

Illustrations abound from both business and governmental experience to support the wisdom of such an approach. The perceptive store manager spends much of the time on the floor. The good city manager may appear anywhere. The capable general never loses touch with his troops. With the advent of large bureaucratic organizations, it is easy to remove one's self from this kind of reality. The responsible executive must constantly remind himself not to lose touch with what is going on.

Professional Personnel Assistance

Executive time is one of the company's most important assets and, like any resource in short supply, it must be used prudently. Recruitment of managerial talent, whether from within or outside the organization, needs the help of professional people.

"Personnel as usual" is not good enough. Often the personnel staff is so overburdened with the details of its day-to-day operations that management thinks of it as a counseling or clerical operations unit. If the job is a big one, the organization may need help from the outside, or the special assignment of others from the inside with known competence.

A number of companies are available to assist in placement matters. In recent years also, management consultants have increased their services to include specific placement assignments. Small or medium sized organizations cannot afford to spend a large amount of executive time on the mechanics of finding and checking out candidates for key positions when experienced placement people can be obtained to do the job for them.

Promotion Boards

Use of promotion boards or assessment centers has the advantage of bringing a variety of points of view together. Ordinarily, this results in a broader look at the problem. Promotion boards are not, of course, without their weaknesses. Some of these are likely to become institutionalized. Military and Foreign Service boards provide a case in point. Sometimes, the "old school tie" tendencies these represent can be lessened by having one or more members of the board from outside the organization. Their influence can often be important.

References a "Must"

In any kind of promotional action, regardless of whether it involves someone inside or outside the organization, references are a must. The compiling of such a record may seem *pro forma* to many, and some of the time it may be, but it has hidden virtues which strongly recommend it. Consider the following:

1. It provides an orderly method of inquiry into a person's past job performance.

2. It creates a record so that others may judge the virtue of the selection.

3. It is an indicator of "good faith" on the part of the appointing authorities. (This is very important where promotions are likely to be questioned.)

4. It provides a vehicle by which unfavorable comments may be brought to the attention of those who might not otherwise get them.

Anyone with experience in evaluating others—the reference check is really a part of such a process—will be encouraged by the helpfulness of those of whom inquiry is made. Sometimes, even, the information-giver is penalized by frankness.

Although most organizations are delighted to be rid of their lemons, they are not likely to use the deliberate lie in doing so. People will sometimes fail to volunteer pertinent information, if derogatory, but will ordinarily give it if asked directly. Sometimes, by way of amelioration, they will explain that the person in question has had difficulty on the current job but is not wholly at fault. The nuances of language are many. The professional ear will distinguish most of them, but even an amateur will not have too much trouble if trained to listen carefully. More than one check should be made, sometimes as many as seven or eight. The reference check may be basic, but it is surprising how often people use it casually or not at all.

Summary

Every organization has its horror exhibits of executives who have gone steadily, if not spectacularly, up the ladder from one failure to another. Many of them are fine fellows, pipe smoking and tweedy looking with a fund of good stories and excellent judgment in whiskey. Some are recognized for their foibles and failures, perhaps even by those who installed them in the first place. Others are known only to their subordinates and God. They are at best a burden to the organization and at worst a positive force for its disintegration.

They come from many sources. Because of this, the job of keeping them from getting into important organizational posts is likely to be a continuing one. This is no reason, however, for failing to face up to the problem. If common sense will not solve it—and it hasn't seemed to—there are some procedural steps which can help. Each new job opening is a reminder that the filling of it will be viewed by those in the organization as a test of management's real intentions.

The better Japanese companies have set an excellent example in this. Western observers have been impressed with the amount of time that is spent in the recruitment process. It is, of course, time well invested. Those who join the company, whether as professionals or as part of the labor force, are seen as lifetime employees, and neither company nor government wants to make mistakes.

If we wish to avoid some of the problems we now have, we should regard each new vacancy as an opportunity for reasserting the theory of meritorious choice. It is high time it was paid more than lip service.

FOOTNOTE

[1] For a report in full of this study, see David S. Brown, "Subordinates' Views of Ineffective Executive Behavior," *Academy of Management Journal*, Dec. 1964, pp. 288-291.

CHAPTER XVIII

SHAPING THE ORGANIZATION TO FIT PEOPLE

It is not as difficult to shape an organization to the needs, skills, abilities, and values of its members as many believe. A growing number of organizations has done so consciously—and successfully—and an even larger number without realizing it.

Even so, the concept has found only limited acceptance among administrative planners. The reasons can be explained by a variety of factors. In the first place, most managers have not really given much thought to the problem. They accept without question the conventional organizational precepts of departmentation by function, by product, or geography, or client without considering alternatives.

This myopic view of the universe is reinforced by the manager's strongly held ideas of his or her role. The manager is the chief, the director, the person who gives orders which others are expected to carry out. To endorse the idea of subordinate *rights*—which the doctrine under discussion seems to suggest—is to downgrade the principle for which one has so long labored in getting to the top. As one manager bluntly put it: "I broke my back to get to the top, to be able to run things. I don't propose to give it all up now that I'm here."

But even if one were committed to the idea of shaping the organization so as to reflect the characteristics of its members, there would still be the problem of what to do and how to do it. Old ideas die slowly, and new ones are often untested. What assurances are there that the theory is applicable? How does one go about shaping an organization to the characteristics of those in it—presuming one could know what these characteristics are?

The Adaptive Manager

Too often, we think only of the formal organization, the organization portrayed in the organization chart and described in the procedures manual. The organization is rarely this—and always more than this. Basically, organization is a system of relationships involving two or more persons concerned with the satisfaction of needs or the achievement of objectives. Such relationships occur in a variety of patterns, determined by need, convenience, status, sociability, and individual preference. The dimensions of the real organization will be better understood by reference to what one writer calls the "varying composite" structure system and another identifies as the system of "overlays." The "varying composites" include, in addition to the command-action (formal) structure, the problem-solving, communicational, social and process structures. The system of overlays, which is much the same, includes the sociometric (the special friendships), the functional (the manner in which specialists relate to operations), the decision-making (the manner in which significant decisions are made), the power, and the communicational. Sayles, in a revealing study of managerial behavior, emphasized this point:

> The individual manager does not have a clearly bounded job with neatly defined authorities and responsibilities. Rather he is placed in the middle of a system of relationships, out of which he must fashion an organization that will accomplish his objectives. There is no "standard" interface; rather, the relationships differ, depending on the objectives and the position of the other groups with whom he must achieve a working pattern of give and take.[1]

This idea is underlined by the manner in which the individual makes allowance for—indeed, adjusts to—the behavioral patterns of others. Such situations occur at all levels and in all walks of life. They are part of the process of membership in the societal organizations we require for survival.

The Real Organization

Actually, much that is being suggested here has already been done, often without conscious appreciation, in the small, personally-oriented organization or work group. Whether reflected in the charts or not, the operational organization has been substantially modified by individual and group behavior. The manner in which those workers with inabilities or disabilities are employed is a case in point. The handicapped person is not expected to do more than his or her infirmity permits, nor is that person who does not get along well with others likely to be selected for public relations tasks. Allowances, in fact, are made at all levels of the organization—at the bottom for typists who cannot type, in the middle-management areas for engineers who cannot engineer, and at the top for managers who cannot manage and leaders who do not lead. A few years ago, Fortune reported at some length on the unwillingness of large companies to fire their executives. Instead, they were left, like blighted fruit, to hang from the tree while business went on as best it could around them. This is, of course, only the beginning of informal adjustment. It does, however, provide examples common to all—practices followed because the organization has chosen to live with its square pegs rather than without them. Others of a more constructive nature can be cited. A number of studies have pointed out that the best supervisors are those who adjust their supervisory approach to fit the needs—personal as well as job needs—of those they lead. Thus, the management lexicon comes to include such new verbs as coach, develop, support, supply, help, show, counsel, and assist, as replacements for the less satisfactory, and less successful, tell, order, and direct—all carryovers from formal organizational theory.

The Formal Organization

It is not enough to concern one's self with the informal organization, however real it may be. The formal organization also should reflect the characteristics of its membership. This is the blueprint, the master plan, to which people look for direction and guidance and to which reference is inevitable when conflict occurs. For good or ill, it has influence on what, how, and how well things are done. And, of course, it does reflect in a limited way the characteristics and capabilities of the members of the organization, the protestations of those who claim "scientific detachment" to the contrary.

There is evidence, as well, that other behavioral considerations have had influence on organizational design. Even the formula for determining the proper dimension of span of control has begun with the "people" factor as its starting point. So also, in more recent times, have the revisions of basic military patterns with respect to the size of a squad or the organization of a division. If one examines closely the premises of much of the traditional in design, one will discover *at its root* (although often artfully hidden) a recognition of the importance of the arrangement to the behavior of those who will be called upon to fulfill it. The emergence of unionism and the possibility of strikes, among them wildcat strikes, has triggered organizational remedies for lessening the possibility of work stoppages that would immobilize the company. Nothing could be more rational.

Considerable attention has been given to the experience of merchandisers who impose organizational patterns on their firms to emphasize individual selling or producing units. Headquarters-field office relationships and sales organizations in particular have been the objects of experimentation, where new arrangements for the performance of staff service functions are being tried experimentally. The placement of scientific and research personnel to encourage creativity yet assure optimum contribution to the organization has been the subject of a great deal of study.

All of this, however, is a mere scratching of the surface, the exception rather than the rule. For the most part, the specialists in administrative planning and design have continued to plod along well-established paths rather than to venture into areas which modern social science research has shown to be well worth exploring.

Influence for Change

The situation, however, is changing. The literature of management currently reflects two major lines of emphasis. The first is concerned with identification of the characteristics of the individual. The second is with their application.

Although it is difficult to state precisely when or how the behavioral movement began, one of the major and most articulate spokesmen is Argyris with his landmark book, *Personality and Organization*, which appeared as long ago as 1957. In calling for renewed research of the problem, he put forward the thesis that a conflict exists between the normal healthy individual of today's society and the organization of which he is a member.[2] This approach has been vigorously pursued by others. Among its results has been a focus upon the development of new patterns of leadership, as illustrated by McGregor's celebrated "Theory Y," in which the leader (or manager) attempts to create an environment conducive to increased individual participation. The emphasis which McGregor places on the self-fulfilling prophecy provides us with further evidence of the importance of individual behavior in organizational arrangements.[3] Such terms as consultative, participative, supportive, and democratic leadership are being used increasingly in management circles.

Likert's studies of work group behavioral patterns and his identification by means of the "linking pin" of relationships between individuals and groups has provided substantial data for this approach.[4] But many others have shown increasing concern for organizational change. Leavitt, for example, in a chapter of his *Managerial Psychology* on "Adapting Organizations to People," says:

> The problem can be looked at this way: Organizational factors like authority and pyramidal shapes force management people toward paternalistic, subjective, and more or less concrete, short-term, and often defensive behavior; but the changing business environment de-

mands the opposite behavior. It demands that the businessmen make multiple decisions and more objective, long-term, planful decisions. The problem is how to modify the organization so that it makes the second kind of behavior more likely.[5]

Golembiewski says quite bluntly that *"Organization is a moral problem,"* (his italics), and suggests a number of patterns which help to bring organizational behavior more in line with the Judaeo-Christian ethic.[6] More recently, the professional journals have produced a number of papers and articles pointing to ways by which organizational shape can accommodate—indeed, encourage—the normative forces within the individual. No attempt will be made here to identify all or even a significant portion of these, but the trend is significant. Their titles suggest the direction of the thinking of their authors—"Adapting Organizations to New Technology," "Engineer the Job to Fit the Manager," "Adaptations of Scientists in Five Organizations: A Comparative Analysis," "Organizational Size and Job Satisfaction," "Organizational Structure: A Framework for Analysis and Integration," and "Design for People, Too."

Shaping the Organization

As these and other writings suggest, there are a number of ways by which the organization can be patterned to make more effective use of member contributions. In general, they emphasize a wide variety of values associated not only with the Judaeo-Christian ethic and American behavioral patterns, but also characteristics which our society and its institutions over many years have encouraged. These include (but are not limited to) a belief in the dignity and the contribution of the individual, the need for opportunity for self-development, the willingness of the individual to commit himself or herself to group effort and common purpose, a desire to be creative, a need for self-identification, and a willingness to accept responsibility and take risks.

I have never been able to understand why so little attention has been given by social scientists to the area and/or national characteristics of a given population. They seem to prefer lumping all people together, whatever their cultural backgrounds, to arrive at generalizations concerning their motivations. This, it seems to me, compounds an already difficult problem.

Many of the most prevalent American characteristics were identified in Chapter II as a Theory A approach. The idea behind it, as I tried to make clear there, is that the values felt and expressed in the society at large will also be revealed in the marketplace, the office, the factory, and the laboratory. Is it too much to expect that those who design organizations and organizational systems take these factors into account?

Organizational adjustments to the needs and attributes of people are suggested in the following sections.

Job Enlargement

Basic to all organization patterns is the individual job. For years, management has sought to specialize and to simplify work under the theory that this led to greater worker mastery of the processes of production, greater ease of training and performance, and increased efficiency and economy of operations. In many instances, it has. But as simplification has proceeded, it has become apparent that dysfunctions were also being produced. Suddenly workers became aware of the fact that they were capable of more (in a qualitative way) than they were being asked to do, that jobs were no longer challenging, and that, in fact, they were being dulled and deadened by them.

Happily, the problem has now become a matter of organizational concern with the result that attention is being given to ways by which the job can be made more meaningful, more interesting, and more intellectually rewarding. Management science has not been without productive ideas once its focus has become clear.

Making Organizations More Manageable

Students of organization have known for some time that beyond a certain point, size increases rather than lessens overhead costs. They have been aware also of the growing burden placed by large organization on the processes of communication, and coordination. More recently, they have become concerned with the relationship of size and individual job satisfaction.

Industry has responded by the creation of a number of new types of networks, the effect of which has been to reinstate older patterns of entrepreneurship. By use of the franchise system, service organizations have been able to provide their participant members with a greater stake in the total enterprise. The military departments have gone outside the Pentagon with the creation of "R and D" organizations. Work of many types has been "farmed out." Internally, the effort has been made to cope with organizational size by the creation of semi-independent divisions and departments which have been granted a considerable degree of autonomy so long as they maintained general standards of performance and cost. The matrix organization is now an established thing. All of these have had their uses.

The Increased Span of Control

Although the span of control in most organizations is still limited by concepts developed in another generation under other conditions, there is a growing tendency today in both industry and government to enlarge it. I have visited factories where there is one supervisor for 50, 60, or more. This suggests a whole new way of thinking. One can also be encouraged by the broadening of the span in such areas as sales, field operations, and research. A corollary to it, of course, is the application of changing supervisory techniques which emphasize general rather than specific direction, mutual agreement on standards of performance, and greater acceptance at operational levels of individual responsibility.

The Shortened Hierarchy

The broadening of the organization results also in its shortening. Not only does this demonstrably lessen the distance between top and bottom, but it reduces the number of status distinctions and hierarchical levels as well. Thus, such arbitrary distinctions as those between "policy" and "operations" and "officer" and "employee" are reduced in a manner consistent with prevailing community patterns. The shortened hierarchy also shortens and simplifies the communicational system and facilitates the establishment of horizontal relationships which must take place if the organization is to do its job properly.

Patterns of Member Participation

In the past twenty years, a variety of organizational patterns has institutionalized systems of member participation in the decision-making process. The precursor of many of these was the Scanlon Plan, which provides for the establishment of worker-office committees for consultation, advice, and recommendations on a variety of problems faced by the company. Similar arrangements devised to encourage members of the organization to feel a greater sense of proprietorship and participation have appeared in scientific and research organizations and, of course, in universities. From an original advice-giving role, many of these have now become firmly established as sources of agency policy. There has also been a modest, if nonetheless clearly identifiable, trend in both industry and government during recent years to identify products with organizational units, thus encouraging greater employee teamwork. This is in contrast to the fragmented structure in which the focus is upon parts rather than the whole.

Americans are also experimenting with adaptations of the Quality Control circles which have proven so useful in Japan. Among other things, these invite the factory-floor worker to contribute to the resolving of problems which in conventional systems are turned over to engineers or executives. There is also an effort to apply some of the assembly techniques used originally in Sweden by Volvo. Whether these efforts will achieve here what they have elsewhere remains to be seen.

Recently also, new developments in staff-line theory have suggested a pattern by which *both* staff and operational units are held responsible for the accomplishment of particular objectives and judged together rather than separately. This illustrates one of the uses of the group or committee system in administration. Recognition of the group system as an important tool of objective-achieving management tends to establish it as part of the organizational structure. There is less fear of committees and greater recognition of their unique contribution than a generation ago.

Growing Emphasis on Decentralization

Management has come to appreciate in recent years the values of decentralization. By assigning certain functions to the field, thereby removing them from close supervision, it has been able to achieve some of the same response from its employees that has long marked the smaller, more personal organization. There is also the profit center which provides its own initiatives. The argument for decentralization was strongly put by Goodman nearly 20 years ago. It has not been improved upon:

> Throughout society, the centralizing style of organization has been pushed so far as to become ineffectual, economically wasteful, human stultifying, and ruinous to democracy. There are overcentralized systems in industry, in government, in culture, and in agriculture. The tight interlocking of these systems has created a situation in which modest, direct and independent action has become extremely difficult in every field. The only remedy is a strong admixture of decentralization.[7]

The decentralization called for is being accomplished by the creation of field units with a large degree of autonomy in which individuals find not only a means of self-identification with their tasks, but also an opportunity for the freedom which would not be possible in a head-quarters-dominated office. Moreover, the creation of advisory and service units which are permitted to exist as long as others make good use of their services suggests another, though related, approach to the same problem. There remains, of course, the matter of standard setting and oversight, but once these problems have been surmounted, decentralization (and delegation, which it implies) contribute substantially to the total organization product.

Summing Up

This listing is intended to be illustrative only. It suggests the number and variety of possibilities for shaping the organization to fit the characteristics, values, and needs of its members. There are many other directions which organizations can and, in fact, do take. What, institutionally, can be done to increase a stake in one's own performance? How can creativity be encouraged without damaging fiscal responsibility? In what ways can advice be used to replace direction and control? How can the many different professionals in the organization be related more meaningfully to each other? In what ways can organizational design help to meet workers' individual needs?

Such questions offer fruitful fields for inquiry and need to be addressed. The human factor must be recognized for what it is—one of the major determinants of effective organizational performance. It should, accordingly, be given its proper place, along with function and objective, among the leading patterns of departmentation.

The architects of a building take into account the qualities of the material—the bricks, steel, concrete, wood, and glass—that go into it. So must the organizational architects take into account the characteristics of the people they work with. The building architect is fortunate that the strengths and weaknesses of his materials are relatively fixed and can be readily learned. The architect of human organizations has a much more difficult assignment. The qualities of human materials, although we have lived with them over the centuries, are still only partially known. They also have the enormously frustrating habit of changing their properties and even of shifting about once the mortar of the organizational system has been applied.

This does not mean, of course, that one cannot generalize concerning human characteristics. Rather, it emphasizes the need for understanding all that current knowledge permits us of the qualities themselves, the nature of the differences between them, how they function, and, if possible, *why* they do as they do. We must give more attention to fitting organizational patterns to those who are a part of them. Only in this way can the individual contribution to the whole be optimized.

FOOTNOTES

[1] Leonard Sayles, *Managerial Behavior*, NY: McGraw-Hill Book Company, Inc., 1964, p. 27.

[2] Chris Argyris, *Personality and Organization: The Conflict Between System and the Individual*, NY: Harper & Brothers, 1957.

[3] Douglas McGregor, *The Human Side of Enterprise*, NY: McGraw-Hill Book Company, Inc., 1960.

[4] Rensis Likert, *New Patterns of Management*, NY: McGraw-Hill Book Company, Inc., 1961.

[5] Harold J. Leavitt, *Managerial Psychology*, Chicago: University of Chicago Press, 1958, p. 275.

[6] Robert T. Golembiewski, *Men, Management and Morality*, NY: McGraw-Hill Book Company, Inc., 1965, p. 291.

[7] Paul Goodman, *People or Personnel: Decentralizing and the Mixed System*, NY: Random House Inc., 1963, p. 3.

PART V

MANAGING AND LEADING

CHAPTER XIX

RETHINKING THE SUPERVISORY ROLE

Once upon a time, supervising was simple. The work to be supervised was relatively uncomplicated, subordinates knew what was expected of them, and there was no doubt as to what would happen if their responsibilities were not met.

The supervisor was a person with both expertness and experience. He (and sometimes she) had probably come up through the ranks; he had learned the job the hard way; and because of this expertness and loyalty to the company, he was chosen for a position of honor and responsibility.

The supervisor was also close to those being supervised. When they failed to produce, he was immediately aware of it and could do something about it. He had little to worry about in terms of either union or governmental interference. By and large, he knew he would be supported topside.

This is the way things used to be. But somewhere along the line, something changed. Today most supervisors feel caught in the middle between management and labor—the rock and the hard place—and are unsure of the support of either. A consistent complaint supervisors make is that they are bypassed from below as well as above.

What Has Happened?

The fact is that the decades since the 1930s have seen many significant changes in the supervisor's role. Technological changes have had their impact, but of even more importance have been societal changes. Today the supervisor is not only a supervisor; he or she must be a lawyer, counselor, social worker, training specialist, and P.R. man as well.

Of course, I was overstating the case when I said that supervision was once easy. Being a *good* supervisor has never been easy. But in comparison with some of the requirements that today's supervisor must meet, it was certainly much simpler and a great deal more rewarding to be a supervisor a couple of decades ago than it is now. It is time these changes were recognized, and *it is also time for management to stop blaming supervisors for the kinds of problems that exist at office and factory floor levels and to develop more constructive approaches to them.*

Why has the supervisory role become so difficult in modern business and government? Why are there so many problems and so few solutions?

Changes in Society

First of all, there have been great changes not only in the society and in the workforce but also in the nature of the work to be done. The social pot may have come to a boil in America during the late 1960s and early 1970s, but the fire under it had been there for a long time. The basic American credo—in which all of us have so long professed to believe—promises life, liberty, the pursuit of happiness, and, by implication, much else. In addition, we endorse the view that *no one* should be excluded from these promises any more. It is, of course, only a question of time before promises become expectations. That time has now arrived.

Let me elaborate on this statement. In recent years, television and other communications have made available to everyone the values and ideas once shared by only a few. The affluence of the middle and upper classes has been made highly visible to those who do not share it—and there are many people in that category as national income figures make inescapably clear.

Those who watch television see the many new forms of power available to the have-nots. There is the power of people in the streets, of mass demonstrations and marches, of confrontations, and of work slowdowns and stoppages. If television does nothing else, it reminds the viewer that by being action-oriented, one is only being American. One uses one's tongue, one's fists, one's guns to support the demands that are made. The approach that overcame the forests, crossed the plains, and breasted the mountains is now being applied to internal problems.

The motor car has also underlined and added to this feeling of American independence and activism. It made it possible for the Okies to go west and for those in the Southern cotton fields to get to the large cities. But it has also done something else. It has provided a mobility to the American population that has deprived it of roots and to a certain degree also of stability. The automobile has become our national "get away" vehicle, with all that this implies.

But no changes in American society have been greater than those in education. Not only do children stay longer in school than ever before, but they are also targets of a different kind of education than their elders received. This begins with the basic idea—consistent with American philosophy—that each of us should have the opportunity to develop our capabilities to their fullest. It encourages each of us to discover ourselves, to seek our own way and our own identity. And it often does this with little attention as to whether or not there is any place, once we are "developed," for us to go.

Changes in the Workforce

Paralleling the changes in society, major changes have taken place in the national workforce over the last three decades. The majority of today's workers are white- rather than blue-collared. Indeed, the term blue-collar has lost much of its original meaning. Many of those who fill what would have once been described as blue-collar jobs now resent the classification and, in effect, try not to identify with it. Thus, we have such terms as stationary engineer (for janitor), sanitary engineer (for garbage collector), hygienist, and the like.

Additionally, nearly 42 percent of today's workforce are women and more than 50 percent of all women, in fact, are gainfully employed outside the home. And of those workers entering the labor force in the next few years, the majority will be women. Also, the educational level of those who work for a living is rising. Over 80 percent of those between 20 and 29 are high school graduates, and currently a record thirteen million people are in college, which presages a much more educated workforce for the future.

Another major change in today's workers is that those who will make a career of one job in one organization are clearly in the minority. Figures indicate that nearly 20 percent of all American families change their place of residence each year, indicating a high job turnover rate as well. The 20-year-old, whether male or female, who enters the labor force this year may well be in eight to ten different lines of work before retirement. This places a major burden on training systems.

The workforce of the future can be expected also to include larger numbers of blacks and persons of Spanish origins than in the past. Each will bring its own cultural characteristics to the workplace.

Changes such as these, testifying to the new nature of the workforce, are also a reminder that there are major changes in worker-held values as well. In fact, the "work culture" is a considerably different one from what it was a few decades ago.

Generally, work is seen today in a variety of ways, depending upon those who are looking at it. There are some who regard it as a major life objective; others, however, see it merely as a means to some other end. Still others think of it only as a burden to be suffered. By and large, Americans still work hard—harder than workers in most other countries—but they have in recent years become more selective in terms of the things they will and will not do.

These workers' views are shaped by the society in which they live. While it is not easy to generalize about these views, such studies as the Department of Health, Education, and Welfare's task report on *Work in America* (1973) make clear some of the demands that workers at all levels are laying before management. These include dignity, a challenge, a certain amount of independence of action, an opportunity to associate with others of similar backgrounds, and appreciation for what is done. Like their higher level associates, lower level workers want to be able to feel that they are masters of their environment.

No one should be surprised by sentiments such as these. The American nation has endured a turbulent decade and a half, marked by demands for greater freedom of the individual, a fuller expression of human rights, greater opportunities for personal development, and a larger share of the affluence around us. Never a placid or serene society, we have become increasingly a loud and demanding one. The worker at the lathe or behind the counter is not to be excluded from his (or her) entitlements.

Changes in the Job

Not least among the changes that have affected supervisory practices are changes in the nature of the modern organization. No longer is work performed in traditional ways. Factors having to do with space (that is, distance), specialization, client relationships, and power patterns have all had their effect.*

The Distance Factor. There is no factor that changes the rules of supervision more drastically than that of distance. Distance diminishes direction, so a subordinate out of sight of supervisors has a freedom not shared by those who sit at desks or work at machines under their watchful eyes. The former may be held accountable for performing a given amount of work (when it can be calculated), but also has a large degree of freedom in terms of how this work is to be done. This is why so many journeyman jobs, such as mailman, garbage collector, bus driver, and serviceman, are eagerly sought by those who understand their own and society's limitations.

The Specialized Job. Those who become highly proficient in the performing of a task earn the right to free themselves from the close

---

*This idea is developed more fully in Chapter III, "The Fifth Freedom—Freedom from Supervision."

and watchful attention of their supervisors. Because of the nature of the job, the supervisor is often incapable of providing the guidance that was once given. Sometimes, the individual's work area is seen as a private domain only to be entered when things go wrong. Some supervisors manage to keep well-enough informed so that they will know what to do in the event of the subordinate's illness or resignation, but they make a point, for good reason, of staying well out of the way.

New Processes and Equipment. New tools produce new practices. This is particularly true when new processes are introduced or new equipment installed. Not having established guidelines to direct them, those who are involved with the new systems tend to develop their own. They can be counted on to argue for those guidelines that insure them the greatest independence for individual action.

Special Sources of Power. Power may be acquired and wielded in a variety of ways. It can be acquired by subordinates as well as by superiors and can even be legitimized when so held. That this is usually spoken of as countervailing power does not make it any less real.

The existence of a union—or even the fear of unionization—is a threat to managerial power. The supervisor may have the legal right to recommend an adverse action but may be persuaded not to do so for obvious reasons. There are many other forms of power that limit the ability of supervisors to do some of the things that are expected of them.

There is, for example, the job with its own constituency. In these cases, the subordinate enjoys so close a relationship with the client that management fears to disturb the situation even when it is dissatisfied with some of the things the subordinate is doing. And there are those who do jobs no one else cares to do and, by so doing, free themselves from supervisory restraints.

Implications for Management

Changes in the workforce such as these are not minor; the whole nature of the managerial system is affected by them. They help to explain why today's supervisor is finding supervision in its traditional pattern so difficult to carry out. Not only is the average employee less willing than ever before to be directed, but the changing nature of the organization has produced jobs that are virtually unsupervisable as well.

Does this mean that supervision as such is going out of style? Hardly. But it does mean that older patterns are being replaced by

newer ones that emphasize larger acceptance of individual responsibilities at all levels, including those at the bottom; a greater measure of
individual freedom on the job; a fuller appreciation of individual worth
and dignity; and the need for improving the quality of working life.

These factors call for something more useful than the usual
simple—and simplistic—diagnosis that the root of most personnel problems lies with first-line supervisors. What is really needed is a better
understanding at all levels of what is taking place in the American
workforce and a new approach that is intelligent, relevant, and doable.
It is of no value to continue to recite homilies that have long since
outworn their usefulness.

A New Meaning for Supervision

There needs to be, as a point of departure, a better appreciation by
managers of the supervisory role. Traditionally, the first-line supervisor
has been held responsible for whatever goes wrong. This is no longer a
tenable approach. What is needed is a rethinking of the supervisory role
at *all* organizational levels, because this role, in its traditional form, no
longer enhances the work system nor is it really acceptable to those
who fill the majority of American jobs. This applies not only to those
who are supervised but to those who supervise as well. Being a supervisor is the price one must pay in most organizational systems for
"getting ahead." And so it is endured if not always practiced.

In the long run, it may be more useful to try to *reduce* the supervisory role rather than "improve" it. This is not fantasy. It can be done.
In fact, it is already taking place, as the examples given above of jobs
with minimal or no supervision suggest. That this has occurred in an
evolutionary, rather than in a more dramatic, fashion makes it no less
substantial. The cumulation of small changes often produces effects of
a revolutionary nature.

Management has been an active if unsuspecting partner in the process. It has done this by granting increased autonomy to those at lesser
levels. It has created profit centers where individuals and groups can
pursue their own initiatives. It has developed systems of licensing, job-
bing, and subcontracting. Many executives have voluntarily broadened
spans of supervision (or control), fully realizing that, since supervisors
have more people to watch over, each worker will be supervised less
closely. Many an executive has learned that the best supervision is often
the least even if unwilling to admit it.

This suggests that there is a need for a rethinking of the word
"supervision" in favor of some more acceptable term. In its present

form, it implies the idea of superintendency, oversight, guardianship, and control, which so many people find objectionable. Certainly a nation that has gained so much from an individualistic ethos can make greater use of it in its organizational systems.

A number of institutions have indeed found other ways of approaching the problem and use terms with fewer emotional connotations. The problem, however, is more than a terminological one: it involves the development of more useful forms of institutional action.

Influence vs. Control

"Are we not more interested," Chester Barnard once asked, "in influence than in control?" The question answers itself. We seek to extend our influence: this is what management is all about. Control is only a means to such an end, and there are other means that are usually more effective.

The manager, whether a high-level executive or a first-line supervisor, will already have discovered as much. But it is an easy idea to forget as pressures mount. When something goes wrong, the lights begin to flash and the bells to ring. The system demands *action*, and action usually takes the form of directives and controls.

Managers must learn to cultivate ways by which their influence can be increased. They must understand why they are what they are. They must be articulate in putting them forward. They must be willing to hear what others at all levels have to say.

They must know their people, including those several jobs away who are important to the health of the enterprise. They must be able to generalize from what they see and hear.

Managers need to think of themselves as persons whose life is involved with learning and teaching. They are, in fact, committed to persuading others that what they seek is important.

CHAPTER XX

CHANGING ROLES AND FUNCTIONS OF THE MANAGER

"Of all of the performing arts," Professor Peter Vaill has reminded us, "management is the most important." A perceptive Frenchman, Jean-Jacques Servan-Schreiber, puts it even more strongly. "Management is, all things considered," he writes, "the most creative of all arts. It is the art of arts. Because it is the organizer of talent." It is, of course, the essence of the pragmatic. The building of a dam, the assembly of an automobile or TV set, or the running of an airline, a primary school, or a church, all require managerial inputs.

What is so surprising—and also disturbing—is that the basic approach to organizing and mananging has changed so little over the years.

Major changes have taken place in the past half century in almost every area of human endeavor—art, architecture, engineering, medicine, chemistry, physics, aerodynamics and education—to mention some of the more significant. We have changed also from an agricultural to an industrial society, from one of small towns to one of great cities, from a highly isolationist to an interdependent world, and from one in which individuals were of little consequence to one in which they are paramount. Yet in its basic concepts, management theory is not greatly different today from what it was when the "scientific management" movement first emerged over 75 years ago.

To be sure, the post-World War II period has emphasized a humanizing element long since overdue, and remarkable new equipments have been devised and put to work, but organizational structures and management precepts still continue to direct themselves towards control when what we are really seeking is *performance*. As Mary Parker Follett observed more than 50 years ago, "The object of organization is control, or, one might say, organization *is* control." A large majority of the textbooks continue to accept such a goal, and a large majority of the practitioners to seek it.

Professor Dwight Waldo, public administration's most distinguished spokesman, has noted that "any institution that doesn't adjust to the constantly changing milieu of the contemporary revolutions will not be effective in terms of its purpose or assignment." "Long range," he goes on to say, "it will not survive." The same may be said for a profession, a system, or a philosophy. This is why it is so important to re-examine old concepts and old habits and to determine whether they still are sufficient to the day thereof.

A new, long, hard look at the role and functions of the manager is certainly needed. To repeat what Fayol laid out for us a century ago, no matter how prescient he was; to search for a key to greater efficiency; or to recite once more an outworn POSDCORB prescription is hardly enough. We need to come to grips with modern requirements of managing.

There is, first, the matter of who the manager is. By definition, managers have a wide variety of titles, and sometimes no title at all. They are people with responsibilities which are sometimes imposed upon them but often voluntarily accepted. Much of the time these are greater than the legal authority or the power or resources to carry them out.

Surely, a president is a manager (as well as a leader) and so is a minister or director. Staff people are also managers, as are those who fill a wide variety of positions in what is euphemistically called the middle-management area. The first line supervisor (or foreman) is one as well, but so are those who have a responsibility for, and a voice in, any of a large variety of undertakings—economic, political, social, and familial. Managers may or may not supervise others. They may not have the right to command. But they have—or need to have—influence, and how this is acquired and exercised has major bearing upon what is achieved.

Managers in the 'eighties, surely—and also in the longer period ahead—face far different requirements and must perform a greater variety of functions than their predecessors only a generation or two ago. While changes have, in fact, taken place in the managerial role, they have occurred incrementally for the most part and often with so little éclat that some of them are yet to be perceived even by those who practice them, and their implications are still not fully understood. Among the most important is the proliferation of "outside" relationships which have become so vital to the achievement of organizational—and managerial—objectives.

This chapter identifies six of the most important of the current functions (or roles) of the manager. They apply to all levels, and basically to all types of work. They build upon conventional managerial wisdom, but because of the new demands placed upon men and systems, go well beyond it.

To fulfill their responsibilities, managers today must prepare themselves in each of these areas. The larger the organization, the greater the need for doing so. While the attention each requires will vary both with the situation and the capabilities of the manager, all of them are important to managerial performance. The six are:

1. The manager as manager.
2. The manager as negotiator.
3. The manager as leader.
4. The manager as developer.
5. The manager as innovator.
6. The manager as human being.

Only one of the above is traditional, but others have been recognized for their contribution to organizational achievement.

1. *The Manager as Manager.* This is the traditional role, the subject of all basic texts. In fulfilling it, the manager becomes the person "in charge," the one who in the face of uncertainties or indecision, decides—or helps to decide—and then, sees to it that the decision is carried out. In this role, the manager is expected to be fair, firm, insightful, and, above all, prudent. We may expect more, of course, depending upon the level, the experience, the circumstances, and the history of similar situations. Traditional managerial training attempts to prepare the manager-in-being to meet these requirements. Given ever-changing scenarios, this is not an easy task and even the more rigorous and conscientious of our institutions are sometimes at a loss to know what should be learned or how the learning process should be undertaken.

Certainly, the manager must know the tools of the trade. These as might be expected are increasing in number, but there are basics around which academicians cluster in schools of business administration, public administration, engineering administration, and management. They involve such subjects as planning, organizing, budgeting or financing, accounting, auditing (including internal auditing), personnel, training and development, communications, work measurement, and the like. The modern manager is also expected to know something about computers and their potential, as well as information and control systems. There may or may not be sessions in supervision, human relations, or in the newer but fast developing field of organizational development (OD), or, as Gordon Lippitt identifies it, organization renewal.[1]

The importance of these subjects should not be under-rated. The manager should know as much about the business of managing (or at least what is conventionally seen as managing) as the physician about physiology or pharmacy. Such a knowledge is expected by one's associates and to be found wanting is an almost certain harbinger of failure.

This, however, is only one of the requirements of the job. Its focus is largely upon the manager's subordinates—the "control" factor which Mary Follett has identified for us—and neglects the variety of other relationships so necessary to the achievement of objectives.

2. *The Manager as Negotiator.* A managerial function that has increased in geometric proportions during recent years is that of negotiating with others the many vexatious issues and problems which involve a variety of people, offices, and organizations. At higher levels, the majority of the executive's time is spent in external relationships. There are matters to be worked out with governing bodies, with other organizations which share an interest in the problem, with clients, with suppliers, with associations (supporters as well as opponents), with unions, with the media, and even with the courts. There is also the matter of one's competitors to be taken into account, and while laws may vary from country to country with respect to what is and is not permitted, what *they* do has a major bearing upon what we do. All organizations have competitors, whether in a service or product field, or, if in government, in contention for the limited resources available.

What is so obvious in the instance of a cabinet minister, or a company director, occurs also at lesser levels in the organization. Few managers are so fully hidden from view that they are able to escape contact with others. The director of a field station or branch office is in constant communication with an environment that has grown increasingly large and demanding. Even the first-line factory supervisor must, if he's to be successful, develop continuing contact with others outside of the unit. That they may be elsewhere in the organization, rather than on the outside, does not change the fact that one does not have the control over them that one likes to think one has over one's subordinates, and must negotiate the performance of services essential to effective operation of the unit. This is a recognized aspect of the matrix organization, and, indeed, one of its strengths.

As Leonard Sayles has pointed out (in *Managerial Behavior*), the success of the supervisor/manager depends to a large degree upon the success of these negotiations. By acting as a facilitator of the workflow processes, by getting maintenance people to the spot as needed when breakdowns occur, by knowing how and where to obtain the services the unit requires, by "trading-off" where this is useful, and by attempting to service those who receive the unit's products, the manager is clearly performing a more important function than as if the equivalent time were to be spent in direct supervision of subordinates.

Yet most management courses give little attention to the development of acceptable working relationships by the manager with others. What is learned is learned on one's own, often by trial and error.

3. *The Manager as Leader.* Effective managers are more than managers. They are also leaders. The two roles, however, are by no means the same, and the greatest achievements come from a combination of the two.

The manager is the expert in the processes of administration. We look to managers to combine people and resources in ways that will achieve objectives within established limits. They see their role as that of perfecting the system and then making sure that it continues to perform as wanted and needed. They are selected by those higher up to perform these tasks.

The leader, on the other hand, is someone chosen by those who follow his or her example because, for whatever reasons, they approve it. We identify leaders by their followership, by the fact that others *voluntarily* accept their influence. The leader need not be a part of the organization's authority system, in fact may even be outside it. The leader becomes a leader because others accept his or her objectives, values, ideas, enthusiasm, and wisdom. The great leaders of this century—people like Churchill, Gandhi, Einstein, Roosevelt, Freud and Ford—were leaders because so many others identified with and supported them.

One of the advantages of leadership is that it is not restricted to subordinate constituencies. The true leader has influence with his associates (the horizontals), with higher-ups, with those outside the organization, and often with those at governing levels. We may not always understand how influence is acquired but we can identify its effect. As Professor Lindeman has reminded us, "The leader is a stimulus, but he is also a response."

Managers are most effective when they are also respected as leaders. The position they hold provides opportunities for leadership but does not automatically assure it. In fact, it sometimes detracts. The title one holds makes one conspicuous, and managers often fail as leaders because they rely upon power rather than persuasion or example to get things done. It is a temptation difficult to resist.

Managers should understand the importance of leadership to the managerial function. "Real leaders of men," Churchill once wrote, "do not come forward offering to lead. They show the way."

4. *The Manager as Developer.* As the requirements of the organization become more complex and more demanding, the need for a work

force able to cope with them increases also. The marketplace cannot be expected to supply more than the raw talent, if that, which is required to meet these needs. It is, accordingly, part of the manager's job to see to it that people are recruited and trained to do what is needed not only for the present but for the future as well.

The manager's success in this role will be determined more over the long than the short haul. The development of able and dedicated employees is an assignment that can hardly be achieved overnight. There is no immediate payoff, and many headaches and heartaches occur in the process. But, like other forms of planning, manpower planning and development is an assignment that must be undertaken.

Not only will good managers insist that there be training programs which will meet the future needs of the organization but they must be trainers themselves. It is part of their ongoing assignment to make sure that others understand and support the purposes of the organization—its immediate and long range objectives—and also that they are prepared to undertake specific roles in it. The effective manager helps to train others at all levels.

Chester Barnard, whose *The Functions of the Executive* is so insightful, argued strongly for organizational change through the molding of the system by means of appointments and the "educating" of subordinates. He puts it this way:

> An executive is a teacher; most people don't think of him that way, but that's what he is. He can't do very much unless he can teach people. He does it not by any formally organized classes or seminars, but that's what he has all the time. He has conferences that are seminars in which either he or other people who are involved do instructing. That's absolutely essential. You can't just pick out people and stick them in a job and say go ahead and do it. You've got to state the goals; you've got to indicate the limitations. . . .the methods.[2]

Learning is, of course, an individual matter. This means that each member of the organization must be given the opportunity to see, understand, and do what will later be required. It is the manager's responsibility to see that this happens.

5. *The Manager as Innovator.* In 1969, Peter Drucker, one of the keener observers of management, wrote in a landmark article in the *Harvard Business Review* that ". . .in the period ahead, entrepreneurial innovation will become a very heart and core of management."[3] This has, in part, already been borne out by some of the workplace innovations, strongly encouraged by management, which have been reported

from Japan. This is why it is included here among the new functions of the manager.

Managers themselves do not, of course, need to be the primary source of organizational innovation. What is suggested here is that innovation *per se* be seen as the important contributor it is to productivity, and that the manager become one of the major catalysts in producing it. This is developed more fully in Chapter XXIV.

The great merit of creativity lies not only in its potential for the improvement of products, tools and equipment but methods and systems as well. Yesterday's common sense is today's dogma, and, understanding this, we must find new solutions to the problems we currently face and also be able to anticipate those ahead. There is no limit to the potentials of such an approach. There is first of all invention—the development of recognized new devices, products, or formulae, the value of which can hardly be estimated. Most of us will produce few patentable products, but much is possible if we use another term, innovation, which recognizes new uses for existing equipment, new methods for making existing goods, the value of novelty, renovation, deviation, modernization, and adaptation. Artists and writers have always been highly creative, but other professions, including that of management, have more often placed greater value on iteration and repetition. Events of the past two decades, however, have suggested that we have lost sight of one of the individual's and group's greatest potentials.

All of us are capable of considerably greater creativity. Emergency creates in many an opportunity for doing something differently. (Necessity has long been recognized as the mother of invention.) But we now know that creativity can be nurtured and encouraged, and we also know how it can be done. As philosopher Alfred North Whitehead has observed (in *Science and The Modern World*), "The greatest invention of the nineteenth century was the method of invention." The manager has neglected this area for far too long a time.[4]

6. The Manager as Human Being. There is, finally, the matter of the humanness of the manager. Managers are not machines, nor are those who work for them. Being human is the commonality we all share.

Because some occupy high office amid elegant surroundings and draw large salaries while others work in heat, grime, and noise for a pittance, does not change the situation. We are all members of the family of man, brothers and sisters under the skin.

In a world which is increasingly emphasizing the importance—and rights—of the individual, the manager needs to be seen as someone who feels for others, who shares their hopes and expectations, who understands—or at least tries to understand—their problems. This does not relieve one of making difficult and often painful decisions, or for deciding, as one so often must, for the group rather than for the individual. It is merely a reminder that in doing so, one must not overlook the human implications of what is done.

It is sometimes said that a manager is "tough, but also fair." The toughness goes down better when fairness, or considerateness, is also present. Those at lesser levels, given the opportunity, are aware of the play of events over which one has no control. The least they ask is understanding and compassion.

The history of the world is a struggle for independence of the forces which are attempting to subvert one. It does not suffice to win independence in one area and to lose it in another. A transfer in the ownership of a company, or a change in government, avails little if the individual on the job is still subject to the kinds of controls which existed before.

It is important, therefore, for the manager to understand how others feel about the managerial role. These feelings, we know all too clearly, have major effects on one's performance. Their greatest importance, however, is to remind the manager that to be effective one must understand how others look upon one and how they feel about the work they are asked to perform. The manager must be first, last, and always a human being with empathy with others.

In Summary

Sir Stafford Beer whose work with systems has won him international standing has said (in *Platform for Change*):

> Man is a prisoner of his own way of thinking, and of his stereotypes of himself. His machine for thinking, the brain, has been programmed to deal with a vanished world. This old world was characterized by the need to manage things—stone, wood, iron. The new world is characterized by the need to manage complexity.[5]

If this is so—and the arguments for it are persuasive—that day has already arrived.

The tools we have used, and the theories we have held, are no longer adequate to the tasks we face. It is no longer possible to think in simplistic ways of direction and control, whatever power one may have.

If there is any message which comes through clearly for those with managerial responsibilities, it is that they need the support and cooperation not only of people at all levels of the organization but with a variety of "outsiders" as well. New and better methods must be found to obtain them.

The requirements of the large and complex organizations which mark our age will no longer permit our managers to do the things that were prescribed a half century or more ago. The several functions described above offer new possibilities and new hopes.

FOOTNOTES

[1]Gordon L. Lippitt, *Organization Renewal: A Holistic Approach to Organization Development*, Englewood Cliffs, NJ: Prentice-Hall, Inc., 1982.

[2]As quoted by William B. Wolf in "Conversations with Chester I. Barnard," ILR Paperback No. 12, New York State School of Industrial and Labor Relations, Cornell University, Ithaca, NY 1973, pp. 7-8.

[3]From Peter Drucker, "Management's New Role," *Harvard Business Review*, Nov.-Dec. 1969.

[4]Alfred North Whitehead, *Science and the Modern World*, NY: Macmillan, 1931, p. 141.

[5]Sir Stafford Beer, *Platform for Change*, NY: John Wiley & Sons, Inc., 1975, p. 15.

CHAPTER XXI

LEADERSHIP AND FOLLOWERSHIP: TWIN INGREDIENTS

Most people yearn to have influence with others. Some come by it with little effort. Others go to great lengths to achieve it. Some are satisfied to influence only a few and in limited ways. Others are not fulfilled unless they have influence with many.

Influence is, of course, the essence of leadership. We are leaders because others are influenced by—and follow—our instructions, our suggestions, our example. *We become leaders because we have followers.*

To no one is this truth more important than to the manager. He or she may have learned well the tools of the profession, but their fulfillment depends in the final analysis on this something we call leadership.

Leading is not the same as managing. "Managing," as the term is commonly used, is the systematizing of behavior so that certain preselected objectives can be achieved. The manager is given the "right" to command, to seek and get performance from others as part of a contractual arrangement which brings them to the organization. The manager issues orders with the expectation that they will be followed.

Such arrangements are very important, but they constitute only a part of the process. They can be minimally as well as fully met. Leadership, because it can obtain greater-than-contract fulfillment, is thus an important adjunct to managing or directing. It is the factor which puts flesh and blood on the skeleton of the organization. The manager who is also a leader has demonstrated something beyond the specifics of the role. Such a person has shown that one can have influence beyond what one can command.

Leadership has other virtues as well. Leaders are not limited, as managers are, by the dimensions of the organization or the *mores* of organizational behavior. They can encourage followership wherever it exists—from "higher ups," from peers and also from clients and others outside the organization. They are not limited, as are managers or supervisors, to those at lower organizational levels.

In today's fluid world, this is an enormously important point. The only limit to influence is the willingness of the person to whom it is addressed to accept it. One need not have command, or share its paraphrenalia, to have influence. One need only to meet the criteria that those who are potential followers require. And yet how often do we seek to *control* instead!

On its surface, all this may seem simple enough. Unhappily, it is not. It is important, therefore, to look more deeply into the meaning of leadership and how it may be acquired.

Leadership and Followership

Perhaps the most significant learning to come from the many studies of leadership is, as we have suggested above, that it is determined by followership. There can no more be leadership without followership than there can be compass north without compass south. The follower determines the leader. If we do not have followers, we do not have leaders. It is as simple as that.

Followership, however, must be voluntary. When it is induced by power, by the fear felt by those who fall into line, it is not leadership. It is coercion. This is more than semantics. Those who count as leadership something that is coercion-induced are fooling only themselves. As General Eisenhower once pointed out:

> I happen to *know* a little about leadership. I've had to work with a lot of nations, for that matter, at odds with each other. And I tell you this: you do not *lead* by hitting people over the head. Any damn fool can do that, but it's usually called "assault" and not "leadership.". . .I'll tell you what leadership is. It's *persuasion*—and *conciliation*—and *education*—and *patience*. [Emphasis his.][1]

Employees do have choices and they exercise them. They can support vigorously what is asked of them and go to great lengths to see that it is done. They can give lip-service support only and in practice remain indifferent to what they do. Or, they may even oppose, citing legal, moral, or physical reasons for doing so. They are a reminder of the existence of countervailing power and the willingness of people to exercise it.

Leaders and Headmen

The nature of leadership cannot be fully understood without distinguishing between *real* and *titular* leaders. The titular leader (the headman) is the person with the official title or role. He or she is selected by someone higher up to fill a position or role and thereby invested with organizational authority. The headman may be a leader, or one of the leaders of the organization, but, again, may not be. One may have influence in some matters but not in others. The headman has power, or a certain amount of it, because it is part of the trappings of the office, but that does not mean that one is automatically a leader. I distinguish between commanding, which is an organizational role, and persuading, influencing and inspiring which are quite different.

Holding a position of honor or respect—or even of power—will usually encourage followership. There is a desire on the part of most people to want to do the things their organization wants them to do. (What we call the organization is actually a conglomerate of relationships of which those in the hierarchy are only a part.) The manager must compete with others for influence. Sometimes they are peers, sometimes subordinates, and sometimes outside the organization.

There is also the matter of situational or functional leadership. Few people are leaders in all areas. This is not surprising, given the increasingly complex nature of our world. And yet, the higher up the pyramid the manager is, the more likely one will presume to be "the" leader of it. Also, the more "command power" one has been given, the greater the temptation to use it and the more this happens, the less one is seen as a leader.

One should not be surprised to discover that each group, let alone each organization, will have a number of leaders. It is a mistake, even in a small group, to think in terms of single leadership only. One person will be looked to for one thing, another for something else. Some will be seen as having more information on a given subject than others, some as having better judgment, some as having greater compassion. All of this is observed, noted, and taken into account.

There will be changes in these judgments over time. Some who have influence today will find that they have little or none tomorrow. And some who have little or none for the present will come to be greatly honored—and followed—years later. Influence can be immediate and specific, or it can be long-lasting and future-oriented. Acquiring followership for many is an event. For others it is a process. Someone who has little impact on the present can have major impact on the future even though no longer physically there to profit from it.

Why We Follow

If leadership is determined in the final analysis by followership, what determines this followership? What causes people to give, voluntarily, their support? There can be no final or definitive answers. They will vary with the individuals involved, the time, the circumstances, and the need. But we do have information on the subject.

We give our support to others because we agree with the objectives they espouse. We support them for their compassion. We follow them because they have the support of others; because they know how to "make things happen;" because they have shown they are people of judgment and strength. We accept their leadership because we like them, and we like them because of the way they work with us.

I have, for example, asked nearly 1000 supervisors and managers over the past several years what they felt to be the qualities they most preferred to have in those they regarded as their leaders. From a list of 27 items, these men and women were asked to select the *five most important*. Their answers can be classified into three basic categories:

- Knowledge and skills.
- Personal attributes and characteristics.
- Ways of relating to others.

Five of these have consistently rated above the others. They are the following:

		% Selected
1.	Respect and feeling for others.	48.6
2.	Knowledge of the subject.	46.4
3.	Willingness to accept personal responsibility.	45.2
4.	Willingness to support me.	43.0
5.	A quality which indicates strength or confidence.	40.8

Two of these ("Respect and feeling for others" and "Willingness to support me") are examples of ways by which the leader relates to the follower. Two are personal attributes ("Acceptance of responsibility" and "Strength or confidence"). Knowledge or skill is represented by "Knowledge of the subject." From the beginning of the survey, now in its eighth year, these choices have always been part of the top five.

They tell us much about our own values as individuals as well as organizational members. If one wants to know the characteristics of the leader or manager, look to the values of those who will be asked for support. We choose leaders whom we feel are like ourselves, although more capable than we are in certain areas.

We want respect from our leaders for both ourselves and our ideas. We want them to show this by their willingness to support us as need be. We want them to have knowledge of the subject because we value knowledge. But they gain our support also because they show qualities which indicate personal confidence and strength. And they must be willing to accept responsibility for what they do.

These are all learned characteristics, whether acquired consciously or unconsciously. Some of them are, of course, more difficult to achieve than others. Not all persons will be able to gain the knowledge required of them, but all of us should be clear that knowledge is a precious thing and will in the long run be respected. Not all of us will have sufficient personal charisma to satisfy everyone, but one is reminded that charisma comes in a variety of forms. Much of it, of course, is determined by the eye of the beholder.

We have listed above the five most preferred characteristics of leaders. The next ten are worth noting also. In general, they support our earlier thesis that we look to the leader for particular knowledge and skills, specific personal attributes, and ways by which they relate to us.

		% Selected
6.	Interest in developing others.	32.8
7.	Deep integrity.	31.4
8.	Willingness to innovate.	28.3
9.	Ability to plan.	26.0
10.	Willingness to roll up one's sleeves and help out.	19.8
11.	A sense of realism.	18.0
12.	Basic reliability.	17.8
13.	High intelligence.	17.0
14.	Willingness to use the power one has.	16.2
15.	Great drive and energy.	16.2

It is instructive to note that near the bottom of the list are such characteristics as "Has been designated as leader" (2.6 percent), "Control over rewards" (1.4 percent), and "Seniority" (1.1 percent).

Why We Reject Leadership

If this is why we select our leaders we ought to look also to some of the reasons we reject them. Too little attention has been given to this subject. Rating high on a number of preferred characteristics can always be counterbalanced—and undercut—by other things which the leader is seen to be or seen to be doing. Good works can be undone by examples of selfish or hypocritical behavior.

I once interviewed a number of mid-management people on the subject of the "bad behavior" of persons above them. I was shocked by some of the incidents and actions involving superiors. Further, during the period, 1971 to 1978, 1107 persons were asked to select from a list of 33 items the *five characteristics* which they regarded as most likely to cause them to "reject those in positions of leadership." Following are the 15 most frequently selected responses. Nearly all of the persons surveyed were in supervisory or higher positions, and the majority were from the public sector.

Summary of "Rejection Factors"

		% Selected
1.	Inability to delegate; couldn't accept subordinate ideas.	40.7
2.	Dishonest or deceitful; lied to others.	36.3
3.	Did not support subordinates.	34.1
4.	Unable to make intelligent judgments or decisions.	29.6
5.	Reversed self often; indecisive.	27.0
6.	Completely inflexible.	25.3
7.	Lacked respect for or trust in others.	23.8
8.	Egotistical; interested only in self.	22.5
9.	Weak; no self-confidence.	21.5
10.	Inability to act; passive.	19.1
11.	Would not communicate with others.	18.1
12.	Unwilling or unable to give constructive help or guidance.	17.2
13.	Over-controlled others.	14.6
14.	Over-involved with details.	14.4
15.	Played favorites.	14.1

These responses speak for themselves. There are persons high in organizations who have risen, in Dr. Peter's words, to the levels of their incompetency. And there are others who irrespective of ability are seen by those who work with them as dishonest, deceitful, mendacious, and hypocritical. (If you want additional support for this, read Studs Terkel's great book, *Working*.) Small wonder that so many have little confidence in others. Small wonder that such managers must turn to command and coercion for whatever action they need to have.

The "rejection factor" which has always occupied first place in my questionnaire responses is "inability to delegate." What it suggests is an expectation of work and decision-sharing on the part of subordinates which has not been fulfilled. We *say* we delegate, we give lip service to the idea, but for a variety of reasons we do not, or at least not to a sufficient degree to satisfy those who are being addressed. The word itself, "delegation," is an easy one to say, but a difficult one to define. As someone has observed, "There is a great deal of disagreement between the lion and the lamb over the meaning of the word 'liberty.' " So too there is much disagreement between superior and subordinate over the word "delegate." The manager/leader should be aware of this and the problems it creates.

One needs to note how often "support" and "trust" also become items of controversy. Subordinates need to feel that those in higher positions are communicating with them, understanding them, and trusting and supporting them. Managers/leaders should appreciate also how others react to their ways of thinking about and doing things. Negative impressions are often easier and quicker to form than positive ones. This may help to explain why those in higher positions are so often judged as being inflexible on the one hand or, on the other, indecisive; egotistical or weak; and passive or over-controlling.

The Leader Should Want Something

The preceding discussion has suggested some of both the positives and the negatives which followers find in those who seek to lead them. This knowledge is useful but it by no means tells us all we need to know.

People do what the situation calls for—and usually what the leader has suggested—not because they are directed to do so, but because it makes sense to them.

"Real leaders of men," Winston Churchill has said, "do not come forward offering to lead. They show the way, and when it has been found to lead to victory, then they accept as a matter of course the allegiance of those who have followed." Of himself, he later said: "I did not inspire the nation. . .I merely found the words to express the feelings others held. . .I had the luck to be asked to provide the lion's roar."[2]

Many have remarked that it is the leader's duty to lead. Clyde Ellis, a leader in the rural electrification movement, puts it this way:

> It is the duty of leaders to lead, to study, to think and then take the facts to their people; once the people know the facts, they can be trusted to make the right decisions. Sometimes those decisions will not be the ones the leaders think they should make, but more often than not they will prove to be wise ones.[4]

Let us see how we can apply this advice.

The manager at whatever level should want something beyond minimum requirements of the office. The manager is not fulfilling his or her responsibilities unless they are enlarged upon. One should want to achieve goals that are not now being achieved: such things as a better quality product, greater productivity, reduced costs, a broader distribution of benefits, improved community relationships, the development of the system and its staff, the encouragement of individual growth, and the protection of the environment.

One might seek also, as a concomitant to whatever else one does, improvement of the quality of life. Ours is a beautiful country which with hard labor we have made ugly in so many ways and places. I would hope that one of the things the manager might want is to make our workplaces more pleasant and more desirable. This may not increase productivity, but there is no evidence that ugliness improves it either.

My point is that the leader should establish and set out achievable goals for self and associates. These should parallel organization goals; they should, in fact, build upon them. And they should be goals which in both the planning and the doing can be shared with those who will inevitably be involved with them. The manager/leader should lose no opportunity to talk about them, to provide their rationale, to see that progress is being made towards them, and to give support to (reinforce) those who make major contributions to them.

As each goal is reached, new goals can and should be set. Leader as well as follower should be able to have the feeling of accomplishment which goes with their being met. Thus, organizational dynamics are fulfilled.

The Changing Nature of the System

How one leads depends upon whom one is leading, when, and where. Its ingredients are the leader, the led, the job, the objectives, and the values each supports. "The test of leadership," John Buchan reminds us, "is not to put greatness into humanity, but to elicit it, for the greatness is already there."

The organization, or more appropriately the system, is far less monolithic than conventional theory and experience have led us to believe. There is a greater concentration of power at lower levels than at first appreciated. This has now become obvious in many ways: through strikes, job actions, slowdowns, violations of policy and procedural guidelines, and the like. But it has also been emphasized on the positive side by actions, risks, and commitments which individuals have taken well beyond the call of duty to make good organizational responsibilities. Individuals at all levels are choosing whom to believe and whom not, whom to follow and whom not, and what to do and what not.

Free choice, insofar as it is possible, is the hallmark of our society. We should not be surprised that behaviors present in the voting booth or the market place are present in our organizational systems as well. We make choices wherever we are. Among our rights is that of choosing whom we wish to be influenced by.

This does not leave those with organizational responsibilities without tools, influence or power. It merely refines their task. Holding a position within the organization provides one with many opportunities to influence others. These should neither be overlooked or undervalued. A name and title on the door and a place on the organization chart requires, in fact, that the holder use whatever is available—knowledge, skills, experience, and personality—to persuade others of the course they should follow. But one should be careful not to take either a title or a position too seriously. Others may not.

In the final analysis, as we have noted, the follower determines, when not being coerced, whom to follow. The leader, therefore, should respect the views and values of others wherever they are in the hierarchy. Otherwise, one may discover with Franklin Roosevelt who had made a highly unpopular foreign policy speech during the period of American isolation, that ". . .it's a horrible thing to look over your shoulder when you're trying to lead—and find no one following."

The idea presented here is not new, only the emphasis and interpretation. Lao-Tzu, in the sixth century before Christ, wrote:

> A leader is best
> When people barely know that he exists
> Not so good when people obey and acclaim him,
> Worst when they despise him.
>
> Fail to honor people
> They fail to honor you,
> But of a good leader who talks little
> When his work is done, his aim fulfilled,
> They will all say, "We did this ourselves."

FOOTNOTES

[1]As quoted by Emmett John Hughes in *The Ordeal of Power*, NY: Atheneum, 1962, p. 124.

[2]From Winston Churchill in his biography of his father, *Lord Randolph Churchill*, 1906.

[3]Clyde Ellis, *A Giant Step*, NY: Random House Inc., 1966, pp. 97-98.

CHAPTER XXII

THE MANAGER AS A CHANGE AGENT

(This is an adaptation of a presentation made to the International City Management Association, which explains the references to city managers. The points that it makes, however, are applicable to all managers, public or private. Its purposes are to show the manager as a whole person.)

The American penchant for method and system has, without doubt, been responsible for much of the world bountiful we have assembled about us. The attention we have given to such mundane matters as organizational design, position specification, work simplification and measurement, and methods and procedures has rewarded us with a level of productivity that has been the marvel of much of the rest of the world. Anyone who has the opportunity to examine the approaches of others, particularly those in the countries we call "developing," will be at once impressed by the differences between their production processes and ours. One will also be reminded of the extent to which system and order have become a part of the American soul.

Now, I am not against orderliness, or at least a certain amount of it. What I object to is the notion many seem to have that orderliness is the same as godliness and that conventional and time-hallowed ways are necessarily the only ones or even the best.

Indeed, there is growing evidence that we have permitted management to become much too stylized, and much too mechanical and catechistic. There is evidence that we have put too much emphasis on method rather than on goal, that we have given more attention to form than to substance. We have accepted too readily precise and symmetrical organization charts, standardized patterns of delegation and subdelegation, foolproof (or nearly foolproof) systems of accountability, and new and costly mechanical systems such as the computer. Of course, I am for the computer. When it functions properly, it is doing things that we could not otherwise do. My problem with it is that it often causes us to lose sight of the human factor without which no system can survive. That is our fault, not its.

In the past few months, several city managers have shared with me a sense of frustration and failure that they have not been able to do some of the things the management blueprints seemed to prescribe. It is clear that some of them feel privately self-conscious because they are only recently into data processing or have not yet been able to install a PERT which I gather, makes them feel less pert around city hall. The responsibility for such failures, I have no doubt, really belongs to city councils, but managers have, nevertheless, bravely borne the shame.

Too great a preoccupation with the tools and methods of management is, of course, dysfunctional. Dysfunctional also are ways of thinking and habits of acting that find us more concerned with the "fine print" of administration than with the achieving of organizational and societal goals.

Functions of Management

Let us see how this applies to the area of management. Let us begin by asking who the manager is and what he really does. If we take the narrow view of it, the manager is *someone who manages*. He is someone who plans, organizes, staffs, directs, coordinates, budgets, and, occasionally, reports. And who is the best manager? Why, the one whose organization runs most smoothly, is least conspicuous or troublesome, and runs on the least gas. The latter is particularly important. People who are insensitive to nearly everything else are quite sensitive to gas.

Such a gauge of management effectiveness is, of course, nonsense. The best manager is no more the manager who is, mechanically speaking, the most orderly or the best organized than the best physician is the one with the tidiest office.

The manager's job is much broader than the name implies—which may be why we might consider another title. His or her job is that of *helping others to achieve goals*. The "others" may be within the organization, or they may be outside it. People achieved goals long before modern ideas of management were heard of, before "principles of management" were invented, and, unlikely as it may seem, even before computers made their appearance. Management should be thought of as a method, not a goal. When it helps us, let us welcome it. When it gets in the way, let us revise it. We must ever be critical of our own work processes.

Role of Change Agent

Let us see what happens when we define the manager's role broadly. Let us see how we behave when we think of ourselves as leaders rather than as directors, as counselors rather than as commanders, as change agents rather than as supervisors and controllers.

Let us examine the "change agent" concept. What happens when we see ourselves as agents of change?

For one thing, we behave in a quite different way than when we see ourselves as directors or manipulators. We recognize the "authority" of those at all levels in the organization. We know that the job will not be done unless others do it. Instead of ordering them about, we try to encourage and inspire them. We seek to help them find ways by which the work will be done on a continuing, self-sustaining, and self-correcting basis. Any father of growing children knows how limited are the real bounds of his control. He seeks to perpetuate his influence by doing the kinds of things that will enable those younger than he to make use of the best not only of what he and others have to offer but also the best of what they have within themselves. This is the real change agent role.

The change agent concept has important implications for the total organization. The manager focuses downward along carefully drawn organizational lines toward subordinates or, more specifically, those in the *sub*orders below. The change agent, on the other hand, is bound by no such rigid rules. He or she has no vested control over anyone. The members of the board of directors or the council, the public, those in other organizations, or even subordinates two or three times removed are as fit objects of attention as are those immediately below.

This is hardly a new concept. On the contrary, it is quite an old one, but one that we are not accustomed to applying to organizations. We know, however, the values our society has placed on its innovators, its instigators, its trail blazers, its agents of change. We know the debts we owe them for their ideas and their discoveries. Is it unreal to suggest that they have an important role in the office or the shop?

When someone cast doubt on the role he saw for the presidency, Woodrow Wilson replied: "The President is at liberty, both in law and conscience, to be as big a man as he can." If there is nothing in the Constitution to limit the greatness of a President, there is nothing either in the city charter to keep the city manager from being as big as he is able to be. As to the need for change, there are plenty of targets in most American cities for doing things differently—and better—than they are now being done.

There is another advantage to the change agent role, and that is the scope or range of its application. The manager is limited. Like the Maine farmer whose tombstone recorded, "He et what was sot before him," the manager is limited by precedent and rule to a circumscribed agenda. The change agent, on the other hand, is controlled only by what others will accept. If one is intelligent and considerate in the way one approaches the task, this may be quite a lot. If a *city* manager, one might conceivably give time and attention to such matters as urban renewal, city planning, encouragement of industrialization, reduction of crime, human rights and integration, improvement of community health, development of recreational and cultural facilities and beautification. Certainly these are as important to the life of the city as a tax billing system, a new method of examining fire department recruits, a zoning hearing, or a parking program.

This does not mean that managers should pre-empt the functions of others or assume that theirs is the only responsibility for good government. If the functions mentioned above are shared with others in the city—say, the council or the planning board—they will always be involved. But let the manager be sure he has fulfilled his part in the process by helping them and others to perceive and understand the nature of the situation, to hear what the experts are saying about it, to see what those elsewhere are doing, and always to provide the support, both moral and material, that will be needed. These are certainly managerial responsibilities. They are also a part of the change agent role.

I can imagine a number of managers reflecting bitterly on their experience in encouraging the most modest of urban improvements. Perhaps they are thinking of specific people back home—people whom Adlai Stevenson described as having been dragged "kicking and screaming into the Twentieth Century"—those of little vision but of strong will and great power. I can imagine their asking a number of pertinent questions: How are we going to go about becoming change agents? How can we get others to do things differently than they are now doing them? How can we be the leaders we want to be and still survive?

Guidelines for Change

The processes by which people change—not only changes within the group but, more importantly, in the ways individuals themselves behave—have received a great deal of study in the last few years. From this research and observation useful ideas are beginning to emerge.

We know, for example, that the individual's conscious behavior is grounded upon a set of satisfactions which in turn is based upon established value patterns. We know also that a given action may be judged against more than one value. For example, we desire to satisfy our superiors, but we also want to satisfy others—the public, or specific persons in it; professional associates whose approval we value; and even our subordinates. We also have personal standards which we feel should be met. When there is agreement among all of these, there is no problem. Much of the time, however, there is disagreement. So we are forced to choose among values. Such knowledge is useful to us in understanding why people do what they do.

We must be aware also of the variety of factors that relate to action and, in particular, our own role in it. These will include:

- A general understanding of goals.

- An appreciation of the costs of change; what, in effect, the changed relationships will mean in terms of time, loss of present values, retraining, and actual monetary outlays.

- A knowledge that a change in one part of the organization, or even in one person's role in it, will have an effect on other parts as well.

- An awareness that once change has taken place it must be helped to establish itself, so that it does not revert.

- An understanding of the need for establishing effective client-change agent relationships.

- The need for helping others to help still others to change.

Let us look at some of these precepts a bit more closely.

Understanding Goals. More and more, as we come to understand the nature of complex organizations, we realize that those who are members of them have differing needs and, consequently, varying goals and objectives. Sometimes these fit reasonably well together; sometimes they are in open conflict. The change agent must understand this. One must understand also what the objectives of the organization are and must help to keep them before the group one is working with.

Costs of Change. Inducing change can be costly—costly in time spent in encouraging it, in outright money outlays, in loss of existing benefits, in the opposition that is likely to be encountered. It is well to understand this before embarking upon a change program. One should understand also that the failure to change, or the pursuit of irrelevant courses of action, can be even more costly.

Effects of Change. Life is a process of trying to adjust to our environment. When change occurs, the environment is altered and new relationships must be created. Sometimes this will be easy to do; often it will be difficult. Much depends upon how those within the organization react to the change. Is it seen as needed and welcome? Is it self-serving? Have the opinions of those concerned been sought before action took place? Or was it foisted upon them? Answers to such questions as these will have marked bearing on the manner in which change is accepted.

Preserving Change. Once change has taken place, it must be given an opportunity to establish itself lest it revert. This is an important point, but one that is often overlooked. New behaviors that are unsatisfactory will ultimately be abandoned. Compromise is always a possibility. Once change has been abandoned, the possibility of future change becomes less likely. So it is up to the change agent to understand the need for a stabilization of the new behavior pattern until the time is ripe for the next step forward. This calls for reinforcement and support until the change is a matter of habit and practice.

Establishment of Effective Change Agent-Client Relationships. Studies of change agents in our society—doctors, teachers, psychiatrists, consultants, and others—have revealed the importance of effective relationships between the change agent and the client. The doctor cannot heal the patient. The patient will follow the doctor's advice only when there is faith in that advice. So it is with the teacher and the student, and the manager and his or her associates. Influence is enhanced as each increases basic trust in the other; as a climate for discussion and inquiry is provided; and as the free acceptance, or rejection, of ideas that are put forward is made possible.

Helping Others to Help Still Others. This is probably the most difficult task of all. Not only must change agents establish effective relationships with those with whom they work, but they must also help them to do the same with others. In the case of the city manager, it is not enough to be on good terms with the city council. The council members themselves have clients, and their failure to work effectively with them will have repercussions in their relationships with the manager. The manager, to be an effective change agent, must understand this and, as part of the strategy of change, help to create a framework where the council member can work easily and freely with those whose support is so essential.

Strategy for Change

Given such factors as these as a starting point, a general strategy of change can be constructed. One such strategy, put forward by the eminent social psychologist, Kurt Lewin, focuses upon an analysis of the "forces for" and the "forces against" which are present in all social situations. The traditional approach to change is to add to the "pro" forces—the power factors such as reward, punishment, praise, ridicule, and the like—which move the individual to take certain courses of action. Lewin has pointed out that emphasis on these often increases the "anti" forces, which now rise to carry the day. Is it not more reasonable, he asks, to try to lessen or remove the anti forces? No strengthening of the pro forces will then be needed. Such a course calls for an understanding not only of the reasons why the change should be desired but also why it is likely to be resisted. Thus the individual or the group is encouraged, in keeping with its own sense of values, to find a more satisfactory solution to the problem.

Change can also be encouraged by the introduction of new people to the organization. Although their coming may be resented by those who hoped for such positions themselves, the new ideas and new energy which the newcomers are likely to bring to the organization will usually have a positive effect. Management, however, must be prepared to give them freedom to act, and also support them in what they do. New blood is important to all organizations, and in large ones it can be acquired from other areas within the organization as well as from outside.

There are also times for change, and times when it will be successfully resisted. Great leaders are sensitive to this, and managers should be also. There is no formula one can offer, merely the suggestion that as attitudes change, as the moment becomes ripe, the manager should be prepared to act. Lincoln waited for a Union victory to announce his Emancipation Proclamation. "Public opinion," he once said, "is everything," and, being sensitive to it, based many of his actions accordingly. But he also helped to develop that same public opinion by both his words and his actions. The model is a useful one.

In our daily life, the individual assumes a variety of roles. Each is likely to call for a different pattern of behavior. Contemplate, for a moment, the roles a city manager assumes in a day's time: The role toward a member of the council; toward the head of a department; toward an ineffective subordinate worker; toward an influential member of the public; toward a hostile member of the press; or toward your clergyman or your wife and family. Perhaps the role that has been used is not a satisfactory one. Why not try a different role? Need we play only the role that custom has established? The change agent is willing to experiment with roles and to help reinforce others in support of the change that takes place.

There is another major approach to change—the training function. Training, of course, is the process of helping others to find ways of improving their skills, knowledge, attitudes, and behavior to the end that they can more adequately do what is needed of them.

Other approaches to the inducing of change have in common the fact that the role of the change agent is one of encouragement, of clarification, of development, and of support rather than of direction or command.

Awareness of Surroundings

Two more suggestions may be of value. The first of these is a reminder to the manager to be alert to the forces already at work in our society. The city hall, to those who occupy it, may seem so completely the political arena that one fails to realize that sometimes it can be a political fallout shelter instead. An illustration of such a phenomenon is the matter of civil rights. This idea has burgeoned not through our political institutions but around them. It is no less significant a fact because of it. Its germination and development could have been observed in the press and literature, through TV, and in the shaping of individual points of view—in short, in the growing sensitivity of our times to the needs of all.

These are the kinds of factors the keen observer is alert to. One's ears and eyes need to be as finely attuned to what is taking place nationally and internationally as to what is happening locally. One should also be aware of what *ought* to be. The last entry in Victor Hugo's diary was this: "There is one thing stronger than all the drives in the world—and that is an idea whose time is come." Those of us who serve the public will need be aware of the ideas that are about to be born. Such sensitivity will always do yeoman work for us.

We must think in terms of broad rather than limited perspectives, the long-range rather than immediate goals. One should be neither ebullient in success nor jarred by failure. I was recently reminded by a friend of mine how often we lose the victory but salvage the defeat. We are familiar with the comment that "So-and-so snatched defeat out of the jaws of victory," but we are less likely to recall Frederick the Great's lament that "another victory like this one and I am undone."

Too often, such things happen in our own affairs. Defeat can even lead to victory depending upon how one accepts it. The solid case, the good fight, and the graceful acknowledgement that the choice has gone against us can reset the stage for a more satisfactory ending another day. Indeed it is important for managers, like lobbyists, to realize that one of their most precious assets is their ability to be heard again.

It is essential, in terms of the large needs we have today, to see the manager as a major partner in the governmental processes, to see him or her as a leader as well as an administrator, and always as an agent of change. No less will really do.

PART VI

LOOKING AHEAD

CHAPTER XXIII

IDEAS ON DEMAND: A NEW APPROACH TO PROBLEM SOLVING

There is no such thing as "management on the cheap," as many a manager has discovered to his or her dismay. The closest to it, however, may well be an investment in new ideas.

The case for creativity is really a simple one. It is based on the proposition that it is easier—much easier, in fact—to develop new products, systems, equipment, methods and approaches than it is to try to increase the efficiency of existing ones, or even to try to change old habits. This has, in part, already been borne out by the workplace innovations which have made their appearance in the past decade.

Wanted: New Ideas

There is no need, in fact, to depend on serendipity, or chance, for the innovation that modern management requires. New ideas can be produced *on demand.* How to do this has long been known. It is now being adapted and used in industry, government, and the community. The task of managers everywhere is to learn to apply this knowledge. Witness the following:

Item. By the time the Seattle, Washington county government undertook the building of an indoor stadium, skyrocketing prices had seemed to put the stadium it was planning beyond the reach of the Seattle taxpayer. Almost, but not quite. A group of engineers was put to work to find ways of saving money and time in the new venture. They succeeded on both counts. By the application of ingenious new planning and scheduling programs, they put together their 65,000-seat structure at a cost only slightly higher than that of the 50,000-seat Houston Astrodome, which was constructed eight years earlier when the dollar was worth much more.

Item. The willingness of the Japanese to innovate not only with the goods they have introduced to the world's markets, but also with the management methods required in producing them, is one of the marvels of our times. But American companies have shown that they, too, can be innovative. The supermarket in its many forms is a monument to new ideas, as are the food service chains such as McDonald's, Colonel Sanders and the like; and so are American earth-moving machinery, household equipment, self-service devices and merchandising methods.

Item. On a note of personal observation, many of the managers I have worked with in training programs have shown they are inventive. A number of them hold patents in their own name. One man while in the Navy developed what is now the approved way of removing a ring from a swollen finger. Another invented an artichoke puree which, while it probably won't replace onion soup, nevertheless has its own merit. Others have invented such widely varying items as a means of advising customers what their company has done as a result of their complaints; a system of training employees in jobs other than their own; a more satisfactory approach to tree-trimming; a new way of handling meter reading; and a waterproof explosive.

Which brings us to an important point. To innovate does not require that one produce a totally new idea or product. Nor does one need to have invented a product himself. Applying an old idea or an old tool in a new way will do as well.

A new method is often more valuable than a new product. New sources of supply, different uses of old tools, new ways of reaching and servicing clients, new sources of manpower, new ways of training and using existing manpower—these are all innovative and useful. The person who discovers an easier, less expensive or better way of performing an old task is an innovator. A suggestion which saves labor or money, however modest, or helps to produce a better product, has its own merit. One does not need to have invented the wheel to have made a contribution.

New Ideas

There are many opportunities in most organizations for the application of new ideas. Indeed, one of the functions of trade publications has been that of calling new ideas and new needs to the attention of their readers. Let us use energy problems as an example.

There is need for new and readily available sources of energy. There is need for energy sources which do not at the same time pollute the environment. (Can waste products be used for other purposes?) Ways are needed for storing electricity for future use. There is always the challenge of finding better ways of providing service. How can this be done without increasing costs? What tools are available for bringing the supplier and the consumer into a more harmonious working partnership? Are there ways of involving the customer (as has been done in cafeterias and supermarkets) in helping to serve himself? How can the company provide service and goods but still protect the beauty of the countryside?

These are clearly areas for innovation, but so is the managing of the company. An associate of mine conducted a survey which revealed that 15 percent of the time on the job of first-line supervisors with local power companies was spent in transportation to and from assignments and another substantial block of time was spent in "standing by." This is the equivalent of one day a week. How can such time be reduced or better used?

Training has become increasingly a managerial responsibility. How can this be done more effectively? How can employee safety be improved? Is the organization getting its share of the talent available in the labor market? What can be done to provide more attractive careers? How can employees be made to feel greater responsibility?

Many jobs need to be redesigned. Perhaps some can even be eliminated as jobholders reach retirement age. Better use can undoubtedly be made of modern equipment (the computer, construction equipment, the telephone, radio, and the like) as many companies have already shown. Much can surely be done to make management systems more workable—and also more responsive to the needs of the time.

Questions such as these, if asked in the right way and of the right people, will produce useful and sometimes even revolutionary results. Actually new ideas are not as hard to come by as one might think, *provided they are really wanted.*

Producing New Ideas

Large organizations (such as *Fortune's* top 500 businesses or major agencies of government), generally have R & D units. A variety of experts is assembled to find new and better ways of doing what the organization is now doing and to explore what may be useful in the future. Its terms of reference are likely to be broad. Its mandate is to research, explore, experiment and invent.

Where a company doing business with the U.S. government has not already done so, Federal contracting procedures may even require setting up a program of "value engineering." The work of such units has resulted in many new products, along with new ways of merchandising, new markets, new methods, new types of equipment, new organizational systems and even new clients.

R & D staffs are likely to be out of the reach of many companies but they can certainly avail themselves of the *problem-solving group*. In fact, this approach fits so neatly the approved newer approaches to managing that it recommends itself in a variety of ways.

Faced with a problem it wants to resolve, management assembles as needed a group of employees and puts the problem before them. Members of the group are urged, making use of brainstorming and other techniques, to come up with as many ideas as they can, all of which are carefully recorded. Building upon someone else's ideas is encouraged. So is trying to relate conventionally unrelated ideas and issues.

Several meetings may in fact be held with the participants invited to explore the problem on their own as well. These are followed by review sessions in which the most useful ideas are distilled from the bulk of those put forward. It is hoped that they will be improved upon.

The group asked to find a solution to a particular problem may be put together for a specific purpose, or it may simply be a regular staff meeting. If the latter, its agenda should, of course, be the problem for which the solution is sought. Such meetings are likely to have considerable appeal. In fact, being asked to join one is usually seen as a compliment.

The tools of the brainstorming meeting are a room free of interruption for at least a two-hour period; a number of newsprint sheets; marking crayons; recorders (two people are suggested for this assignment) to make sure that all ideas are recorded; and a "group moderator" sufficiently knowledgeable in revised brainstorming techniques to get the kind of participation needed. The moderator makes sure the objectives are clear to all—"ways of improving client relations," "cutting costs in maintenance," etc.—and then invites individual contributions.

The "best" group will contain six to eight persons but more or fewer can be used. The moderator encourages building upon the suggestions of others. Whatever is proposed should be written on the sheets and *not* criticized or otherwise evaluated at this time. That will come later.

"Far out" ideas are not to be discouraged. The objective is to produce as many suggestions as possible. Participants can be encouraged to think in idea-producing ways:

  – The use of existing tools in new or different situations.

  – The "borrowing" from what others have done.

- Involvement of people (staff, clients, members of the public) in new combinations and ways.

- Using surplus (or easily available) materials in new combinations.

- The suggestion of "short-cuts" which eliminate steps once thought necessary or desirable.

- Fantasizing: thinking in terms of "I wish I could do this."

- Putting apparently unrelated ideas together. (This is called "synectics," a widely used approach.)

It is often advisable to provide a lapse of several days between Meeting One and Meeting Two when the effort again resumes. Have the lists typed up and made available to the participants. This will encourage more ideas.

After the larger list of ideas has been achieved, a third meeting is held to determine the five or six most useful ideas. It is at this point that they can be criticized. The moderator, however, should try to keep the meeting on a constructive plane, suggesting the modification or revision of ideas where possible to achieve acceptability. Authorship is unimportant; in fact, most people won't be able to remember who suggested what anyway.

Further refinement can be undertaken at this or a fourth meeting to achieve the one or two *best* ideas; or the four or five most promising can be passed on to management for its choice. A by-product of the system is that often several ideas will be found to be useful, sometimes in quite different situations from those first intended. This is group problem-solving.

The Individual as Innovator

Another by-product, perhaps even more useful, is encouragement of individual innovation and creativity by the problem-solving group. All of us are inventors of sorts. All of us have a considerable amount of creativity. We take pride in our solutions to the daily problems we face: emergency motor repairs, home improvements, cooking, and the like. Most of us will admit that we enjoy the creative process, whether as individuals or in working with others.

Alas for the organization, most of us often are at our best in outside-the-job situations. There is something in most jobs which encourages conformity rather than creativity. In fact, the inventive man or woman may even be seen by both supervisors and associates as something of a "kook."

Individual creativity, however, can be increased both by the individual and the organization. Creativity can be encouraged in the organization by letting it be known that it wants and values new ideas, and by rewarding those who produce them.

Necessity undoubtedly has been the mother of a great many inventions but not so many as the creative climate. Inventions result from a combination of need with something else, such as the challenge the need provides and the satisfactions to be derived from successfully meeting this challenge; or the patient, often plodding effort of someone who will not be deterred from a private goal because he or she feels it is worthwhile to pursue it.

To get new ideas, management must make clear to one and all that *it wants them.* It must encourage experimentation. It must reward the idea-producers, not neglect or punish them. It must, in short, provide an innovative climate. This is as important in the obtaining of ideas as a fertile soil and warm sunshine are to the growth of the plant.

An innovative climate cannot be created overnight. It is a process, developed and encouraged in a hundred different ways at all levels, but most of all by those in the organization's upper echelons.

Recently, as if to underline the importance of this point, the results of the Japanese experience with Quality Control Circles has received international attention. What the Japanese have done, of course, is to institutionalize the ideas that were basic to the provision of innovation in the organization. Their major contribution is to make clear that those at the lowest organizational levels—the factory floor work force— have important contributions to make to problem-solving and are willing to make them if given opportunity and encouragement. This an enlightened management has done, and the results are now apparent to all.

It did not, of course, occur overnight, but was the result of decisions reached at the highest national and organizational levels and strongly supported within the company. What has happened reminds one not only of the usefulness of approaches that invite creativity from the entire work force but also of the importance of, over time, building it into the system in an organizational development mode.

CHAPTER XXIV

"REFORMING" BUREAUCRACY: WHAT CAN BE DONE

High on the list of promises made to the American people in the last three or four presidential campaigns has been the pledge to do something about what Jimmy Carter, in his bid for the nation's highest office, called the "horrible Washington bureaucracy." Ronald Reagan was even more positive about it. In his inaugural address, he said: "In this present crisis, government is not the solution to our problem; government is the problem." As if the point had not been strongly enough made, he said in his Economic Report to Congress that "waste and fraud in the Federal government. . . is a scandal we are bound and determined to do something about." This, according to columnist Joseph Kraft, got the loudest applause of any of his pronouncements.

In this, both men—and Richard Nixon before them—probably reflect what a high percentage of their fellow citizens believe. Irrespective of the benefits they receive from what that bureaucracy does, they hold it, for a variety of reasons, in low esteem.

There is no question that there are problems with large, bureaucratic organizations, whatever their virtues may be. These exist whether one is talking about the Department of Housing and Urban Development, the FBI, the Cleveland Department of Sanitation, or the American Telephone and Telegraph Company. Large organizations may be necessary, as indeed they are, and they have their strengths—and also their virtues—but that does not make them *per se* economical, efficient, or sensitive to client needs. Jefferson opined that "eternal vigilance is the price of democracy." If alive today, he might have added that bureaucracies need our attention too.

The trouble is that our political leaders usually come up with simplistic and, on the whole, less than effective ways of dealing with them.

Jimmy Carter talked frequently of "reorganizing" which for him meant anything from creating a Senior Executive Service and introducing zero-based budgeting to establishing a couple of new departments and increasing a White House staff which under Ford and Nixon he had complained was already much too large. Ronald Reagan, on the other hand, has opted for less government. He or his associates have indicated an intention of dismantling some of the agencies already there, and have proposed drastic cuts in funds across the board. In general these can be expected to reduce the cost of the Federal establishment but will probably do little to improve the administration of the many programs which remain.

The concern of our presidents with the nature and functioning of our administrative systems is, of course, to the good. In fact, an examination of what is happening within large organizations is clearly long overdue. However, what concerns many of those who share the view that the vast Federal system is not working well—or at least not well enough—is that they have so often underestimated both the enormity and complexity of the task they have promised to undertake.

Bureaucracy's Fall From Grace

At few times within memory have the agencies of government fallen to such low esteem as now. They are openly and strongly criticized not only by those who are their traditional enemies—the political right—but more recently, from both the center and left as well. The latter have hitherto been their strongest supporters. The deficiencies are being constantly cited in the press, on the airwaves, in car pools, and over backyard fences. Even those who draw salaries from them are often among their sternest critics.

Some idea of the low esteem which the Federal bureaucracy has reached can be gained from a comparison of the public's views of President Nixon and Federal agencies a month or two before his resignation in 1974. At a time when he was at his nadir (a 20 percent approval rating), trust in the *agencies of government* was only a few points higher! (This is not the report of a single survey but of several). Mind you, the bureaucracy was not involved in Watergate, nor were any non-political officials.

Popular distrust is not limited to the bureaucracy as such. Government officials score poorly when compared with other professionals such as doctors, lawyers, clergymen, professors, and the like. While nonelected public officials—for want of a better name, bureaucrats— rank higher than elected ones, and military officers higher than their civilian counterparts, the differences are not really substantial.

Nor is the bureaucratic malaise a disease only of the Federal government. State and local agencies are afflicted as well. As other surveys show, they rank even below those in Washington. Members of the general public, it must be clear to one and all, have considerable doubt about their public servants.

No government, of course, can hope to survive without a strong and effective administrative system, nor can an administrative system exist without the support of those it was established to serve. Presidents Carter and Reagan were right that government administration poses a problem which must be addressed, but they and their associates would have been well-advised to move prudently, cautiously, and, as Chief Justice Warren advised the country in an earlier affair, "with all deliberate speed."

No Single Solution

There is, of course, no single—or simple—solution. This is because we are addressing a collection of problems which has developed over the years. And yet there is undoubtedly sufficient agreement about some of the major deficiencies of the bureaucratic systems we have created that, if properly planned and prepared, much can be done by way of improvement.

First and foremost, the President and his advisors will need all the help they can get. They will need help not only in resolving the problems they face but, before that, in determining their nature.

They will need to understand also that an undertaking of this kind is not easy and will certainly not be quick, even though cuts in size are achieved. The agencies of government were not created in a day and they will not be reformed in one either. Or in a year or, even, in a single presidential term. Bureaucratic reform involves long-range commitments and will require patience, perseverance, insight, and wisdom. Not only must the President have such qualities—and his management staffs along with him—but the American people must have them also. It is part of the President's continuing task to remind his impatient and impetuous countrymen that what he is about is vital to the national interest and for that reason must have their strong support. Given the public's notoriously short memory, such advice will need to be repeated time and again.

Perhaps a useful starting point for any new administration is a "sorting out" process. It will need to consider carefully what it proposes to do—and what some of the repercussions will be. There are some important caveats to be observed, including a number of "don'ts" which the failure of many earlier reform efforts underline.

Some Key Caveats

The first of the caveats which a President and his staff will do well to observe is to separate program criticisms from administrative ones.

Those who are opposed to what government is doing will often focus upon *how* it is being done instead. Critics of this kind will not be satisfied by mere administrative reforms. They will, however, urge them anyway often to the extreme.

A second caveat: those who seek to revitalize Federal administration must be selective in what they do. There are many bureaucracies within the Federal system, and these are neither equally efficient or inefficient. There are also able bureaucrats as well as poor ones. It is no service to the capable and committed public servant to lump him or her with those who are interested only in getting by. There should, therefore, be an understanding of the *specific bureaucratic behaviors* which must be changed, and an effort mounted to modify or eradicate them.

Bureaucratic reform should be approached with due consideration to the nature of the burdens which agencies of government are asked to bear. Many times they are expected to take on jobs without either the resources or the experience necessary to successfully carry them out. If one would like an example, the Immigration and Naturalization Service is such. Unlike the FBI which by comparison is lavished with money, INS is asked to perform superhuman tasks with few resources. Too often an agency is charged with doing the undoable and then blamed because it fails.

A final caveat: reformers should take care that in their efforts to remake the system they do not throw the baby out with the bath. The ability of bureaucratic systems thus far to survive massive public criticism should not suggest that this capability is unlimited. The critics of bureaucracy sometimes forget the contributions of old and well-ordered systems which, day after plodding day, collect the garbage or the taxes, deliver the mail, send us our car registration forms or Social Security checks and process our responses. We must be careful not to destroy the advantages of the bureaucratic system before we have found a replacement.

After all, some of the ablest men and women in our society work for government, and the record of their achievements is great. That present systems of administration need modification and change, as do all human institutions, is no reason for dismembering them. Nor should those who operate them be threatened in the process.

Some Important "Don'ts"

A number of remedies suggest themselves not so much because they have previously proven successful as because they are still part of the "conventional wisdom." The President is warned that, whatever their political merit, they are partial remedies only and more likely to produce dysfunctional than positive effects. More specifically, Reform by Legislation, Reform by Budgetary Controls, and Reform by Reorganization are by themselves closer to being nostrums than cures.

Reform by Legislation

Americans are notable for seeing the "passing of a law" or the voting of funds as solutions to societal problems. We have, in fact, tried to reform our administrative systems by statute many times over the years. These efforts have had some success where specifics are concerned, as witness the Administrative Procedures Act and the Freedom of Information Act. They have not been greatly productive, however, where the objective has been the overall improvement of bureaucratic performance.

Individual Members of Congress as well as certain committees or subcommittees can become powerful forces for new ideas, but one should not expect too much of the Legislative Branch in matters of this kind. To put it bluntly, this is not its forte, although clearly within the range of both its power and interest.

This does not mean that Congress should be ignored, however. Quite to the contrary, as events have already shown. What it does suggest is that the basic changes that will undoubtedly be necessary in administrative forms and practices are, first and foremost, an executive concern, and initiatives should be undertaken at the White House end of Pennsylvania Avenue.

Reform by Budgetary Controls

Cutbacks in agency spending may well reduce program dimensions if that is the objective, but they provide no assurance that agency efficiency has been or will be improved, nor do they hold great promise for bureaucratic reform. In fact, quite the opposite may occur.

The most recent proposals via the budget have the alluring name of sunset laws. This is a device which would cut off appropriations at the end of a given time unless Congress can be convinced that the program should be continued. (One may presume that in the majority of programs Congress can and will be convinced.) As previously noted, the Carter administration favored a system called zero-base budgeting which required a unit or agency to justify in cost-benefit terms all of its budget request, not just the increase over last year's appropriation.

Neither of these ideas has done what was expected of them. One is reminded that in the final analysis, budgets control only money.

Reform by Reorganization

"Reorganization," Harold Seidman, a former head of the Bureau of the Budget's Division of Administrative Management, has reminded us, "has become almost a religion in Washington."[1] It is too frequently looked to, particularly by new administrators; too much is claimed for and expected of it; and too little usually happens as a result.

Reorganizations have their uses, of course, and management consulting firms have made noteworthy contributions to organizational performance. But there is increasing doubt that the so often widely-hailed reorganization does all or even most of the things claimed for it.

Reorganizations are usually announced as efforts to modernize and to "streamline," however that may apply to large organizations. (Has anyone ever tried to streamline an iceberg?) Rarely do they deal with the kinds of problems for which large organizations are so frequently criticized. On paper the new arrangements look impressive, but, as the French say, *Le plus ça change, le plus c'est la même chose.*

Reorganizations also have their costs. These are usually high, albeit hidden. They often produce severe dysfunctional effects. This is not to argue that agencies from time to time do not need to be regrouped. They do. The generally haphazard manner in which new institutions are created requires that there should be a continuing examination of what has happened and how it is working. The reorganization approach by itself, however, has limited utility and should be used cautiously and infrequently.

A Suggested Approach

The successful approach to bureaucratic reform is likely to be multiple. Many are responsible for what it is today—its strengths along with its weaknesses—and many will need to be involved in its regeneration.

First among these, of course, is the President himself. If war, as Clemenceau has reminded us, is too serious a matter to be left to the generals, the reform of the governmental system must not be left to the technicians. The President must be involved, deeply involved. And why not? It is not enough to set a policy course: the truly great leaders have shown that they must concern themselves with how—as well as how well—it is carried out.

Accordingly, a seven-point approach is suggested here:

1. *Understanding the Limitations of the System.* There is growing doubt among both practitioners and scholars that a "revision" of traditional bureaucratic patterns will provide the answers we are seeking. The heart of this argument is that the bureaucratic form is already approximating the limits of its capability (where it has not already exceeded them) and the usual methods of revising or reinforcing will not really resolve the difficulties. What is needed, they suggest, are *new* organizational patterns and arrangements.

The problem is not only bigness, but also one of kind. As organizations have grown in size and workload, large and complex new requirements are being placed on old and primitive structures which, simply put, are not adequate for them. There are practical limits to organizational size just as there are limits to the size and height of buildings. Beyond a point, it is both impractical and uneconomic to add to them. New demands add up to an overload which increasing the size of the organization does not remedy.

What kind of organizations should we attempt to create? Such a question is more easily raised than answered. Nevertheless, it is useful for the President and his associates to engage in some futures thinking. It is useful for them to understand that no piece of machinery, custom, or organizational form can survive more than a few years at best, and that the age of the towering multi-purposed organization may well be ending. We learned in the Vietnamese War that systems which had served us so well in other wars had limited utility under the new conditions our military faced. We should not be surprised to find that the organizations we have so laboriously, and on the whole skillfully, constructed are running out their life-force. The search for new ways of doing things is a difficult and also an endless one, but it must be pursued. The Reagan Administration would do well to see that there is a suitable investment in research and exploratory efforts. The operation of organizational systems is a skill at which Americans excel. We should build upon what we already know.

A study done by McKinsey and Co., management consultants, and reported in the July 21, 1980 issue of *Business Week,* contains a list of eight organizational attributes which have marked 37 selected companies with a reputation for excellence and a history of achievement. They include: a bias toward action; simple form and lean staff; continued contact with customers; productivity improvement via people; operational autonomy to encourage entrepreneurship; stress on one key business value; emphasis on doing what they know best; and simultaneous loose-tight controls. This is the kind of attention organizations should get and from which real intelligence emerges. There is no reason why bureaucracies cannot be looked at in some of the same ways.

No one, of course, should expect to see the end of the large organization within the immediate future. Despite its defects, it is still greatly needed. But because it appears in many forms and is administered in many ways, it is useful to explore those which are productive and those which are not.

2. *Involving the Bureaucrat.* Members of a system are usually thought to be enemies of its reform. If one believes this of the government employee, however, he/she has considerably less than a full understanding of the Federal bureaucrat.

It is true that the resident bureaucrat has done many of the things that are so widely criticized. It is true also that he/she has opposed many reform efforts. But it is equally true that these same bureaucrats have kept the system going.

There is ample evidence that the career employee will be an eager and willing participant in any major improvement efforts that are serious in objective, reasonable in their approach, and have any real hope of success. After all, this same employee is the personal target of those who distrust government and its agencies, is well aware of this and, anonymous or not, hates every minute of it.

No reformer can afford to be without support. Yet it is a shocking fact of life that in the age of consultation the career employee has rarely been consulted or his/her advice sought on matters so vital as this. For all the pious platitudes of the Kennedy, Johnson, Nixon, Ford and Carter administrations, such programs as PPBS, MBO, and productivity improvement were launched with little consultation beyond the highest levels. No wonder they met with so little success.

The point is that the support of those within the system must be obtained if "reform" is to succeed.

3. *The Matter of Congressional Support.* The Congress' support must also be obtained. This must be more than lip service which is, of course, easily and quickly given and often as quickly forgotten.

The individual Congressman or Senator, whether of the President's party or not, must be sufficiently convinced of the virtue of the Administration's efforts that he or she is willing to forego a part of the critic's role which historically Members of Congress have so often assumed. More importantly, the Members of Congress should be encouraged to help in the process. After all, it is his or her government as well as the President's.

A significant part of this contribution will be to understand that Congress itself has helped to overload the system by asking it to do more than it can do. Happily there seems to be a growing appreciation of this fact.

Large, bureaucratic organizations can, of course, do some things better than others—and some not well at all. By asking too much, legislators have created unrealistic expectations. Too little has been provided by way of guidelines. Statute has been added to statute with little concern for the manner in which one modifies or displaces the other.

How a law is administered affects what that law is. Congress may not have the ability to reform the administrative system, but it can, and often does, make it more difficult for others to do so. It is part of its responsibility to see that this does not happen. It is part of the President's responsibility to advise Congress.

4. *The Client, the Citizen, and the Bureaucrat.* There will be no solution to the organizational problems we now face without attention also to official-citizen relationships. These are not one way relationships either.

There needs, first, to be a better appreciation by those in large organizations that many of today's problems are due to citizen attitudes about bureaucrats which they themselves have helped to engender. "Bureaucrats" are seen variously as high-handed, autocratic, captious, trivial, unhelpful, and self-serving, and doubtless many have earned such disparaging descriptions.

Clients and citizens, on their part, however, often demand too much of government and too much of their public servants. Along with their representatives in Congress, they have overloaded the system.

There are many ways by which citizens/clients can be related more meaningfully to the government. There are ways by which their views can be heard, by which they can actually be consulted. The organization is not a closed system which only "members" can enter.

There are many ways also by which individuals can become, to their own advantage, a part of the process. Nowhere is this better illustrated than in the system of levying and collecting income taxes. Taxpayers assess themselves, collect from themselves (when employers do not do it), and send what is owed to the government. The taxing authority has only to record the transaction and occasionally—a bare two percent of the time—to audit it. Much the same process occurs when we go to the self-service supermarket, eat at a cafeteria, drive drive-it-yourself cars, doctor ourselves, dial a telephone call, and in many other ways involve ourselves for a variety of reasons in the organizational system.

These and other patterns have application in the organization of the future. We need also to rethink many of the traditional divisions between public and private sectors. They work more closely together today than most of us realize, with little evidence that either is taking over the other.

5.   *Focusing on Bureaucratic Specifics.*   Most of the criticisms of large organizations are actually criticisms of specific bureaucratic behaviors. An example of this is hierarchy. The larger the organization, the more levels. The greater the number, the longer the chain of command, and the longer it takes for a message to go from top to bottom. The greater the likelihood also that one starting at the bottom will never reach the top.

Hierarchy produces redundancy. Messages must be read, even if not acted upon, at each level through which they pass. Because it depersonalizes the system, hierarchy encourages distrust, alienation, and ultimately disloyalty. We have seen much of all three in recent years.

There is really no good reason even in very large organizations for the eight to 20 levels which now exist. Much needs to be done to bring top and bottom closer together. Broadening the span of control and thereby eliminating a few levels can be accomplished in most organizations.

Federal agencies, despite lip service to some of the newer managerial theories, tend to be overstructured. There are far too many people in dead-end jobs. The latter includes many deputies and assistants, too many in positions that have outlived their usefulness, and a great many personal secretaries who much of the time serve in a status rather than a productive role.

Too great an emphasis is placed upon ideas whose time has passed. One of these is the idea that there should be equal pay for equal work. The civilian job classification system is, in fact, built upon this premise—as if it were really possible to determine what is equal work. As a result, we have sought to insure that the same grade job receives the same pay regardless of the part of the country it is in. This rewards those in the boondocks and at the same time encourages job inflation in high cost-of-living cities like Washington, New York, and Chicago. The uniformed services use another system, with rank going with the person. It is, of course, much easier to administer and perhaps even more fair in the long run.

We have insisted also that a Federal statute be enforced equally whether in Wausau, Wisconsin; Berlin, New Hampshire; Paris, Maine; or New York, NY. To do this requires costly control and auditing systems which perform no really constructive service. In a country as large as this one, we might consider the relevance of varying needs, customs, styles, and practices in terms of what government should do. Even a modest change in our way of viewing the problem—and there are ample precedents for it—would help to reduce the administrative burdens we now bear. The point I am making here is that the bureaucracy cannot be reformed without getting at the nitty-gritty.

6.   *The Improvement of Government Productivity.* Each administration likes to leave its mark on the system. The Johnson Administration espoused the Planning, Programming, and Budgeting System (PPBS), but this got short shrift from the Nixonians. They in turn introduced Management by Objectives (MBO) which, without any real support from the Ford or Carter White House, continues a sort of halfway-house existence. So it is with a number of the Carter contributions under Reagan.

Perhaps of greater long-range benefit than either PPBS or MBO is a movement which has evolved from a combination of sources, in part legislative, in part executive, in part outside-of-government, for productivity improvement. The productivity concept is considerably broader than the "efficiency" movement which has so long been pressed by business. It concerns itself not only with the cost of achieving a given objective, but with the nature (quality) of the objective as well. It is thus more adaptable to governmental (service) functions and more acceptable to government people. A productivity improvement program invites those participating in it to consider any of a variety of ways by which performance can be improved.

The time is ripe for a greater degree of "productivity awareness" on the part of those in government. The Arab oil boycott awakened us to over dependency on others for energy. Subsequent events have now made it clear that we have other shortages as well: in other natural resources, in human resources, and in money. Once we acted as if the dollar could resolve all our national problems. Now we know that even if we had an unlimited supply, this would not be so. A new administration sincerely committed to a goal of productivity improvement, would do much to convince both those inside and outside the government that the bureaucracy can improve its performance.

7.   *Systems Analysis and Bureaucratic Deficiencies.* One of the most frequent citizen complaints about the bureaucracy is that it is

impervious to the criticisms of those who work with it. "A primary problem of bureaucracy," Professor Rourke has written, "is seen to be that of administrative inertia—the failure of bureaucrats to deal vigorously and imaginatively with problems that are high on the agenda of public concern."[2]

Bureaucratic productivity may improve and unit costs may be reduced, but its representatives are still likely to remain cold and detached, and it may continue to take a dozen telephone calls to get to the right person and a month and a half to get a reply to a letter. Such problems can—and should—be specifically addressed, and there is a vehicle for doing it. This is systems analysis.

Systems analysis provides a method by which organizational patterns can be better understood and corrected. Each government agency today has systems analysts: their profession is recognized and their contribution to the workings of the bureaucracy is substantial. It remains only for better use to be made of the talent and experience they possess.

We also have the knowledge of experience with another relatively new managerial tool—innovation. In general, government has made far less deliberate use of creativity than has the private sector. There are exceptions and NASA is one of them. Other government agencies, too, even some of the most tradition-encrusted (such as the Department of Agriculture and the Veterans Administration) have made marked use of this approach. In fact, the U.S. Department of Agriculture 1975 yearbook, *That We May Eat,* is a monument to the creativity and imagination of government people at Federal, state, and local levels. What is needed, however, is greater inventiveness in organizational arrangements.

A Thought for the Future

The carefully designed and well-administered bureaucracy we once thought to be the answer to society's needs. It was, and is a system whose virtues, in the words of Professor Blau, are "precision, speed, unambiguity, knowledge of the files, continuity, discretion, unity, strict subordination, reduction of friction and of material and personnel costs."[3]

Experience has shown that while it may still do all or most of these things, it does other things as well which we would prefer not to have. And it does all of these at a cost we are no longer willing to pay.

The remedy lies neither in abolishing government nor in its becoming significantly smaller—at least not as long as we continue to make great demands on it. Old bureaucratic habits which have developed over many years must be changed. There are ways to do it, if one has an understanding of the problems, a willingness to pay the costs, and the resolve to see it through.

Because bureaucracy is not an ordinary or a simple system, simple remedies will not do. Bureaucratic change is a process, not an event. A President seriously committed to improving the performance of government can make substantial progress even with the roadblocks which both friend and foe are sure to place in his way.

FOOTNOTES

[1]Harold Seidman, *Politics, Position and Power*, NY: Oxford University Press Inc, 1970, p. 3.

[2]Francis Rourke, *Bureaucracy, Politics, and Public Policy*, Boston: Little, Brown & Co, 1969, p. 29.

[3]Peter M. Blau, "The Dynamics of Bureaucracy," *American Social Patterns*, Robert K. Merton, ed., NY: Doubleday & Co Inc, 1956, p. 252.

CHAPTER XXV

THE CONSULTATIVE APPROACH: AN ACHIEVABLE GOAL

Much has been said and written in the past twenty years about participative management. Wishing it, however, and achieving it, are two quite different matters.

Where real participation, at whatever level, has taken place the results have, by and large, been positive. The costs of such an approach—and it has both costs and dysfunctions—have undoubtedly been more than compensated by results. The problem is one of introducing participative management into systems which are at best unreceptive and at worst hostile.

Participation, of course, takes place in a multitude of ways in all our daily activities. Even those most ready to decry it as a managerial approach apply it in part. Nevertheless, it is an idea that has been accepted more in the breach than in the actual performance.

It is antithetical, in fact, to conventional approaches to managing. Whatever we may have preached, we have practiced a doctrine that holds that the boss is boss and that initiatives should come from above. As if to underline this point, we have given names to those high in the hierarchy which emphasize their *macho* content: director, executive, administrator, manager, commander, controller, governor, president, master, headman, and chief, to indicate some of the most common of them. There is little in these titles to suggest a willingness to share the helm.

If one has doubts as to the norms such positions produce, a reading of the business press should relieve them. *The Wall Street Journal* which covers as fully as any newspaper in America what is happening within the business community, reports the achievements of the tough-thinking, hard-driving, risk-taking executive who has seen his company through difficult times and has now captured a major share of the market. So also do such reputable publications as *Fortune, Business Week,* and *Forbes. Time, Newsweek,* and now such important metropolitan dailies as *The New York Times*, *The Washington Post*, and *The Los Angeles Times* provide us with some of the same information in their business sections.

We structure our organizations in ways that leave no doubt that we believe specialization and compartmentalization are the ingredients of success. We talk of delegating (which in effect is decision-sharing) but are more likely to demit instead. (Demitting is giving to others those assignments we are pleased to have out of the way.) We develop rules and regulations which restrict and standardize the ways our subordinates are expected to act. When they are permitted responsibility, it is with the understanding that they will be held accountable for results. The word "subordinate" itself suggests a sub-order. There is no doubt where subordinates find themselves in the pecking order.

Small wonder that participative management is so hard to come by. Small wonder, given the nature of our large and complex organizations, that it is so difficult to arrange. Anyone who has explored the difficulties of delegation—a concept as difficult to understand as it is to arrange in an organization of four or more levels—should have no doubt on this score.

And yet, participation does take place. It is more often a by-product than an objective, and achieved more frequently by able and aggressive subordinates than by plan or intention. There is a saying that if one doesn't pay the cook, he will pay himself—and the cost of a good meal is often the result of the cook taking matters into his or her own hands. This is participation of sorts but not, I think, what is being sought by those who urge either Theory Y of Theory Z upon us.

Consultation: An Achievable Goal

It is always more realistic to undertake organizational patterns which are in keeping with established ways of doing things than those which are not. The simpler should always come before the more complex. We learn to crawl before we walk, and we walk before we run. Participation may be the desired objective but there is something which precedes it, and is also much easier. In fact, most of us do it with little forethought—consulting with others.

Consultation is, in fact, a form of participation, and because it reflects the mores of our times, is much easier to manage.

Most of us will readily acknowledge that it is satisfying to be asked for either advice or information even if it is not used. Under most circumstances, we are ready to give it. The fact of someone else asking what we think—and of seriously listening to it—is an indication that our suggestions are respected and wanted even when we surmise that they may not always be agreed with or followed. When the advice-seekers are of higher rank or status, we are even more appreciative of their coming to us.

The giving of advice does not necessarily require that it be accepted. As one matures, one recognizes that there are differences of opinion even among men of good will and that, for a variety of reasons, the advice-seeker has responsibilities that will often preclude agreeing with what we have to suggest. Even so, we are usually pleased to have been asked our opinion and appreciate the opportunity to have had our say before a decision was made.

For the advice-receiver, the advantages are multiple. Not only is much of the information that is being offered of potential value to the organization—and to him as a manager as well—but it is also, if one is a receptive listener, a means of learning how those at other levels view what is going on. The advice one gets often contains feedback as well.

In his monumental study of management, *The Managing of Organizations,* Bertram Gross speaks of the age-old precept philosophers have laid down for rulers. Simply stated, it is: "Be well advised."[1] It is found in the Bible, in the Koran, and other great religious documents as well as in philosophy. Proverbs 13:1 is an example: "Where no counsel is, the people fall; but in the multitude of counsellors there is safety." Machiavelli in his most notable work underlines its importance. Managers, like princes, may decide not to heed the advice they are given— and may be right in doing so—but at least they should have it.

Some of the more significant examples of consultation are from the military, strange as many civilian executives may find this to be, when the highest of all possible stakes are at issue. The most autocratic of commanders have found it not only prudent but essential to consult with their associates before undertaking campaigns, battles, or even skirmishes. Nor is the military, despite popular views to the contrary, the respecter of chains of command where advice or information is really required. The staff system itself is, in fact, a way around it. And of course, where operations are concerned, the wise officer seeks out those who know best the enemy, the terrain, the state of the troops, or the weather, whatever their rank.

The American Civil War, which is probably the best researched and reported of all wars, provides us with detailed information on the consultations which occurred—between the leading military figures of that war and also among lesser officers and men. World War II reported the pattern on an expanded scale. Not only did generals like Eisenhower, Bradley, MacArthur, Alexander and Slim consult in detail and at length with their staffs but this was a characteristic of both the Russians and the Germans as well. Had Hitler paid more attention to what officers like Manstein and Guderian were telling him, he might have avoided some of the disasters he suffered. Even so, they often had their say and at times it had its effect on one of history's most autocratic leaders. Stalin, be it said, listened carefully to the likes of Zhukov and Rokossovsky and much of the time heeded them.

Advice for the Advice-Seeker

There is a Turkish saying that "he who speaks frankly should have one foot in the stirrup." Sometimes, as history is witness, this is undoubtedly so. More often it is not. There are still those, of course, who will hear only what they want to hear, but in today's increasingly complex world, we are likely, sooner or later, to get the bad news along with the good, and most of us are practical enough to prefer it sooner rather than later.

There are many ways of getting advice. The most common is to ask for it from those we respect or trust, on a person-to-person basis. Some do this easily and as a matter of course. Others may be more reluctant. Americans seem to feel both a need and a responsibility for advice-giving, and are no respecters of rank when the urge is upon us.

But even so obvious an approach as seeking out the opinions of others whom we know and trust has its limitations. Some believe that advice-asking is a sign of weakness which undercuts the executive role. Others feel so self-sufficient (or so morally secure) that it usually does not occur to them that advice is needed. Still others are embarrassed to ask either advice or assistance in areas where they are presumed to be knowledgable. There is also, one knows, a concern on the part of the advice-asker that he or she will be given more assistance than is being asked for. (Advice, yes; feedback, no, is a not too uncommon fear.) Advice is asked—and will continue to be asked by most of us—but it will usually be limited not only by our previous experience in consulting with others but also by a kind of line-of-sight vision. Still, it is much easier to achieve than participation and, because that is so, needs to be encouraged.

In the large organization, size, complexity, specialization and territorial dispersion have placed practical limitations on both advice-giving and advice-getting. Those who are part of the process are always more likely to be strong supporters of what is ultimately decided than those who hear about it later on. Ways must be found, accordingly, of institutionalizing the consultative approach for it to perform satisfactorily.

Such ways do exist. Most of them are a part of well-established organizational systems. To use them effectively, however, we must rid ourselves of a number of mind-sets.

The most important of these is the mind-set against committees. Americans are a gregarious people as earlier indicated. We live and work in close association with each other. Much of our life is spent in groups; yet when we call such groups "committees"—which, of course, they are—they and their accomplishment are derided.

Committees and committee service are, in fact, part of the American pattern, and to suggest a Theory A approach without recognizing this is to do no justice to establised ways of doing things. Nevertheless, a great many Americans have doubts about committees and will cite any number of examples to prove their point.

In particular, we deride the idea that they are useful for managerial purposes when actually we could not get along without them. Committees keep minutes, we note cynically, but waste hours. The best committee is one of three with one vacancy on it and a second member at home ill. A camel is a horse designed by a committee. (Here, that is. In the Sahara it is the other way around.) There are few monuments to committees—the Laocoön aside—but this is because stone is difficult to work, and a single figure may well exhaust the sculptor when it does not bankrupt him. There are, however, innumerable paintings which reflect the fact that our best and most important work is done in relationship with others.

If we take the broad view that a committee is a meeting of two or more people, whether formalized or not, we see that organizations are actually collections of committees. The organization, in fact, is itself a committee. No matter how much we talk of single man direction, the organizational idea itself is one of cooperative effort.

That many organizations are badly run is not an argument against organizations. That many committees have not performed as we would like is not an argument against bringing people together. We have simply looked at the half glass of water and pronounced it half empty. We could instead have described it as being half full.

Several years ago, I listed in an article some of the pluses of meetings of a committee nature.[2] Here they are:

- They bring to bear a wide variety of intelligence on a problem.

- They provide a useful and efficient device for information sharing.

- They encourage teamwork.

- Where the product of a meeting is a true group product, those who have participated in it usually feel committed to it.

- They provide for representation of a number of differing views, both with the organization and the larger community.

- On the whole, Americans have a great deal of faith in committee/group action—for example, juries, legislatures, corporate boards, advisory committees, and councils of various kinds.

- Membership on committees has a number of valuable by-products, including individual learning and development, acceptance of new ideas, and respect for others.

- They are useful for moderating and healing differences of opinion.

- People like to work with others and service with a group provides a useful opportunity.

- Setting up such a group is an obvious way of consulting with others about a plan, a policy, a procedure, or a problem, and, if honestly done, is seen by others in that fashion.

All of these are important reasons for working with others, but the last is of particular importance in today's climate. Consultation is, in fact, one of the basic requirements of our times. We need only to consider how best it can be achieved.

The Getting of Advice

Skillful managers are ones who get advice from many quarters. Their ears are always open and their minds at the ready to sift the important from the trivial, the good from the bad. There is no single source, no one way by which information can be acquired.

One's associates are a useful fountainhead of facts and opinions as long as one recognizes their limitations. Those higher up can also be consulted—and should be—depending on the matter at hand. Outsiders can also be involved. Clients, customers, and suppliers often fall within these categories.

At lower organizational levels, it is useful for the manager to circulate at intervals among those who are doing the basic work of the company or agency. The Japanese factory system incorporates the idea that the manager should be available to rank and file employees. Westerners are startled to observe the frequent intercourse between them.

It also happens here. A useful definition of a large organization offered by a company president is one in which the chief executive officer no longer knows the first names of those who make day-to-day operational decisions. His idea is that such a company has already become too large.

A reading of interviews which *Nation's Business* has conducted, with company presidents over the years reveals the value which a high percentage of them place on informal contacts with their employees. Pascale and Athos have written at some length of the relationships of senior American managers with those at operational levels.[3] No less an autocrat that Harold Geneen, for years the guiding force behind ITT, is quoted as saying that "the first requirement of a senior executive is instant availability."[4]

Small talk, as many have discovered, can without much stretch of the imagination become consultation. The manager is not so much intruding upon the chain of command as personalizing an interest in what is actually taking place. One does not even need to take an initiative in asking advice. There are those with suggestions to make who will venture them when given the opportunity.

The ombudsman also has its uses—although advice-soliciting is hardly one of its major ones—as does the suggestion system and the "open door policy." No one should be misled into thinking, however, that these are primarily consultative. They merely provide an occasional vehicle for communication.

The Use of Meetings

Consultation occurs on a continuing basis in both American business and government but it is probably done best, many will be surprised to learn, at the higher levels. For some reason, subordinate managers are much less likely to talk over their problems and objectives with their associates, let alone to ask their advice. Consultation occurs least of all at the first-line supervisory levels. Perhaps this is because the latter feel they have so little authority that it is dangerous to risk sharing it.

What is needed in most organizations are ways by which those in managerial and executive positions can reach employees at lesser levels in a continuing and productive way.

Perhaps the most useful approach is via the committee, or if another term is preferred, the meeting. These meetings, however, should be conducted in a planned and systematic way. If consultation is the purpose, they should be designed with that in mind. This means that they should be conducted within a fixed time frame with attention given not only to membership but to arrangements as well.

The Information Sharing Meeting. As organizations become more complex, there is an increasing need for information at all levels. No longer is it sufficient to "tell them only what they need to know." Large-scale meetings can be held occasionally where, in addition to the information exchanged, they give managers the opportunity to be seen and heard. Smaller scale meetings should also be held for exchange of information. No decisions need to be made at such meetings. The manager can take the suggestions which are proffered as advisory.[5]

The Internal Advisory Committee. This is a new device only in name. It has frequently been used informally by managers who wished to try out some new idea or proposal on those who would ultimately be involved. On other occasions, self-appointed representatives of the work force ask to meet with those at higher echelons for the discussion of mutual problems. Usually, these meetings are of an *ad hoc* nature.

We suggest that the internal advisory committee (or committees) be institutionalized. This can be done in a number of ways. Individuals of known interest in and knowledge of the matter at hand can be brought together. Mid-managers can be involved with their associates, or separate committees can be formed of each. In order that a few do not dominate the committee, a part of the membership can be changed each year.

Or, members can be selected at random. This provides for a broad mix, enabling high level managers to learn at first hand what is going on in their organizations and how people feel about it. It serves the same purpose as a public advisory committee except that its membership is internal.

There is no reason, however, why advisory committees cannot be established in specific areas and at various levels. They have their uses wherever ideas and advice are wanted. These may have to do with such matters as safety, absenteeism, the environment, retirement systems, working conditions, equipment purchases, or any of the many problems the organization faces. Their primary purpose, however they may be organized, is to hear the views and gain the suggestions of those who ultimately will be involved. They not only produce ideas, but also contribute to a greater feeling of unity. They "personalize" the organization.

Such committees should be seen more as a sounding board for the expression of views than as a device for resolving problems. They should not be encouraged, at least not until the manager is comfortable with them, to reach group conclusions or to take committee positions. Where problem resolving is wanted, there are other ways.

Time allocated to advisory committees should be limited, and there should be an agenda. Consensus is not necessary, nor should the committee become a power center. Those who call or chair these meetings should not use the committee to gain support for specific programs or undertakings. Members will usually be supportive if listened to, but resent becoming a captive or manipulated audience.

The Ad Hoc Committee. The work group, *ad hoc* committee or task force can be useful.[6] Unlike the QCCs which have a permanence about them, the *ad hoc* committee is limited to a specific problem and when this is resolved or recommendations are made it goes out of existence. Members can be selected irrespective of level or occupation—there is considerable merit in variety. Generally, they are relieved of other assignments to work with the committee but this practice may vary. Where the committee is long-term (several weeks, for example), a specific amount of time may be assigned.

Most people enjoy working on such committees. It is a distinction to be asked, there is an objective to be addressed, and the committee adds variety to one's experience. The major criticism of such committees is that they are not used often enough.

Quality Control Circles (QCC). The literature of management is giving a great deal of attention at this time to a committee called the Quality Control Circle.[7] Its overnight popularity underlines its significance.

QCCs may not be the source of Japanese productivity but there can be little doubt that they have contributed to it. It is important to take a long hard look at them. They are widely used in Japan and increasingly in the Untted States. Experience began several years ago in selected Japanese industries. That the idea behind them appears to have originated in the United States is beside the point: they have fitted readily into both Japanese cultural and industrial patterns.

A QCC is made up at the factory floor level of those employees who are engaged in a particular operation. The foreman acts as chairman and the Circle is dedicated to the improvement of work performance. To enhance its contribution, it has certain prerogatives: it can, for example, stop work in many companies in order to look into certain operational procedures. The reward the members feel are neither the citations nor the small financial awards they may receive so much as the satisfaction which comes from the feeling that one has contributed both to company and to national goals.

The usefulness of the QCCs in the United States depends upon attitudes. They undoubtedly hold considerable potential, but miracles should not be expected.

Brainstorming a Problem. Brainstorming meetings are creative. A group is assembled, usually one with considerable variety in member experience, and is asked to address a particular issue or find a solution to a given problem. No limitations are placed on what members can suggest: all ideas, no matter how far-fetched, are welcome. Sometimes several meetings take place to give people a chance to think between-times about the mission. Later, there may be a session which tries to distill from the suggestions the most useful ideas.

The record of brainstorming sessions is a good one. In addition to the ideas they produce, there is a feeling on the part of those involved that they have contributed, as indeed they have.

The Problem Meeting. This is another device by which the views of those at lower levels can be heard. While not in wide-spread use, it has appeared often enough to have earned recognition.

The problem meeting may be distinguished from ordinary staff conferences in that attendance is limited at a given meeting to representatives of a single division or section who meet with a half dozen or so from the organization's top staff. Meetings are scheduled well in advance, so that time can be given to preparation. This is important because the agenda, which is always the same, is to ask those who represent the subordinate unit to indicate the kinds of problems they see six months or more ahead—and what they are doing about them. The time for the presentation is limited (say, half an hour) with another half an hour for discussion. The meeting is not an occasion for decision-making—decisions should be made in the normal process—but to alert topside to what operational units believe they may be facing.

Public Adivsory Committees. There is no reason why the private as well as the public sector should not be able to consult with customers, clients, suppliers, and others whose support is so important to the success of the undertaking. Certainly, those "outside" the traditional organization are often as concerned as those "inside" with both its performance and its survival.

Public institutions have for many years availed themselves of adivsory groups—committees made up of those of either specialized or general interest who meet, either as individuals, as *ad hoc* committees, or as committees of the whole to learn of what is happening, and of problems to be faced, or as sources of advice. Business has been more reluctant to share its concerns or to turn to others for assistance. It need not be.

More and more we are coming to understand that the environment is also a part of the organizational system and must be taken into account in whatever we do. How fitting, then, that we should consider ways by which those in that environment are consulted and the advice of "outsiders" heard.

In Summary

What has been suggested above are ways and means of involving those with a concern for the organization and its objectives in matters concerning both it and them. It suggests what is both a conservative and a doable approach to one of the more pressing problems faced by large organizations. By consulting with others, the manager is not passing decision-making to those who have previously had little experience with it. One is not shirking the responsibilities of the position. One is simply involving in a more meaningful fashion those who are bound to be involved anyway.

The patterns suggested for advice-seeking are in keeping with established societal practice. The formal organization and the top-down approach have, like the coelacanth, survived well beyond the period in which they developed. Their efficiency and effectiveness are now being challenged, and clearly traditional approaches need to be reexamined. Consultation as a means of participation is urged here as a peculiarly American approach which has long been under-utilized.

These initiatives are a starting point to achieving more substantial forms of teamwork.

FOOTNOTES

[1]Bertram M. Gross, *The Managing of Organizations*, NY: The Free Press, 1964, pp. 104-106.

[2]For a more extensive discussion of what committees can do, see David S. Brown, "Capitalizing on Committees," *The Federal Accountant,* Winter 1965, pp. 58-73.

[3]Richard Tanner Pascale and Anthony G. Athos, *The Art of Japanese Management,* NY: Simon & Schuster Inc, 1981, pp. 88 *et seq.*

[4]*Ibid.*, p. 75.

[5]David S. Brown, "How You Can Use the Management Meeting," *Management Review*, July 1961, pp. 62-66.

[6]For those who wish to know more about it, see, L.W. Bass, *Management by Task Forces*, Mt. Airy, MD: Lomond Publications, Inc., 1975.

[7]Quality Control Circles are described by William Ouchi, *Theory Z: How American Business Can Meet the Japanese Challenge*, Reading, MA: Addison-Wesley Publishing Company, Inc., 1981, pp. 261-268. Also Dudley Lynch, "Circling Up, Japanese Style," *American Ways*, April 1981, pp. 36-41. Robert E. Cole, "Made in Japan–Quality Control Circles," *Personnel Journal*, Oct. 1979, pp. 682-685, 708. Yoskitaka Fujita, "The Workers' Autonomous Small Group Activities and Productivity in Japan," *Management Japan*, Summer 1981, pp. 16-18.

CHAPTER XXVI

THE MANAGER IN THE YEAR 2000

If someone were to ask me what the middle-aged man will be wearing 20 years from now, I would confidently predict that it would be a pants suit with shirt, socks, and also perhaps a tie, and that he would look pretty much as he does now. The suit would probably be made of a mixture of old and new fibers, some yet to be developed, but the style, given differences in cosmetics which include color, width of lapel, cuffs (or not), pockets and vests, would not be greatly different from what has been with us for well over 100 years. The suit will keep us warmer (or cooler) than now and possibly both; and it will certainly be more coffee-, whiskey-, and cigarette-burn-resistant. It will also, of course, cost much more than now, but in basic appearance it will not have changed greatly.

So it will be, I predict, with the manager. In general, in the year 2000, managers will look very much as they do today and will do many of the same things. As long as there are organizations, there will be organizational problems and there will need to be managers to resolve them. As the late Paul Appleby, a scholar as well as an administrator, was fond of remarking, "It is the manager's job to make a mesh out of things." There should be ample opportunities in the decades ahead to test this proposition.

In fact, the managerial role should grow in importance over the years. The differences between what one will be doing then as against what one is being asked to do now will reflect the differences between the nature of society then and today. To understand what these are, we will need to appreciate some of the funny things that are happening to us on our way to the Twenty-first Century.

Looking Into The Future

There can be no serious prediction of the future that is not a projection of past and present performance. Man is gifted with hindsight, not foresight. To suggest what the future will contain, one must understand what has gone before and, indeed, what is happening now, and be able to project the trends thus observed towards some future target date.

This is, of course, neither as simple nor as easy as divine revelation, but given the infrequency with which divinity reveals itself, it is probably a good bit more likely.

My own approach is to do as the weather forecasters do: to note what is moving our way, what it may encounter en route, when it is likely to arrive, and what, based on past experience, all this will produce. On its face, this is reasonable enough. The problem is that society contains both forces and counterforces in substantial numbers. Any one of these, in fact, is potentially able, like a line squall or an unexpected low, to dominate the whole.

Herman Kahn, one of the more thoughtful and articulate of the futurists, reminds us that the future will hardly be "surprise-free." He says: "The most surprising thing that could occur is no surprises." Still, the effort must be made to look ahead. Man's greatness lies in trying to foresee and overcome the problems he will face.

The manager of the future and what is done will be determined in large part by the organizations one serves. And these, in turn, will be shaped by client groups and publics, by the kinds of demands they make and by the nature and expectations of those with whom one works. Let us examine these in some of their specifics.

People And Their Demands

Organizations are formed to meet needs. People demand goods, services, comfort and protection. The list seems always to be both endless and growing.

But before we conclude that the job is impossible let us reflect a moment on some of the things that are already happening. The past decade, if it has taught us nothing else, has reminded us that there is a limit to what we can ask for and reasonably expect to get. That limit is controlled by the resources we have available or are willing to commit. We have already discovered, for example, that we are short of energy, or more specifically, energy in the forms we most want. We know also that we suffer acute shortages in time and money and such other things as water, good weather, clean air and living space. We have shortages in housing, lumber, coffee and much else. We need more engineers, social workers, parameds, craftsmen, fruit harvesters and household workers. Good managers are also in short supply.

We are learning, slowly to be sure, to reduce or limit some of our demands. The housewife whose husband's income should have assured her of the availability of a cleaning woman has had to relearn the doing of her own housework. We no longer expect mail deliveries to be up to what they were 25 years ago, despite a 500 percent increase in first class postage. We have become accustomed to the fact that doctors will not make house calls anymore, and as we grow richer as a nation, we are moving towards smaller cars because they consume less gas. We may have reached the moon but "really fresh" eggs and fresh-fresh vegetables are likely to be beyond our reach.

We do not expect those who mug us or hold us up to be sent to prison because we know that most of them won't even be caught. We have learned to live with long delays in the arrival of the service man and the delivery truck. As clients, we accept the fact that the doctrine of the customer being always right is passé. We expect more and more of computers but one thing we don't yet expect of them is that they can be programmed to repair themselves.

I make these points to suggest that the future, whatever breakthroughs there may be, will not be one of unlimited largesse. Far from it. The lessons of the past are that we must be more selective in our requirements. We are already learning to rethink some of our "needs."

Managers in the year 2000 will be faced with the fact—already occurring—that their role is increasingly one of ascertaining what our real resource capability is, of protecting the future against future requirements, of making hard decisions concerning them, and of negotiating among those whose demands conflict with one another.

The manager in the years ahead will be less a producer than was traditionally the case and more of an innovator, a developer, a negotiator, an arbitrator and a conservator. The manager and his or her associates must be able to deal with a variety of problems in a highly complex society which are frustrating, pervasive and essentially unresolvable.

No longer is the manager someone whose primary job is to "get the work out." Rather, one will be expected to determine how limited resources (energy, for example) are to be made less limited and also how they can be shared equitably. One of the problems with not having enough is that what is available becomes the more sought after by so many.

How is one, for example, to divide between rich and poor? Between the wasters and the conservers? Between industrial and residential users? Between those who are "old customers" and those who are new ones? Between those bent on achieving personal goals and those who would serve the community? It is not enough to cite national goals or organizational policies. It is the individual manager who must help to determine and administer them. This becomes a primary responsibility.

All of this is far cry from the "push button" world so many crystal gazers have seen for us. There will be new machines, of course—more computers, more word processing equipment, more "instant communications," more automation. But I do not see them dominating us. Increasingly, I believe, they will emphasize the integrative aspects of the manager's job and make that person even more vital to their use than now.

The Changing Organization

Organizations reflect not only the requirements laid upon them but also their times. They are far from static. They may change slowly (as men's outfits change slowly), but they do change.

Among the more important changes in organizations today is that they have become more fluid and more flexible. This may not be immediately apparent, but over a decade or two I believe it can easily be observed. There will be a greater interchangeability of parts and also of personnel between institutions. Specialization will continue to take place but it is likely to be of a different nature: we will know more about more things, and how they go together.

Organizational leaders already are speaking less positively of "company loyalty." There is a lessening of authoritarianism. Those who work with organizations have noted the shared loyalty which members feel for other institutions and objectives. Traditional marketplace enemies may still be enemies (as the law seems to require), but they have begun to accept each other and even on occasion to work together in this over-crowded world of ours.

All of this may not greatly alter the formal appearance of the organization, but it does change its characteristics. Divisional lines are becoming less sacrosanct as matrix organizational structures are tested and affirmed. The importance of staff, as against line (or operations), has at long last been recognized. There has been an erosion of time-worn shibboleths. Harlan Cleveland, author of *The Future Executive,* sees an expanding span of supervision, a lessening of hierarchy, and a greater accessibility of the executive to both internals and externals. "The future," he suggests, "is horizontal." The temporary organization (Toffler calls it "ad-hocism") is proving its usefulness as new arrangements are devised within the parent structure to meet new demands.

We are no longer as committed to bigness, or perhaps I should say conventional forms of bigness, as we once were. The doubts we have long held about public bureaucracies now include private bureaucracies as well. And for good reason. Just because a company or an agency is big doesn's mean that it is either efficient or economical, and it certainly doesn't assure us that it will be well behaved. The celebrated English economist, the late E.F. Schumacher, has pointed out in his landmark book, *Small is Beautiful,* that the advantages of littleness are substantial. Smallness, he observed, is being born again.

Bigness, of course, will not disappear overnight, nor do we want it to. What seems more likely is that the organization of the future will combine bigness with smallness. This is not as ridiculous as it may sound. It suggests a confederational approach, a network, a system or some similar arrangement into which smaller units can be plugged in (or out) as the situation may require. The franchise system made famous by McDonald's has provided us with an example of a way in which local capital and initiative can be involved in a national network. McDonald's—and those who have emulated it—are both big businesses and little ones. We may not yet be able to apply this to automaking but the good word from Detroit is that General Motors is already attempting new work designs, along with the mini-Cadillac, which are likely to be part of the future. And it should. The old order organization, like the gas guzzler, needs rethinking.

Changes in form suggest changes in behavior. Not only is the network (or system) substantially different from the family business with its autocratic controls (or even, for that matter, the traditional stock corporation), but there are changes also in how these systems function. No longer is the manager the "bull of the woods" with life or death power over subordinates. Rather he (or she) has become, as the supermarket manager has shown us, someone who "keeps things going." He greets customers or helps them locate hard-to-find items, he initials checks (if an assistant is not available to do it), he watches for shoplifters, and he may even check groceries or bag them if lines have formed and customers are not being served. A generation of management advisors who have held that the manager's job should be limited to managing is already revising its catechism.

The Changing Individual

Collectively and individually, the work force is changing also. Collectively, there are, and will be, more women in it, more blacks, more persons of Spanish and other minority group descent, and probably in the years ahead, a larger percentage of old people as well. Along the way, people are becoming more highly educated, more professional, and, correspondingly, more demanding.

Nearly half of those in gainful employment today are women, and more than 50 percent of all women are gainfully employed outside the home. (Married women who work are now over 50 percent.) With an increase in child care centers, the number and percentage are sure to increase. The effect on management is inescapable. While women may ask for the same rights as men, they won't permit themselves to be treated in the same way.

Blacks have long since learned that they are the last to be hired and the first to be fired. They and their leaders are taking legal steps to insure themselves that this pattern is revised. It will be. Many of them, backed by legislation and court decisions, have assumed new patterns of belligerence. They are supported in these attitudes by the "hyphenated Americans" who have suffered with them in the hiring halls and personnel offices of the past.

Not only are there changes in the makeup of the work force, but there are also changes in worker attitude towards work and the work environment. The American, always individualistic, is becoming even more so. He is proud, fiercely independent and self-reliant but increasingly aware of the need for interdependence, and eager to make good both sides of his heritage.

There is a general feeling of resentment by the blue collar worker over status and benefits. Both the number and percentage of the blues have fallen during the past two decades, and white collar workers are now clearly in the majority although many of them are paid less than blue collars and do work which is not greatly different. The blues have in part assuaged their injured feelings by asking for more pay and increased benefits and, recently, a greater voice in the running of things. In several European countries, for example, they have won places on boards of directors, and an American adaptation of the same is beginning to happen here. Witness the case of Chrysler. We joke of the janitors who call themselves stationary engineers, of the garbage collectors who have become sanitation specialists, and the tree trimmers who are now arboreal experts. The message, however, is clear. No one wants to be on the bottom rung of the occupational ladder, and the adjustment in terminology is an effort to remedy the situation.

The educational level of workers is rising also, as has been previously noted. This is resulting in behavioral changes as well. The college-trained man and woman, as the manager of the future is sure to discover, cannot be managed by organizational patterns devised by either Frederick—Frederick the Great, or Frederick W. Taylor, the American engineer. Even more than his blue-collar associate, the professional insists on rights and prerogatives and is in a position to get them.

The O'Toole Report (*Work in America,* 1973) points out:[1]

> Workers recognize that some of the dirty jobs can be transformed only into the merely tolerable, but the most oppressive features of work are felt to be avoidable: constant supervision and coercicn, lack of variety, monotony, meaningless tasks, and isolation. An increasing number of workers want more autonomy in tackling their tasks, greater opportunity for increasing their skills, rewards that are directly connected to the intrinsic aspects of work, and greater participation in the design of the work and the formulation of their tasks.

Workers for years have been tied to one job and one company by pension systems, by lack of information concerning prospects elsewhere, by their own lack of training, by custom and habit, and by the uncertainties of moving into new areas. They have thus been forced to accept whatever terms their employer has insisted upon. They are now finding increasing opportunities doing their own thing.

Nationwide retirement systems make it easy for a man to pull up stakes in, say, Huron, S.D., and move to Biloxi, Miss., or vice versa. Indeed, there is the likelihood that Congress will make it easier still. Workmen, in fact, can look forward to the day when they can take their retirement equities, as they do their tool kits, with them wherever they go. Thanks to instant communication, we already are informed of what goes on in Biloxi or Bloomington or Bakersfield—or for that matter, Baghdad. World War II taught us about moving, and we move on the average every four to five years which makes the moving companies another growth industry. The American is mobile as well as flexible: it is part of our present and future life style.

We also are changing types of work at a remarkable rate. We move from one job to another for a variety of reasons: because there are new needs and requirements; because old jobs have become obsolete; because new jobs offer new opportunities and new "challenges;" and because we enjoy the new experiences which different assignments bring. The average 21-year-old will be in eight to ten major lines of work in a lifetime. The manager must constantly be prepared to train new people—and also old people in new things. Indeed, training is becoming one of our most important assignments.

All this is leading to changes in the work ethic. A new generation has raised serious questions concerning the values it has inherited. A view frequently heard among younger workers is that they have no intention of working as hard as their elders have worked. And they probably won't. Most of us have not delved deeply into existentionalism but we have certainly observed and experienced it.

Work, in fact, is seen in a variety of ways, depending upon those who are looking at it. There are those who regard it as a major life objective. (Happily for the manager, their numbers are large.) But others see it only as a means to some other end and still others as a burden upon them which is to be dealt with as lightly as possible. Many who come from the ghettos have little or no feeling for it at all. The idle rich play golf; the idle poor, basketball.

Americans have become increasingly selective in terms of the things they will and won't do, which, of course, adds to the manager's problems. With workers being always ready to say what they think about both their supervisors and the work system, and the strident and critical always being more newsworthy than the routine, the manager of the future can expect to hear many things one would prefer not to have heard. The feedback on feedback is that there will be plenty of it.

Enter The Future Manager

These are some of the forces that are changing the managerial role. They are already apparent. There can be no doubt that the manager of the future will have to deal with them—and probably with less power and personal authority than one's counterpart has today. Ours is a democratic society which shows increasing intolerance of autocratic behavior in both public and private institutions.

The manager's job as we approach the end of the century will clearly be a bigger one than it is today. The manager will need all the creativity that can be mustered and all the help others can provide. Resources are, in fact, likely to be more limited than they are today and powers more circumscribed. Those who make demands upon those in managerial positions will be more positive in their requirements and their voices are likely to be louder. Both internals and externals will undoubtedly have a larger voice in what is done than now.

Managers 20 Years Hence

Managers 20 years from now will need to emphasize certain skills and capabilities at the expense of others to cope with the changes that have taken place between the 'seventies and 'eighties and the year 2000. Here are some of them.

- There will need to be greater understanding of how and why things happen as they do. There will need to be a greater appreciation than managers have today of the importance of systems and their interrelationships.

- They must learn to deal with complexity in its many forms, and with a constantly changing complexity at that. They will live among new and startling equipments and must find ways of not being dominated by them.

- They will need to be increasingly "people oriented." In particular, they must be able to negotiate in a constructive way with all of those, both inside and outside, who have a hand in the achievement of organizational objectives.

- They must learn new ways of leadership. To be successful in the face-to-face situation is not enough. One can no longer rely on traditional forms of authority. One must understand the difference between being in charge and being in control.

- They must be more innovational and creative in all their meanings than their counterparts are today. Innovation, in fact, is a requirement of success.

- At the same time, managers must concern themselves with the proper use of limited resources. Indeed, these limitations and the increase in the demand for them may well be one of the most difficult problems of stewardship.

- Development both for oneself and one's associates will have become a continuing process. Managers will need to find new ways by which both can prepare for what will be required of them.

The manager's reward, we may hope, will be a better appreciation by his or her fellow citizens of the contribution thus made to their comfort and survival. If past experience is any guide, however, one should not count on it.

FOOTNOTE

[1] *Work in America,* Report of a Special Task Force to the Secretary of Health, Education and Welfare (prepared under the auspices of the W. E. Upjohn Institute for Employment Research), Cambridge, MA: MIT Press, 1973, p. 13.

CHAPTER XXVII

THE THREE BASICS: INDIVIDUALISM, RESPONSIBILITY, AND INCREMENTALISM

Over the years, we have begun to discover that many of the ideas, theories, concepts, and assumptions we have held of organizational systems and of their management are proving not to have achieved what we so desperately need. Some have failed us completely; others seem to be only half truths.

Part of the reason, certainly, for some of these failures is the fact that the views held—the values lived by—of those at all levels of our systems call for something quite different from many of the traditional approaches to managing. As Peter Drucker has wryly but accurately remarked, "Much of what we call management consists of making it difficult for people to get work done."

If we have learned anything at all, it is that what was sufficient for another time and place is not adequate to today's needs. This is always sufficient reason for rethinking the problem, and also at times for going back to the old drawing board.

Even if we cannot clearly see the face of the future, we can be sure that the problems it will bring are large, complex, and serious. We know also some of the requirements that will be laid on us. We will need to be more productive than we now are, more ingenious and resourceful, more respectful of the rights of others, and more sensitive to society's needs. The system that can best meet these and other requirements will be the one we should follow.

We may not know what the future holds but we do know some of the values which must be accommodated. The *individual,* individually and collectively, must be served as client, customer, observer and citizen. The individual member of the system is the one who in the final analysis will determine how well or poorly this is done. The individual is the building block of the organizational system, no matter how automated it has become.

Given the individual as a building block—I have suggested earlier that he *and* she are the rock on which the church is built—we must look to their characteristics and how they can be developed.

I have put forward Theory A, based on the premise that the cultural characteristics of the community in which we live have major impact on how we behave in organizations as well as in home and community life. This would be equally true for Germans or Japanese or Brazilians.

The Responsibility of the Individual

The individual is important as a *responsible* agent. This quality or duty of responsibility is of particular importance to the group. It is also an American attribute. In the majority of American homes the child is taught to be responsible before it knows the meaning of the word. This idea becomes more fully developed in our churches and our schools. Social and professional organizations are built upon it. We speak constantly of, even if we do not always practice, the responsibility of the citizen. Irresponsibility is among the most loathed of our sins.

Responsibility is basic to the American character. Our pragmatic approach implies responsibility of the individual. Our belief in democracy is grounded upon it, our individualism reeks of it.

The growth of organizational size and complexity, however, has tended to diminish both the individual's influence and his feeling of responsibility. This feeling must be reinforced. It is essential to organizational success. I speak of responsibility as a duty. Barnard has called it "the quality which gives dependability and determination to human conduct, and foresight and ideality to purpose." A responsible person is one who fulfills obligations or trust. The word "responsibility" is closely associated with the word "response." It is, in fact, our response to a charge or assignment which has been given us.

Responsibility cannot be bestowed automatically, as if it were a citation from above. In an interview given a few weeks before his death, Barnard said:[1]

> Now the point to responsibility is that you have to have acceptance in order to make it work. I can say, "I now hold you responsible for this," but if you don't accept that then there's nothing I can do about it if you don't. You can dissemble, you can give me the run around, but if you don't accept it, it just doesn't work. . . .[N]early everything depends on the moral commitment. I'm perfectly confident, with occasional lapses, that if I make a date with you, whom I have never met, you'll keep it and I'll keep it. Yet the world runs on that—you just couldn't run a college, you couldn't run a business, you couldn't run a church, you couldn't do anything, except on the basis of the moral commitments that are involved in what we call responsibility. Authority comes second.

This emphasizes, as does much of Barnard's philosophy, the idea of acceptance by the individual involved. It is not enough to assign or demand that responsibility be exercised—it must be accepted as part of the contract that brings the person to the system and without acceptance will usually not be exercised.

The *sharing* of responsibility for what goes on—for clearly this is what it is—raises basic questions concerning the nature of the organization, its authority system, and the style and manner of those in its higher positions. It poses a problem for those who have spent their lives in authoritarian organizations and reflects their characteristics. But problems also have a way of becoming challenges if only we can manage to think of them in those terms, and what often seems from one perspective unresolvable or insurmountable can, under other circumstances, be not only logical but doable as well.

Our gregariousness suggests that we can and do work well together. Our belief in individualism reminds us that we have not forgotten that the individual needs to be served.

The Importance of Incrementalism

What this book is suggesting is that our organizations and organizational systems make better use of the characteristics, values, and habit patterns that mark the American people than we have thus far done. To do so, we must be prepared to change not only some of our methods but also the ideas which support them.

This is not easy to do, given the nature of many of our institutions and the managerial practices of those who fill high offices in them. Winston Churchill declared that he had not become His Majesty's First Minister in order to dismantle the British empire, and most of those who have at last achieved positions of power, often at great personal cost, are not ready either to share or give up what they have achieved.

The price of leadership, however, and one of its requirements, is that one be aware of and sensitive to the forces which bear upon the system. A closer look at what is actually happening, and its cost, should be convincing that great changes are taking place, and that adjustments must be made to them.

Lord Salisbury, one of Britain's prime ministers, in speaking of "effective diplomacy" said that its victories are won by microscopic advantages—a judicious suggestion here, an opportune civility there, a wise concession at one moment and a farsighted persistence at another. They comprise advantages, he said, of sleepless tact, immovable calmness and patience that no folly, no provocation, no blunder can shake.

Perhaps something of the same could be said for dealing with the complex human interrelationships which are so much a part of our modern organization systems. If I have learned anything at all in a lifetime which has seen some of the more remarkable events in the history of mankind, it is that there are few "quick fixes", except for junkies. We *do* change our minds and our habits, but both come slowly. Where many are involved, the changes are slower still.

This has its advantages. Those changes which have been most successful in both our organizational systems and in our society are ones that we have accommodated slowly and often cautiously. A greater monument to Napoleon than his victories on the battlefield is the Code Napoleon which has survived as part of the basic law of France.

There is thus a strong case to be made for *incrementalism*. We need to accept and ingest new patterns for them to work effectively. While there is at times need for haste—and some matters, like a burning building, must be addressed at once—deliberateness has its virtue, unless, of course, it is a substitute for dragging our feet.

What I have endeavored to add to existing management theory and approaches is the argument that the humanizing of our systems is not enough, that systemic relationships must in fact be strengthened and time-honored organizational patterns revised. This will not occur overnight, but the process of change is underway.

All of this will be easier for some than for others. It will be affected by the style and character of those at the top, by the experience of those at other levels, and in particular by the history of the organization and the product or service with which it is involved. Happily, there is a changing environment which is more supportive of the ideas this book has put forward than existed even a single generation ago. There is, in addition, a growing cadre of young and middle-aged managers who are already in sync with what we are suggesting.

There are many ways of introducing change into our organizational patterns and one of these is by way of instruments and equipments. As a people, we adjust readily to machines (our materialism?) and, if they do not actually threaten us, take delight in becoming their masters. I flew a seven ton airplane during World War II, and took great pride that a 150 pound being of no mechanical and little athletic skill could guide such a monster. In fact, those who direct large earth-moving or similar equipment have little need for dominating their fellows because they control the machine.

Americans are thought to be quick on the trigger, with often a "shoot from the hip" style. That is partially true. But there are some things in which it is better to proceed with caution. General Kutuzov, whose assignment was that of defending Russia against the invading French in 1812, could do so only by changing the Russian style of fighting from one of battlefield confrontation to one of drawing the enemy in and then wearing him down. As Tolstoy tells it, the change in the Russian officer and soldier he wrought came about by the application of "time and patience."

Something as large, complex, and important as an organizational system requires the same. But we must not delay in getting to it.

FOOTNOTES

[1] As quoted in William B. Wolf, *Conversations with Chester I. Barnard,* ILR Paperback No. 12, Ithaca, NY: New York State School of Industrial and Labor Relations, 1973, p.35.

OTHER PUBLICATIONS OF DAVID S. BROWN

Those interested in additional writings by David S. Brown may refer to the following:

ARTICLES IN JOURNALS

"Some New Ideas on Decision Making," *Management Quarterly,* Summer 1981, pp. 26-35.

"Power Problems at the Managerial Level," *Human Resource Development: An International Journal (HRD),* Vol. 4, No. 4, 1980, pp. 26-30.

"The Myth of Reorganizing," *Journal of Systems Management,* June 1979, pp. 6-10.

"Rethinking the Supervisory Role," *Supervisory Management,* November 1977, pp. 2-10.

"Barriers to Successful Communication: Part I—Macrobarriers," *Management Review*, December 1975, pp. 24-29.

"Barriers to Successful Communication: Part II—Microbarriers," *Management Review*, January 1976, pp. 15-21.

"Management by Objectives: Promise and Problems," *The Bureaucrat,* Winter 1974.

"Modifying Bureaucratic Systems in the Developing World," *Asian Forum,* January-March 1974.

"The Management of Advisory Committees," *The Public Administration Review,* July-August 1972, pp. 334-342.

"12 Ways to Make Delegation Work," *Supervisory Management,* May 1967, pp. 508.

"Why Delegation Works—and Why It Doesn't," *Personnel,* January-February 1967, pp. 44-52.

"The Businessman and Government Administration," *The MBA,* January 1967, pp. 34-38.

"Some Feedback on Feedback," *Adult Leadership,* January 1967, pp. 226-278.

"The President and the Bureaus: Time for a Renewal of Relationships," *Public Administration Review,* September 1966, pp. 174-182.

"Some Vital New Dimensions for Training," *Training and Development Journal,* March 1966, pp. 21-27.

"Strategies and Tactics of Public Administration Technical Assistance," Chapter 7, pp. 185-224, Montgomery and Siffin, eds., *Approaches to Development: Politics, Administration and Change,* (New York: McGraw-Hill, 1966).

"Capitalizing on Committees," *The Federal Accountant,* Winter 1965, pp. 58-73.

"The Assistant Chief: Asset or Liability?" *Systems and Procedures Journal,* May-June 1965, pp. 22-27.

"Subordinates' Views of Ineffective Executive Behavior," *Academy of Management Journal,* December 1964, pp. 288-299.

"Organizational Man-Trap: The Deputy Chief," *Civil Service Journal,* October-December 1964, pp. 9-12.

"The Key to Self-Help: Improving the Administrative Capability of the Aid-Receiving Countries," *Public Administration Review,* June 1964, pp. 67-77.

"The Importance of Understanding Objectives," *The Federal Accountant,* March 1964, pp. 63-73.

"The Staff Man Looks in the Mirror," *The Public Administration Review,* June 1963, pp. 67-73.

"The Lecture—and How to Make It More Effective," *Journal of the American Society of Training Directors,* December 1960, pp. 17-22.

"Individual Freedom and Traditional Management," *Personnel Administration,* September-October 1960, pp. 3-11.

"Members Have Responsibilities, Too," *Adult Leadership,* June 1960, pp. 49-50, 69.

"Advice on Advisory Committees," *Adult Leadership,* January 1957, pp. 216-219.

"The Public Advisory Board as an Instrument of Government," *The Public Administration Review,* Summer 1955, pp. 196-204.

BOOKS AND MONOGRAPHS

Federal Contributions to Management: Effects on the Public and Private Sectors, (New York: Praeger, 1971) 409 pp. (editor).

A Guide to the Use of Advisory Committees, published by the U.S. Public Health Service, 1959 and 1963, 103 pp.

The Public Advisory Board and the Tariff Study, published by the Inter-University Case Program, 1956, 47 pp.

Monographs published by Leadership Resources, Inc.:

The Leader Looks at the Use of Time, 1972.

The Leader Looks at Authority and Responsibility, 1966.

Understanding the Management Function, 1966

Delegating and Sharing Work, 1966

The Leader Looks at Decision Making, 1961.

INDEX OF NAMES

SUBJECT INDEX